ACPL Laramie, WY
3/2010
39092071324547
Garland, James C.,
Saving alma mater :

WITHDRAWN

D0340199

Sources for Library Materials in FY09
Albany County Public Library

■ Cash Gifts
■ Public Money
☐ Donated Items

2.6%
45.0%
52.5%

Saving Alma Mater

SAVING
Alma Mater

A Rescue Plan for America's Public Universities

JAMES C. GARLAND

The University of Chicago Press | Chicago and London

Albany County
Public Library
Laramie, Wyoming

James C. Garland served for ten years as president of Miami University (Ohio) and for twenty-six years as an administrator and professor of physics at Ohio State University.

The University of Chicago Press, Chicago 60637
The University of Chicago Press, Ltd., London
© 2009 by The University of Chicago
All rights reserved. Published 2009
Printed in the United States of America

18 17 16 15 14 13 12 11 10 09   1 2 3 4 5

ISBN-13: 978-0-226-28386-9   (cloth)
ISBN-10: 0-226-28386-0   (cloth)

Library of Congress Cataloging-in-Publication Data

Garland, James C., 1942–
    Saving alma mater : a rescue plan for America's public universities / James C. Garland.
        p. cm.
    Includes bibliographical references and index.
    ISBN-13: 978-0-226-28386-9 (cloth : alk. paper)
    ISBN-10: 0-226-28386-0 (cloth : alk. paper)
    1. Public universities and colleges—United States—Finance. I. Title.
    LB2342.G37 2009
    378.1'060973—dc22

                                                            2009018829

♾ The paper used in this publication meets the minimum requirements of the American National Standard for Information Sciences—Permanence of Paper for Printed Library Materials, ANSI Z39.48–1992.

Contents

Preface   *vii*
Acknowledgments   *xxi*

Introduction   *1*

**PART I   A PRIMER ON PUBLIC HIGHER
              EDUCATION ECONOMICS**
1   Where the Money Comes From   *11*
2   Market Forces in Higher Education   *23*
3   Why Public Universities Cannot Restrain Costs   *41*
4   The University Prime Directive   *51*

**PART II   THE ACADEMIC CULTURE OF FREEDOM
              AND WASTE**
5   The Faculty Are the University   *63*
6   The Cargo Cult College   *71*
7   The Blessing and Curse of Shared Governance   *81*
8   What Price Shared Governance?   *97*

PART III   RENEGOTIATING THE PUBLIC COMPACT

9   The Shape of Things to Come   *107*
10 Leadership Begins with the Trustees   *115*
11 The Role of Governing Boards in the New Era   *127*
12 Recruiting Presidential Leadership   *143*
13 Reforming the Academic Culture   *161*
14 A Proposal for Deregulation of Public Universities   *189*

Postscript   *217*

Appendix A: The Miami University Tuition Plan   *221*
Appendix B: The Impact of Competition on Public University Tuition,
            Costs, and Revenue   *231*
Appendix C: Suggested Readings   *241*
Notes   *247*
Index   *263*

Preface

In 1996 I was appointed the twentieth president of Miami University in Oxford, Ohio, a well-regarded public university founded in 1809. Before then I had spent twenty-six years as a physics professor and administrator at Ohio State University, about a hundred miles up the road at the state capital, Columbus. One of the credentials that helped me land my Miami job was familiarity with Ohio's unusual public university system—a system that is in fact a loose consortium of thirteen autonomous schools (each with its own board of trustees) that run the gamut from tiny Central State University, the nation's oldest public black college, to giant Ohio State, a comprehensive land-grant megauniversity with more than twenty colleges and professional schools.

But even within this broad field of disparate institutions, Miami stands out as an odd duck. In some respects Miami resembles a private university. The school has a pastoral residential campus of spacious lawns and manicured gardens, carefully coordinated Georgian buildings (a unique shade of red brick must be used in all construction), admissions policies that are unashamedly selective (student SATs average in the 1200s), and a traditional-age student body drawn from all fifty states. Nearly a third of Miami's seventeen thousand undergraduates come from outside Ohio, as do more than half of student applicants. Also like that of many private universities, Miami's undergraduate curriculum is firmly grounded in the liberal arts, with an emphasis on preprofessional training. Miami is the state's largest supplier of premedical and prelaw graduates and is second only to Ohio State in its number of science and math majors. Outside Ohio, many people mistakenly believe the school to be a private university.

But despite this widespread impression, Miami is most assuredly public—not only with respect to state ownership but also because of its mission to serve the workforce needs of Ohio. The university has two open-admissions regional campuses that support their local communities in Hamilton and Middletown, Ohio, an education school, a nursing program, and a large business school. The school's NCAA Division I-A intercollegiate sports program has been a training ground for many of the nation's top college and professional coaches.

To me, all of these qualities—smart students, strong academic reputation, manageable size, beautiful campus, and commitment to the liberal arts—added up to an unbeatable package. As a fledgling president, I therefore began my job confident that my new academic home had the strengths, values, and reputation to "move to the next level," as the trustees wanted. Our budgets were balanced, applications were strong, and the faculty, alumni, and trustees seemed infused with a sense of optimism that sounded very different from some of the grim scenarios I was hearing from other public college presidents.

But I had scarcely unpacked my desk contents when cracks began to appear in the picture. For example, I quickly learned that University Senate leaders were upset about faculty salaries, which had slipped well behind comparable private university salaries and were now barely keeping up with those at our public counterparts. I learned that the maintenance needs of our physical plant had been creeping upward, with accumulated deferred maintenance whose costs would greatly exceed our annual renovation budget. Even more ominously, I learned of chronic declines in our biennial subsidy from the Ohio legislature. With its clunky, rust-belt economy, Ohio seemed forever to be stuck in an economic slump. And even in those occasional years when the Ohio economy upticked, appropriations to higher education never seemed to make up for ground previously lost.

Miami's undergraduate tuition charges also posed an ever-present challenge. With the highest public-university tuition in the state (in 1996, our Ohio students paid $5,100), Miami always appeared as the lead entry in the table that invariably accompanied Ohio newspaper exposés of the soaring cost of a college degree. Furthermore, I soon learned that the case justifying our relatively high tuition—small classes, exemplary student services, historic commitment to teaching, internal cost-saving measures, and the like—had generally fallen on deaf ears. From the viewpoint of many elected officials, tuitions were high because universities, Miami included, had been wasting taxpayer dollars. In their view, universities were hidebound bastions of inefficiency, bloated with administrators (a claim that struck a chord with some faculty members on the University Senate) and also with unproductive tenured professors (a claim that did not strike a chord). Universities had been wasting student tuition dollars on expensive frills like climbing walls, luxurious residence halls, and student unions, while allowing faculty members to fritter away their working hours on research projects that had no possible economic benefit—that did not, as was frequently heard in the Ohio General Assembly, "create jobs in Ohio."

For a former university president it is tempting to dismiss such criticism as cheap shots. For decades, higher education has been an easy target for politicians. But no matter what their motivations, the concerns of Ohio legislators mirrored a growing despair in the Ohio body politic. From the perspective of many families, a public college education in Ohio was becoming unaffordable. To struggling, debt-saddled middle-class Ohioans, the reasons didn't matter a whit. The only relevant facts were that (a) a college degree is a ticket to a better life and (b) the price of that ticket was growing out of reach. Public university presidents and their governing boards ignore such concerns at their peril.

Four years passed, and then the dawn of the new century provided an opportunity for Miami to take stock of its accomplishments and look at its long-term future. In 2000 I launched a comprehensive strategic plan, "First in 2009" (the date being the occasion of the university's upcoming bicentennial). Like most university strategic plans, "First in 2009" set forth general goals to improve teaching and research, upgrade facilities, revitalize the curriculum, increase alumni giving, recruit a more diverse student body, and provide improved support for the faculty. However, the real meat of the plan was a formal commitment to quantitative benchmarking and assessment. Departments and offices were asked to define specific metrics for measuring the progress toward their strategic goals and to keep detailed records of that progress.

Despite some pushback from a few academic departments whose faculty didn't like the idea of administrators keeping tabs on their activities, most of the campus seemed generally tolerant of the exercise, and in some quarters there was actually enthusiasm about it. Soon we were awash in charts, trend lines, and survey results on everything from student opinions about residence hall food, to the number of flu shots administered by Student Health Services, to the trunk diameters of the thousands of trees dotting the central campus. We also, of course, compiled reams of financial information: revenues, expenditures, cash reserves, investment returns, debt-service ratios, scholarship awards, student loan defaults, research grants, federal indirect cost recovery, and so forth.

This was not data collecting for its own sake. Our goal was to map out quantitatively the strengths and weaknesses of the institution and then to use that information as the basis for costing out the university's long-term strategic goals. As part of this exercise, our finance office developed a computer model for predicting future budgets. Inputs to the model included estimates of future interest rates, inflation, endowment growth, changes in state subsidy, and enrollment trends. The projected costs of all the "First in 2009" initiatives were plugged into the model, as were best-guess predictions about future salary and benefits increases, energy costs, tuition charges, and needs of operating budgets. Eventually, after a number of iterations, the model spun out a decade's worth of year-by-year predictions, all aimed at answering the question: would Miami University be able to balance its budget for the upcoming decade, while simultaneously embarking on planned initiatives, meeting the faculty and staff payroll, servicing bond debt, and maintaining the physical plant and infrastructure?

Obviously no financial projection can be more accurate than its beginning assumptions, and there was certainly plenty of murkiness in our model, especially for the decade's outlying years. But even after the uncertainties were taken into consideration, even after a best-case scenario where all the error bars lined up in their most favorable directions was assumed, the results of the exercise were worrisome. It became clear to me that Miami University was headed for trouble down the road, not in the current year, nor even the next two or three years, but over the long haul. Furthermore, it seemed there was no obvious way we could fend off a future budget confrontation, short of altering for the worse the character of the university and compromising the quality of its programs. The problem appeared largely on the revenue side of the ledger. No matter how we crunched the numbers, our projected revenues—tuition and state subsidy being the largest pieces—just couldn't keep up with inflation, projected costs of energy and health benefits, growing litigation expenses, expanding regulatory requirements, equipment replacement, and other semifixed costs over which the university had little control. (In the first five years of the new century, the state appropriation for the university declined 21 percent.)

This information was not well received by my trustees, and at their urging we also looked closely at the impact of cutting expenditures—closing programs, scaling back nonessential services, implementing group purchasing agreements with other universities, and embracing other schemes for reallocating dollars and reducing expenses. Obviously these would help, but in the end I felt they were mostly temporary fixes that would only stay the day of reckoning. Over the next decade, holding down class sizes, serving the basic needs of students, and maintaining the campus infrastructure were shaping up to be major challenges. Restoring faculty salaries to competitive levels began to seem like a distant dream.

The grand challenge of economics is learning to see the forest for the trees, to understand, for example, how a tariff change on textiles in Beijing can cause famine on an African plain. As I reviewed the spreadsheets on my desk, however, the forest gradually came into view: the university had been caught in the grip of global trends that were not of its making and over which it had no influence. The chain of logic was straightforward. Miami could not count on significant increases in state appropriation because the state did not have the money to appropriate. The state was short of money because federal entitlements, roads, prisons, K–12 education, deteriorating inner cities, and the needs of an aging population were depleting the treasury. The treasury could not be adequately replenished because Ohio taxpayers were already bleeding from layoffs, plant closings, growing medical costs, and the loss of jobs to overseas manufacturers. The bottom line was that the university's financial future was being jeopardized by an unfortunate confluence of powerful demographic, social, and economic forces that had nothing to do with higher education.

These same forces were also jeopardizing the financial future of middle-income Ohio families, and the fact that Ohio public college tuitions ranked among the nation's highest compounded their struggles. Tuition in the state was high because historically Ohio's universities had been forced to shift their costs disproportionately to students to make up for inadequate state support. This was not a new development; Miami and its sister universities were slowly marching down a trend line that had started a half-century earlier.

What was particularly worrisome, however, is that we were still only in midtrend with no end in sight. None of these adverse demographic, social, and economic forces would abate in the coming years, and there was plenty of evidence to suggest they would get worse. To me, the combined effect was unambiguous: Miami and other public universities, in a decades-long struggle to remain solvent, had gradually been pricing out low-income families from a college education. With its high tuition, my own university was at the forefront of a movement to price out middle-income families as well.

Our own data were very clear on this point. Miami's financial aid and admissions offices track the socioeconomic status of each year's entering class, and I had observed for some time the growing affluence of our student body. Anecdotal evidence abounded: the private jets that dropped students off at the university airport at the beginning of each semester, the BMWs and SUVs in the student parking lots, the upscale restaurants in Oxford crowded each night with undergraduates—all evidence that Miami was increasingly drawing its students from upper-income families. By 2000, the median family income of Miami undergraduates was over $100,000 per year, and the fastest-growing income segment was the $250,000-and-over category. Obviously, these are not typical numbers for a public university. In fact, in comparison to most public colleges, there is little about Miami that is typical. The large majority of American public universities have nonselective or minimally selective admissions and attract a preponderance of nontraditional adult students who hold jobs, frequently enroll part time, and struggle to raise their families on incomes that are far smaller than those of Miami students.

But despite these differences, Miami shares one thing in common with its public sisters: in the end, all are subject to the same impersonal forces of economics. And if a Miami University sees a looming confrontation with economic reality ahead, what are the facts of life for public colleges not blessed by a growing surplus of applications, upper-income students, and a strong national reputation? To the extent Miami sees problems in its future, many of the nation's revenue-starved public campuses are staring into the abyss.

It seemed to me that Miami had only two obvious options for coping with the new century's fiscal realities—and neither was desirable. (The university had already pumped up its fund-raising and was continuously embracing cost-saving measures and efficiencies; barring fundamental structural changes, future improvements in these areas were likely to be incremental.) The first option was to raise tuition even higher, admit more non-Ohio students (who paid higher, nonresident fees) and scale back on financial aid. While theoretically Miami had the reputation and application pressure to take these steps, I knew the political climate in the state wouldn't permit it. Ohio legislators had a long track record of imposing statewide caps on tuition, and my senior staff and I believed that any large attempted tuition increase or expansion of the nonresident student cohort would play very poorly in Columbus and likely result in punitive legislation. More fundamentally, however, such a step would only aggravate Miami's affordability problem. The trustees and I strongly believed that Miami's public mission required us to provide educational opportunities for all citizens. This first option, I felt, ran the risk of turning us into a boutique college for upper-income families from Shaker Heights and the Chicago North Shore. (Chicago's tony New Trier High School had already become Miami's biggest feeder school.) One of my key goals as president was to make the university more accessible to lower- and middle-income students. Raising tuition while decreasing financial aid would take us in exactly the wrong direction.

However, the second option was even grimmer. If the Ohio legislature would not allow the university to raise tuition enough to cover its costs, and if the university could not plan on making up the gap with state support, then to balance the books, the university would have no choice but soon to begin performing surgery on itself. We would have to replace expensive permanent faculty with low-paid temporary instructors. Class sizes would grow to drive down the unit cost of instruction. We would scale back advising and student support services, reduce maintenance of our buildings and grounds, and eliminate programs that could not pay their own way. Smaller operating budgets would force us to drop some intercollegiate sports teams, reduce the number of student organizations, and curtail public lectures and other campus events. Our faculty and staff salaries and employee benefits would deteriorate, forcing us to fill future vacancies from the shallow end of the job pool. The list goes on and on.

Of course, once we had started down this road, there would be no turning back. These changes would soon begin to undermine the university's reputation and competitive standing, with a concomitant drop in student applications. Because people inevitably shun losing teams, our nonresident enrollments would decline, as would gift giving from upset alumni. Our less qualified faculty would become less competitive at attracting grants and contracts, thus further aggravating the revenue picture. On bad days, I could see Miami heading down the path already trod by a growing number of beleaguered public universities—toward a destination of run-down concrete block buildings, dilapidated lecture halls, crowded remedial classes, frustrated unionized professors, and legions of underpaid temporary instructors.

In point of fact, by 2000, Miami had already taken a few steps down that road. Having sustained a half-century of state cutbacks, the university had nearly reached the limiting point of its ability to sustain revenues. As a result, class sizes had begun to eke upwards, from an average of 20 students to about 25. The number of part-time temporary faculty nearly doubled between 1998 and 2004, and in 2004 these instructors were teaching half of the undergraduate credit hours on the school's Oxford campus. Faculty salaries had slipped, and labor unrest on campus was growing. (In 2004, the university had the first union work stoppage in its 195-year history.) And all of this despite years of tuition increases that had outstripped the Consumer Price Index.

Miami University's woes have mirrored those of numerous public universities across the United States. In 2006, the University of Florida system was hoping for a 7 percent tuition increase, at roughly twice the inflation rate. But according to Mark Rosenberg, chancellor of the system, "that [wouldn't] even put a dent in the university system's needs."[1] By 2008, the financial situation had significantly worsened, and in May of that year University of Florida president Bernie Machen announced a plan to eliminate 430 positions and slash the university budget by $47 million.[2]

In 2006, the *Los Angeles Times* reported that the University of California's star-studded Berkeley campus, regarded by many as the best public university in the nation, "has nearly $600 million in deferred maintenance costs and struggles to keep roofs patched, pipes sound, and heating and ventilation systems working. It no longer washes windows, waxes floors, replaces worn carpets, or paints interior walls."[3] In 2006, the Ohio Board of Regents reported that Ohio's thirteen public universities had accumulated $5 billion of deferred maintenance, an amount ten times the Ohio higher-education biennial appropriation for renovation. Similar stories continue to emerge nearly every month. The deferred maintenance backlog at the University of Maryland at College Park, $620 million; at the University of Illinois at Urbana-Champaign, $500 million; at the State University of New York system, $3.2 billion.[4]

And as the physical plants of the nation's public campuses slowly deteriorate, so does the quality of its faculty. Fifty years ago, professor salaries at public colleges were higher than the salaries of their private counterparts. Today, professor salaries at public universities lag those at the privates by an average of $21,270.[5] Increasingly, students at public colleges are being taught by professors who aren't competitive enough to land well-paying jobs in the private sector.

So the problems at Miami University, although colored by Miami's particular academic niche, are hardly unique. Across the country, the handwriting on the wall is clear: tuition growth is gradually pricing out middle-class Americans from a college degree by imposing a $50,000–$100,000 burden on the families of both traditional and nontraditional students. And paradoxically, even while their tuition charges are soaring, revenue-starved public campuses are in a long-term state of decline that shows no sign of reversing.

There has been no shortage of proposed solutions for these problems. Many books, conferences, and commissions have analyzed escalating college tuitions and have advanced ideas for reining in costs: eliminating frills, overhauling cumbersome governance practices, replacing tenure with employment contracts, requiring professors to teach more and spend less time on research, outsourcing the management of dining and residence halls, and scaling back merit-based scholarships in favor of need-based scholarships.

Other proposals basically amount to pleading for more government support: public relations campaigns about the value of a college degree, lobbying for expanding state and federal grants and loans, and a flurry of presidential and chancellor op-ed pieces during each budget cycle urging lawmakers to bump higher education up their list of priorities. All of these ideas are well-intentioned, some make good sense, a few fall in the wishful thinking department. But at the end of the day, when one adds up the cumulative impact of this creative effort, one has to face the stark reality that little of it has worked. The reason is that these kinds of solutions do not address the problem's root causes. They are like the dying Western town whose city fathers try to turn back the clock by sprucing up the town square, offering tax incentives to businesses, and running ad campaigns in magazines—all of which are fine ideas, but none of which face the fact that the rail line has moved.

There is no turning back the clock. As much as we might all hope for vibrant public universities that are well supported by tax dollars, with fees low enough to educate all Americans who aspire to better themselves, those days will not return. They will not return because twenty-first-century America is different from twentieth-century America. Its population is older and needier, its overseas competitors are smarter and more focused, and its potent manufacturing base is shrinking. America of the twenty-first century is also fabulously wealthy, but the gap between its rich and poor citizens has widened. Many of the country's inner cities have become pockets of poverty and social dysfunction, even while multimillion-dollar homes and luxury car dealerships sprout like gilt-edged dandelions across the suburban landscape.

The best jobs in twenty-first-century America require specialized knowledge—the kind of knowledge that can best be obtained via a college education. The ability to write and speak well, to understand a language other than one's native tongue, to think quantitatively, to grasp abstract concepts, to understand contexts, and to acquire habits of curiosity and mental discipline are key ingredients for success in a knowledge-based economy. Thus, while twenty-first-century America is still a land of unparalleled opportunity, that opportunity comes with educational prerequisites that didn't exist in earlier decades. When a quarter of America's 300 million citizens cannot afford those prerequisites, they are effectively being cut off from the American dream and the hope it provides for a better life. If the great American experiment in democracy ever founders, it will not be because we have failed to solve the problem of poverty. "The poor will always be with us," Jesus observed twenty centuries ago, no doubt correctly. Preserving the equality of opportunity is the core challenge for America's leaders, not achieving a utopian dream of income parity. For this reason, the well-being of the public universities and colleges that educate 75 percent of the country's college graduates is of paramount importance. The stakes are too high to let this important national resource wither by neglect and shortsightedness.

As a step toward responding to these challenges, on April 23, 2003, the Miami University trustees approved a plan that radically restructured the school's undergraduate tuition policy. The goals of the new tuition policy were twofold: the primary goal was to increase the affordability of a Miami education for Ohio residents, and the second was to lay the groundwork for stabilizing the university's future revenue base. On paper, the new tuition plan was deceptively simple: the university would raise the base tuition charged to Ohio residents (at the time, $8,350) to the same amount charged nonresidents ($18,100). To offset this increase of nearly 120 percent, the university pledged to offer scholarships to Ohio students. These scholarships would vary according to an individual's financial need, but all Ohioans would receive a guaranteed minimum award.

Scratch the plan's surface, however, and it turned out to be anything but simple. The plan's announcement had followed an intense two years of development. For the plan to work we really had to understand the university's competitive market position, both inside and outside Ohio. It was necessary for us to upgrade our admission practices, revising timetables, correspondence with applicants, and application reviews. We restructured our financial aid practices. We developed new marketing, recruitment, and public relations strategies. And, of course, we had to lay the political groundwork for acceptance of the concept by Ohio elected officials.

As of this writing, the university has accumulated four years of data on the plan's workings. There is no doubt that it has succeeded in making Miami University more affordable for middle-income Ohio students. In the first year, enrollments from first-generation college-bound students jumped 40 percent and minority enrollments climbed 25 percent, and these increases have held steady or climbed in subsequent years. All information to date confirms that needy Ohioans, on average, pay less to attend the university than they would have before the plan. There were also some positive outcomes that we had not anticipated. Our nonresident applications surged 15 percent after the plan's announcement, even though the new structure had no financial impact on nonresidents. And surprisingly, applications from Ohio jumped 8 percent, not only from lower and middle-income residents but also from wealthier applicants who would be required to pay more to attend the university.

These results were obviously a great relief for me, the trustees, and my senior staff. The plan was a huge risk for the university—a calculated risk, but a huge risk nonetheless. We had worried that our domestic applications might plummet, precipitating an enrollment catastrophe, and that the sticker shock of suddenly doubling our already-high Ohio tuition might scare off the very students whom we wanted the plan to benefit. We had worried about how the Ohio media would react to our announcement, burying the facts about the new scholarships beneath headlines about the percentage tuition increase. We had worried that we had miscalculated the price sensitivity of our applicant pool; we knew that if too many low-income students and too few upper-income students enrolled, we could have an immediate cash flow problem. But in the end, the trustees and I had felt the risk was worth taking because the alternative was so grim. As president, I could not allow the university to drift down a path that would lead inevitably to mediocrity and to abrogation of its public responsibilities. Miami's tuition plan was an action born of necessity.

However, today the job is only partially completed, Miami has taken the steps needed to improve affordability for its own students, but while it may have laid the groundwork for stabilizing its financial future, this second goal cannot be realized in the absence of larger systemic reforms.

Thus this is not a book about Miami's tuition plan. It is, instead, mostly about reforming the economic model of public higher education. This is an important point. I do not want to tout Miami's plan as a template for other institutions. The plan (described in detail in appendix A) is idiosyncratic to my university and its niche in the higher-education marketplace. In fact, of the 643 public four-year colleges and universities in the country,[6] there are probably no more than a dozen that could directly benefit from a similar practice. However, I see the Miami tuition plan as an illustration of several key economic principles that can help states and their public university systems be proactively responsive to the destructive forces acting on them. I am writing this book, therefore, in part because I believe that these forces have not been adequately understood and respected outside academia.

But another part of my message goes beyond economics. Systemic reform of public higher education also requires that public universities allow themselves to be reformed. In my experience, university communities, their faculties in particular, are apprehensive about having change agendas imposed upon them by governors, state legislatures, government task forces, or even their own campus administrations. The academic culture is complex and subtle, to the point of being mystifying to those outside the campus gates. And while that culture, grounded in the protection of academic freedom and the free exchange of ideas, is undisputedly one of the great strengths of American higher education, it is also, paradoxically, a major point of vulnerability. For that reason much of this book is also devoted to the culture of academia and the crucial role of academic leaders—university presidents, chancellors, and governing boards—within that culture. This is a complex subject, with complex problems not amenable to easy solutions. Yet reforming the cultural model of academia is just as important as reforming its economic model. Until both of these challenges are faced with courage and an open mind by academicians, members of the public, and their elected representatives, I am convinced there is virtually no hope that America's public universities can be extracted from their current downward drift.

As one might expect, there is a voluminous research and scholarly literature about higher education and its problems and challenges. Virtually every topic touched upon in this book—marketplace forces and public university financing, the rising cost of a college education, the academic culture, shared governance traditions, the university presidency, academic administration and governing boards, university admissions and financial aid practices, state legislatures and public higher education policy—has been studied in depth by higher education scholars and researchers.

However, this book is not intended to be a scholarly work for specialists. In fact, it is not a research-based book at all. It is rather a personal narrative about public higher education's problems and potential solutions, drawn primarily from my experience as a long-term university faculty member and administrator and intended for readers seeking a broad-brush view of the subject. But because the view from the trenches is necessarily limited, I hope interested readers will turn to the select bibliography (appendix C, "Suggested Readings") of excellent recent works in order to flesh out their understanding and to appreciate more fully the history and larger context for my analysis and recommendations.

Acknowledgments

Top billing goes to Carole Garland, my wife and life companion, who read every version of every paragraph in the manuscript and who subordinated her hopes of exploring and enjoying our new Santa Fe environs while I holed up in my office for eighteen months. I am most grateful for her endless support and patience. I am also greatly indebted to my neighbor, good friend, and former boss Richard Sisson, provost emeritus of Ohio State University, whose critical reading and many suggestions greatly improved the manuscript. Several of my former Miami University colleagues also provided invaluable comments, especially Professors Karen and Adeed Dawisha, who were consistently helpful and supportive even though I know some of the book's assertions rubbed them the wrong way. Miami Professors Marek and Anna Dollar also made many helpful suggestions.

I am particularly grateful for the candid and excellent advice of my former colleague Miami University Provost Jeffrey Herbst, who always told me what I needed to hear, not what I wanted to hear, a pattern that he continued from back in the days when I signed his paycheck. My longtime Ohio State colleague and friend Professor Ronald Rosbottom, now at Amherst College, is one of the best—if most brutal—manuscript editors I have ever known and spent hours stripping out clunky language. Thanks, Ron.

I also want to express my appreciation to the Miami University trustees for their decade of support during my tenure as Miami's president. And special thanks go to my friend and former board chairman Roger Howe, who worked with me on a near-daily basis to clean the bugs out of Miami's unusual tuition plan, the foundation upon which the proposals in this book are built.

Three final acknowledgments: to my daughter, Elizabeth Garland, whose anthropological insights into the university culture proved very valuable; to Deborah Mason, my former secretary and frequent coconspirator, whose good humor, sharp instincts, and common sense I have benefited from for many years; and to my editor, Elizabeth Branch Dyson, whose encouragement, insight, and suggestions greatly improved the final product.

Introduction

Public higher education reflects a commitment by the government to the people of the nation. When the North Carolina General Assembly chartered the University of North Carolina on December 11, 1789, it laid the cornerstone for a sprawling educational empire on a scale unprecedented in history. After the Morrill Land Grant Act of 1862, that empire acquired a uniquely American imprint: henceforth, higher education in America would no longer be the province of only the clergy, the wealthy, and the elite.

During the next century, America's public colleges evolved into an extraordinary resource for all Americans, rich and poor, from all ethnic, racial, and religious backgrounds, and from all social classes. That any citizen with brains and determination should be allowed to benefit from an advanced education became the educational embodiment of the American dream. What made the dream work was an implicit compact between state governments and the schools they had created. All taxpayers would support the colleges, and in exchange colleges would keep their fees low enough to embrace citizens from the most humble circumstances. For a century this concept worked superbly, allowing millions of Americans[1] to lead better and more fulfilling lives and fueling the economic development of what would become the wealthiest nation on the planet.

This historic compact between public campuses and government is what in future chapters I refer to as the traditional "business plan" of public higher education. The central premise of this book is that despite its past success, this business plan has stopped working and that it will not be possible to turn back the clock. After some introductory groundwork is laid, we shall see precisely what is meant by this assertion.

In general terms, a business plan is an economic model that governs the relationship between an organization's income and its expenditures. In public higher education, the income is primarily the money coming from the state and student tuition payments, and the expenditures are the dollars spent to hire professors, maintain buildings, advise students, conduct research, and fulfill myriad other public responsibilities. In any viable business plan, there obviously has to be an equilibrium between income and expenditures, and when commercial businesses fail, it is because something has disrupted this equilibrium. Often, failure results from bad management—an inability to control costs, or ineffective marketing, or poorly designed products. Organizations can have perfectly good business plans and still fail if they are poorly run.

On the other hand, an organization with a bad business plan can never succeed no matter how well it is managed. A defective business plan means that there is a structural flaw in the business's core concept. Once successful commercial business plans typically go bad because of the changing environment: consumer tastes change, or technology advances render a product line obsolete. For companies, the uncaring gods of the marketplace are the final arbiter of a business plan's viability and execution. When revenues begin to fall below expenditures, the laws of supply and demand set the company on a one-way road to the bankruptcy court.

The business plan of public higher education is also affected by a changing environment, but in a very different way from that of a commercial enterprise. For public universities, the marketplace forces of supply and demand have historically had little impact on either revenues or expenditures. The revenues of a public university are determined mostly by what state governments give them (through a state appropriation) and permit them to have (by controlling their tuition charges). Expenditures, on the other hand, are simply matched to whatever revenues a campus receives. If the state gives a university more money, its expenditures climb proportionately. If the state reduces the money, then the university retrenches and cuts spending. Therefore, in public higher education, revenues and expenditures are *always* in balance, by design and not because they are conforming to the pressures of a competitive market. In other words, the performance of a public university is not subject to the laws of supply and demand. Excellent universities and mediocre universities can coexist in the same state, each having a balanced budget, each enrolling students, each receiving revenues, and each enduring in perpetuity.

So what does it mean to assert that the business plan of public higher education is no longer working? By what metrics can one verify this statement? We will consider this topic in detail in chapter 1, but for now I merely note that performance metrics are a mix of quantitative and subjective criteria. One indicator of a successful business plan is whether public universities meet the needs of their students: Are students receiving a rigorous, high-quality education, with small classes and attentive, skilled professors? Do support services—health care, job placement, groups and clubs and other activities—satisfy the extracurricular needs of students? Another performance metric is the quality of the campus infrastructure. Are classrooms and dormitories clean and well maintained? Are campuses attractive and safe? Are laboratories well stocked with modern equipment? Are employees satisfied with their jobs?

However, in and of itself neither of these metrics fully answers the question about the viability of the business plan. A company can have a great product, but if it is priced so high that customers stay away, then it will eventually fail. By analogy, a public university can offer a great education, but if it prices itself so high that most people cannot afford to attend, then the university is also failing—not because its expenditures are exceeding its revenues, since that cannot happen, but in fulfillment of its public mission. Much has been written about the growing lack of "affordability" of a college education. Newspapers are filled with charts showing how college tuition outstrips inflation, and the topic is a favorite among frustrated legislators, government commissions, advisory groups, conferences, and think tanks. In 2007, the average in-state tuition and fees at public four-year institutions was $6,185, an increase of 6.6 percent over the previous year. As noted by the College Board, this increase was actually less than the average rates of growth over the previous five years.[2]

At my own university, over the fourteen-year period from 1989 to 2003, undergraduate tuition increased by 260 percent, or 18.6 percent per year.[3] Over the same period, the Consumer Price Index increased only 48 percent, or 3.4 percent per year. Thus over this fourteen-year span, tuition at Miami University rose at an annual rate that averaged more than five times the rate of inflation! During these years, Ohio public universities instituted unusually rapid tuition increases to try to make up for large cutbacks in state support. For reasons such as this, by almost any measure, the price of attending a public university has skyrocketed in the past two decades, with no sign of abatement.

But what exactly does it mean to say that public universities are becoming "unaffordable"? There is an important subtlety buried in that word. For example, during the fourteen years in which Miami University's tuition was rapidly growing, applications to the university were surging. Furthermore, all across Ohio, enrollments at state universities were climbing despite record increases in tuition charges. Clearly, this growth was not fueled by prosperity among Ohio citizens. Ohio has long been plagued by a lethargic economy. It is one of the few states where the relative standard of living has declined in recent years, with personal incomes that have fallen below the national average.[4] And so the prices charged to attend Ohio's public universities, although among the highest in the nation, were clearly not "unaffordable" in the literal sense, since hundreds of thousands of Ohio college students were willing and able to pay them, often going heavily into debt to do so.

It would be a serious error, however, to conclude that robust public-university enrollments during times of rapid tuition growth mean that universities are merely charging "what the market will bear." In fact, there is no real market. Aside from talented high school athletes and academic superstars, who are always in demand and can write their ticket, state residents who want to obtain a four-year college education have only three choices. They can attend a public university in their home state, where their educational expenses are partially subsidized by the state. They can attend public universities in other states, where they pay much higher, nonresident tuition charges. Or they can attend a private college or university, where they will pay even higher tuition charges. Most students wanting to exercise the lowest-cost option have no choice but to pay what their home state permits its public campuses to charge.[5] And because taxpayers realize that a college education is vital to their well-being in this new century, they are willing to make whatever sacrifices are necessary to pay the going price of admission—even if it means taking out another mortgage on their home, going heavily into debt, or forgoing many of the amenities of a middle-class lifestyle.

In essence—and this the subtlety referred to previously—state universities are quasi-monopolistic providers of higher education. Their public subsidies give them a price advantage that discourages competitors, making it possible for them to lock up the low end of the market in their state. The product they provide—a four-year college education—is increasingly indispensable, and the purchasers of that product—college students—can either pay the price or abandon their college aspirations.

Imagine that your local power company suddenly raised its prices and started billing a thousand dollars a month for electricity. You would be furious, but you would make whatever sacrifices are necessary to pay the bill because you cannot live without electricity. Substitute "college education" for "electricity" and you've captured the essence of the college affordability problem. But we should not push this analogy too far. A power company is a regulated monopoly whose prices, like those of most public universities, are dictated by the government. However, the basis for the power company's controlled prices is the cost of production. In other words, government regulators look at the cost of producing electricity and then use that figure to determine how much revenue the utility will be allowed to collect from its customers.

Public higher education works in exactly the reverse manner. States first decide how much revenues they will permit universities to receive, through controlling tuition charges and setting appropriation levels, and then the universities adjust their costs to match those revenues. Revenues almost always ratchet upward because declines result in campus layoffs, wage freezes, larger class sizes, and inadequate maintenance, none of which governments desire for their campuses. Therefore campus costs— expenditures—also keep ratcheting upward in order to balance the revenue growth. If pressures on state budgets make appropriation increases impossible, then tuition becomes the fudge factor that takes up the slack to prop revenues up into the positive territory.

As the societal needs of an aging population, dysfunctional inner cities, road maintenance, and K–12 education have increasingly depleted state treasuries, tuitions have carried an ever larger share of the university revenue burden.[6] The bottom line is that public universities, state governments, and taxpayers are caught in a chicken-and-egg upward spiral: costs chase revenues chase costs, all buttressed by soaring college tuitions, with no end in sight and no obvious way to break out of the cycle.

One would think that with their revenues growing year after year, fueled by appropriation and tuition increases, public universities would by now have become bastions of luxury. But one of the paradoxical consequences of this cycle is that, despite the money pouring into them, public universities are in a chronic state of deterioration. I will have much to say about this deterioration in future chapters, but the symptoms are everywhere: growing maintenance needs of physical plants, lagging salaries of public university professors, a growing underclass of poorly paid temporary instructors, and a surge in the number and aggressiveness of public university faculty unions. One of the most puzzling aspects of the entire public higher-education dilemma is why campuses always seem starved for revenues, even while those revenues keep climbing. Where in the world does all the money go, and why is it never enough? What keeps driving up the costs?[7]

I was president of Miami University during half of the fourteen-year period when the university's tuition increases grew 18 percent per year, and even though the state appropriation increases were minimal, we still saw significant yearly increases in our total revenues. Each year at budget time we would look at our costs, and it was always discouraging to see how they grew. Energy costs, health care costs for employees, maintenance expenses, salary raises—all of these kept climbing in a relentless upward march. Even though our revenue was also growing, usually faster than inflation, our projected costs always seemed to grow faster. Thus during those years, the university implemented hiring freezes, clamped down on operating budgets, and took other difficult steps to keep our books balanced.

But what we never did in all those years, and what public universities almost never do, was try to save money by *becoming more productive*. It never occurred to us, for example, that public corporations also face increases in health care and energy costs, that they also want to give salary raises to their employees, and that they also need to maintain their physical plants—and that successful corporations can do all of these things without increasing prices of their goods and services at a rate any higher than the inflation rate. In point of fact, public universities are among the least efficient enterprises in America, and the burden of that inefficiency is borne on the shoulders of Americans who desperately want to educate themselves and their families and have no other options.

Half of this book focuses on the inefficiencies inherent in the academic culture of public universities, and the other half focuses on their economic model. However, it would be a mistake to think that the two topics are decoupled. On the contrary, I will show how the economic model drives the culture and how the traditional academic business plan, a plan based on government appropriation and regulation, actually exacerbates and encourages campus inefficiency and waste—in other words, worsening the very problems that it is trying to solve.

This book is a proposal for breaking the destructive cycle that is driving up the price of a college education while at the same time eroding the quality of America's public universities. The concept underlying the proposal is to introduce competition into the equation by expanding taxpayer options for education. If students have other choices, then public universities lose their quasi-monopolistic status, thus freeing the enormous power of market forces to shape their organizational behavior. When an organization depends on a market to provide the money that is its lifeblood, then it will do everything possible to satisfy the needs of that market. If it fails to meet those needs as well as its competitors do, the organization cannot long survive. However, if an organization is buffered from market forces by government subsidies, third-party payments, or other sources of revenue that are not tied to its performance, as is currently the case in public higher education, then it will naturally focus its energy on sustaining those revenues rather than serving market needs.

Of course, markets create both winners and losers, and they impose no moral judgment on the outcome of the contest. Thus, if society depends on a market to accomplish a social good, in this case making an affordable college education available to its citizens, then the market's ground rules must be structured carefully to ensure the desired outcome. For this reason my proposal maintains an important role for government oversight of public universities. It does not advocate privatization of public higher education; rather, it calls for a limited deregulation of the nation's public four-year colleges. This partial deregulation would stimulate competition, redirect institutional energies toward serving students and other external constituencies, enhance efficiency, stimulate responsiveness and adaptability, and hold down costs. With careful planning, all these benefits can be achieved, while the historic American commitment to academic freedom and an affordable, high-quality education for all citizens who desire it and can benefit from it is preserved.

And now to work, because time is running short.

Part I

A Primer on Public Higher Education Economics

1

Where the Money Comes From

Do Universities Have a Bottom Line?

Question: Why do economists predict their results to three significant figures?
Answer: Because they have a sense of humor.

This old joke about the dismal science underscores the fact that real markets do not replicate the simple, idealized models that economists use to illustrate basic principles. For even the most straightforward commodity transactions, complicating factors—taxes, regulations, social costs, buyer irrationality, and so forth—inevitably fog up the quantitative predictions of simple market analysis. In the process of explaining the real world of business and commerce, corrections grow on economic theories like so many Malthusian warts, leading to models that may account for a market's general behavior but have little predictive value. As is sometimes said, with enough variables one can fit a curve to the skyline of New York, but the curve can't then predict the location of the next skyscraper.

But at least in the business world there is an overall metric for gauging success, and of course that metric is profit. While General Motors may use many internal measures of performance—market share, sales growth, customer satisfaction—all of these are in service to the corporation's overall profitability. In the language of mathematics, internal performance criteria are independent variables and profitability is a dependent variable. In the end, only the dependent variable matters. That is the reason stock market investors care so much about corporate profits; the actual line of business being financed by their investments may even be of little interest to them except insofar as it provide insights into profit potential.

By contrast, in higher education there is no bottom line except in the sense that colleges must live within their budgets. However, colleges do have a large number of internal performance benchmarks. Many are quantitative but nonfinancial: student SAT scores, graduation rates, win/loss record of the basketball team, percent occupancy of dormitories, number of National Academy of Sciences faculty members, number of pizzas consumed in dining halls. They have many intangible performance benchmarks as well: personal growth of graduates, beauty of the campus, quality of advising and job counseling, contribution to human understanding by English department poets. Furthermore, one can fill a ledger book with college financial benchmarks, including bond quality ratings, federal grant and contract dollars, endowment investment returns, and growth in alumni giving. But all of the benchmarks that ultimately differentiate good universities from mediocre ones are not rolled up into a single criterion of overall performance. In higher education there is nothing analogous to profit, and without this basic metric it is hard to know whether, say, hiring a Nobel laureate for the chemistry department faculty is a smart investment of institutional resources.[1]

A second factor that muddies the economics of higher education is school-to-school variability. Higher education is an industry in which no two organizations produce equivalent products. This is the problem that plagues college ranking systems, the most widely read being the one published annually by *U.S. News and World Report*. For example, in 2008 the magazine ranked the College of William and Mary thirty-second and the University of Michigan twenty-sixth.[2] But the two institutions are so fundamentally different from one another that this comparison provides little meaningful guidance to prospective students. The fact that most ranking services try to use a quantitative methodology and data-gathering protocol can never overcome the intrinsic apples-to-oranges problem of institutional diversity. And just as there is no bottom line to gauge a university's overall financial performance, there is no qualitative measure of its usefulness to society. Which is better: University A, which has Nobel laureates on its faculty, conducts research valued at hundreds of millions of dollars, recruits students from all fifty states whose SAT scores top the charts, and charges $40,000 tuition, or University B, which admits nearly all applicants, most of whom come from nearby working-class neighborhoods, has extensive remedial programs for underprepared students, offers evening and weekend classes for working adults, and charges $4,000 tuition? The answer is clearly in the eye of the beholder.

Despite their broad differences, however, all colleges and universities share one trait in common: they all need money to survive. And the fact that most of that money is influenced greatly by social, demographic and economic forces highlights the importance of making sense of higher education's complex marketplace. Until the academic marketplace is sufficiently understood, policy makers will be hard-pressed to redress the system's more egregious shortcomings and prop up its shaky financial underpinnings.

The University Balance Sheet

Like all commercial organizations, public universities must pay their bills. Because universities are service providers, their biggest payments each month go to their thousands of employees; typically about 70–80 percent of university budgets are for salaries, wages, and benefits. What is left over pays for a hodgepodge of expenses: fertilizer for campus lawns and gardens, bandwidth for Internet gateways, airline tickets to faculty professional meetings, debt service on construction loans, laboratory equipment for beginning physics professors, service contracts for office equipment, and so forth. The largest public universities write checks that total well over two billion dollars a year. Because these payments don't dribble out at a constant rate, and because income from government and tuition payments arrives in lump sums, universities always keep a balance in their accounts to handle expenditure fluctuations. Depending on the size of the school, this cushion, or "float," can average throughout the year to more than a hundred million dollars; university budget officers invest the float in short-term financial instruments so the funds are not sitting idle until needed. Closely related to the float are the institutional cash reserves. As the name implies, the reserves are not budgeted for any specific purpose but are held back to pay for emergencies, to make up for temporary cash shortfalls, and to pay for unpredictable cost increases. Bond rating agencies closely monitor a university's reserves, because they are a key indicator of its financial health.

When times are tough, as they often are in public higher education, a school's chief financial officer will carefully monitor the sizes of the school's float and reserves, because if they shrink too low the results can be disastrous. One late payroll will precipitate an institutional crisis. Missed payments will drive away suppliers of crucially needed goods and services. Any sign of a shaky financial footing will quickly erode the university's credit rating, raising interest rates and potentially preventing access to capital markets. Because nobody wants to stay aboard a sinking ship, a financial crisis will cause the best faculty and staff to dust off their résumés and send prospective students flocking to their backup schools.

Furthermore, most state governments monitor the cash balances of their public colleges, and alarm bells will sound in the state capitol if these drift too low. In fact, if the situation becomes really grim, state government is likely to step in and wrest control of the institution from management. At this point, the reputation of the institution has been devastated, the careers of its senior officers destroyed, and the education of thousands of students placed in jeopardy.[3] The financial meltdown of a public university would inevitably precipitate a statewide political, financial, and social crisis. Because of this fact, of all the priorities of university presidents and their governing boards—hiring top-notch teachers and researchers, satisfying accrediting agencies, attracting a diverse student body, keeping the curriculum up to date—paying the bills trumps the rest.

For a public university, the money needed to pay all those bills pours out of a very large number of spigots. The largest are state subsidy, student tuition and fees, gift income, and research contract and grant income, but to these one can also add investment returns, interest on student loans, dormitory charges, dining-hall meal sales, room rentals in the university hotel and conference centers, ticket sales to campus sporting and cultural events, merchandise and retail sales, facility rental charges, catering income, parking receipts and library fines, bookstore receipts, TV and radio licensing income (for sporting events), and royalties on patents. The list goes on and on, and if the university is home to a medical school and hospital it goes on and on for a very long distance.

This multiplicity of sources contrasts with the revenue profile of most corporations, which typically receive most of their income from product sales or through billing for services. Dependence on a small number of revenue sources helps a business focus its energies, because all corporate activity can be judged against the potential impact on those sources. Historically, the primary source of revenue for public colleges has been a subsidy from their state government, but because the quality of a university's teaching and research was not linked to the size of its subsidy, this beneficial focusing influence was lost. Unlike corporations, public universities have had few purely financial incentives to improve themselves and become more productive.

Although universities have a great many sources of income, nearly all of them have strings attached. What this means is that with few exceptions, the dollars are not fungible. Income from the university conference center cannot be used to hire the basketball coach. Money intended for construction cannot be used to raise faculty salaries, and tuition income cannot be used to build a new wing on the chemistry laboratory. Gifts from alumni nearly always have constraints; a gift intended to create a faculty chair in philosophy cannot be used to provide scholarships for music students. This lack of transferability often leads to misunderstanding and public criticism: how can the university be building a new ice hockey arena when the dorms for first-year students are dilapidated? The answer is that the alumnus who gave twenty million dollars to his alma mater was interested in ice hockey and not in student living conditions.

The New Era of Tuition Primacy

The relative sizes of university revenue spigots have changed greatly over the past several decades.[4] Although a half-century ago the largest revenue source for public campuses was their state government appropriation, that percentage has been in steady decline for several decades.[5] At Miami University, roughly 70 percent of the campus education budget came from this single source. Today, about 70 percent of Miami's revenues come from tuition and only about 15 percent from state appropriation, a percentage that declines slightly each year. The percentages vary from school to school, but the decline in state support relative to tuition income is a universal phenomenon. Cornell economist Ronald Ehrenberg has noted, for example, that the average state appropriation per student at public campuses across the nation dropped about 10 percent between

1985 and 1995.[6] This drop was compensated for by an increase in the tuition share of college expenditures from 23 percent to 32 percent.[7] By 1998 that percentage had grown to 37 percent, and by 2005 it had soared to almost 50 percent.[8] For most public campuses, undergraduate student tuition is now the largest source of income for educational programs.[9]

This transition to tuition as the key revenue source is having a profound impact on public university operations.[10] Students have no influence over the state appropriation that a college receives, but they have a great deal to say about its tuition revenue. If students have choices about where to attend college, then a college's tuition income becomes intrinsically linked to its performance. (The final chapter of this book contains recommendations for increasing college choices for students.) If the college has the freedom to set its own tuition level, its administrators now have to think carefully about pricing its services competitively. And even if its tuition is set by a state legislature, governor, or an external controlling authority, the college must maintain its enrollments in order to protect this revenue source.

Thus there is now a growing financial incentive for public universities to implement careful strategies for recruiting and enrolling students and doing right by them once they set foot on campus. In contrast to prior decades, public universities are increasingly discovering that their financial future is shaped by student demand. This discovery is requiring a campus gestalt shift that can be beneficial for students and the public but is also causing wrenching changes in a campus culture that evolved under a different set of rules.

How Campus Officials View Tuition

Within public university budget offices, attitudes about tuition charges are gradually changing. During the era when a state appropriation was their primary revenue source, campus administrators knew that enrollments were only slightly dependent upon what students were charged. Because the cost of a student's education was so heavily underwritten by the state, student demand depended only weakly on tuition levels. In other words, low public college tuitions attracted millions of students generally but did not significantly influence their choice of which public college to attend. Nonfinancial considerations, such as academic reputation, curricular offerings, and proximity to home and family, were the primary drivers of enrollment decisions.

Because enrollments were only modestly dependent upon tuition, public universities that had the freedom to set their tuition tended to treat it as an independent parameter that could be used to meet expenses. For example, as a dean at Ohio State University, each year I would submit to the central administration a list of "new program" requests for my area, the College of Mathematical and Physical Sciences. Such requests might include laboratory equipment for new professors, salary lines for additional instructors, upgrades for the college's computers, and so forth.[11] In the central offices of the university, my list and those from other deans were vetted by senior administrators and rolled in with projected salary raises, benefits, utilities, plant maintenance, and other university-wide expenditures. In the end, a budget was constructed that reflected the next year's total university revenue needs.

As part of this process, the university also looked at its various sources of revenue, state appropriation in those days being the list's five-hundred-pound gorilla. In spite of considerable lobbying efforts, however, the university normally had little influence over its future appropriation. In fact, about the only real control the university had over major revenues was setting the next year's tuition increase. But it would be an oversimplification to say that tuition was the fudge factor that enabled the university to bring its income into balance with expenditures. The actual process involved a great deal of expense trimming, scaling back expectations, and making numerous compromises, and as part of this process, the potential ramifications of different tuition increases were explored. A key consideration was avoiding backlash from state legislators and the public. The university's annual tuition increase was always splashed across newspapers in Ohio and inevitably generated complaints. The university was thus careful to keep its tuition increase in line with those at other Big Ten universities so it would not attract criticism by being out of step with its peers. There was also a genuine desire among campus leaders to keep increases as low as possible, in order not to harm struggling low-income students. The final proposed percentage increase was the outcome of a careful balancing act between the university's needs and its public responsibilities.

Often all this agonizing came to naught. In many years, the Ohio legislature simply stepped in at the last minute and imposed a system-wide cap on tuition increases that was inevitably lower than what the university needed. Furthermore, this cap was frequently accompanied by an only minimal increase (or even a decrease) in state subsidy. Faced with this twin blow to its revenue base, the university would immediately abandon its hopes for improvement and move into a retrenchment mode, in some years freezing salaries, laying off workers, cutting operating budgets, canceling searches for vacant positions, and deferring building maintenance.

In strategy sessions at Ohio State, the impact of tuition increases on enrollments was seldom a consideration. In those years, the university admitted nearly all applicants,[12] and while enrollments fluctuated with business cycles and the success of the Buckeyes football team, the next year's tuition increase was not a major driver of the numbers. In other words, of all the many considerations that led Ohio State into setting its tuition, the laws of supply and demand were virtually irrelevant.

But today, public universities are in a high-tuition/low-subsidy environment in which they ignore supply and demand at their peril. From an economic perspective, the downside of this new era is the insecurity of a weakened government safety net. The upside is that public campuses, if they make the right strategic decisions, now have some measure of influence over their destiny. And the practical consequence of this changing era is to send public campuses into a single-minded search for tuition revenue.

Who Decides How Much Students Pay?

In contrast to private colleges, where boards of trustees set tuition rates, public campuses typically have little authority to do so independently. A state-by-state survey of public university tuition policies showed that only five states—Delaware, Illinois, Michigan, Pennsylvania, and Wyoming—granted sole authority to their public institutions to set tuition rates. Thirteen other states allowed individual institutions to set rates, but only within a framework of approved guidelines.[13]

The more common pattern is for public college tuition to be determined by an external authority, such as a governor, state legislature, statewide coordinating body, or systemwide governing board. In some states, tuition-setting criteria are based on an explicitly stated philosophy, the most common of which (sixteen states) is that tuition should be as low as possible. Whether the standard is stated explicitly or not, nearly all states emphasize affordability and access as important considerations in their philosophy. As a practical matter, tuition decisions entail yearly incremental adjustments to a base tuition, and as a consequence the public and the media tend to focus on the announced percentage change rather than examining whether the base itself reflects good value or is comparable to that in other states. State decision makers take into account many considerations before announcing a tuition increase, and these may actually have little to do with any underlying philosophy. Typically, states will agree to larger tuition increases if public appropriations are being cut (and smaller increases if the reverse).

In many states, tuition adjustments take the form of "caps" that are imposed on public colleges that otherwise would be able to set their own tuitions. Occasionally some horse-trading takes place, where colleges are given a choice of either accepting a subsidy increase or raising tuition. In 2007, for example, Ohio governor Ted Strickland proposed a 5 percent annual subsidy increase for colleges that agreed to freeze tuition. Individual universities within Ohio then had the opportunity to weigh the revenue implications of each option and make their choice accordingly. Generally speaking, states do their best to make informed and responsible decisions about tuition adjustments. They factor into their decisions the desires of taxpayers for minimal increases, the needs of the colleges, the level of public subsidy to campuses, unemployment rates in the state, financial aid policies, and other considerations that most reasonable people would agree are appropriate. Furthermore, many policy makers want to be better informed about the issue, giving rise to a flurry of commissions, study groups, and workshops charged with studying college affordability.

What states do not do, however, is to allow the forces of supply and demand to influence their decisions.[14] Thus in nearly all states there is an implicit assumption among policy makers that tuition setting at universities by central controlling authorities will better serve the public good than will the impersonal forces of the academic marketplace. Great philosophical battles have been fought over the relative merits of free markets versus regulated markets, and there is little to be gained by again laying out the arguments. Suffice it to say that economists generally believe that government price-fixing of any good or service seldom accomplishes its purpose without creating corollary problems that ultimately dwarf short-term benefits. Here most of us would agree that history is on the side of the economists. Furthermore, the decaying state of public campuses[15] and the growing costs of a college education suggest that one should at least inquire whether ignoring market influences is really desirable in higher education.

Breaking the Cycle of Mutual Finger-Pointing

For whatever reasons, when a state authority sets a low ceiling on allowable tuition increases, it can deprive a campus of the revenue it needs to cover costs. A school in this situation must then make do the best it can, which in the past has often meant minimal or no salary raises for employees, hiring temporary instructors instead of regular faculty, enlarging class sizes, and cutting back services. Despite such problems, public officials are often reluctant to allow universities to set their own prices, believing that the educational marketplace will not impose the constraints needed to prevent runaway tuition increases. To justify their view, legislators can point to many years in which tuition increases at public universities exceeded the inflation rate. To them, a key reason for these large increases is inadequate cost discipline caused by inefficiency and wasteful practices. Thus they see regulating tuition as a way both to protect taxpayers from painful price increases and to pressure decision makers on public campuses to become more committed to reining in expenditures.

Naturally, public college presidents see the problem differently. They often lay the blame for high tuition charges at the feet of lawmakers, whose perceived lack of sympathy for their schools' fiscal needs has resulted in inadequate public subsidy. Had state support kept up with the growing responsibilities of their campuses, presidents argue, then students would not have been forced to shoulder an ever-growing share of their educational costs.

In my opinion, each side is partially correct: the problem of rising public college tuition is driven by a combination of declining state subsidy levels and the inability of universities to exercise the cost discipline that is common for well-managed organizations outside academia. But finger-pointing only perpetuates the cycle. As I will show in future chapters, neither state governments nor public universities can reverse this trend by treating the symptoms; state governments cannot print dollars to make up for inadequate appropriation levels nor regulate campuses into submission over containing costs; and public university leaders cannot by themselves provide the incentives needed to improve the efficiency of their campus operations. What is required is a cooperative effort to rewrite the fundamental relationship between the two parties.

An important key to that new relationship lies in understanding how the forces of supply and demand operate in the academic marketplace.

Can competition really restrain prices, if public colleges mostly enroll students from their immediate neighborhoods? Would decreased government regulation lead to runaway tuition? How does state subsidy influence student demand? Do tuition controls succeed in forcing universities to curtail expenditures? These are the kinds of questions policy makers need answers to if they are to break the discouraging cycle of rising prices and deteriorating campuses.

Market Forces in Higher Education

A Bit of History

One of the premises of this book is that when it comes to moderating tuition increases, controlling costs, and boosting enrollments, the power of the purse ultimately triumphs over good intentions, hope, and the hand of government. If one accepts that premise, then it follows that any public policy that tries to redress public higher education's growing tuition charges, dilapidated facilities, and lagging faculty salaries, as well as the public perception of inefficiency and bureaucratic resistance, must construct economic incentives to shape the desired outcomes. But public higher education's ills did not pop up overnight. The nation's public university system has been on a long-term downward trend line, and it is thus reasonable to ask what has caused that trend. The answer, unsurprisingly, is fundamental economic forces.

In the decades during which state appropriations underwrote the majority of educational expenses, the cost of college was not a major factor in a student's decision to seek an undergraduate degree. For example, in 1961, the year I was a college freshman, a Minnesota resident paid $213 to attend the University of Minnesota for a year. (By 2008, that figure had grown to $9,621, an increase of 4,400 percent.)[1] In those days, it was common for college students to earn enough in summer jobs to pay for their year's tuition. Students chose to attend a particular public university for a raft of reasons—program offerings, nearness to home, advice from guidance counselors, etc.—but college affordability was not a significant consideration.

This insensitivity of enrollments to tuition also meant that university officials did not have to fear that tuition increases would turn away students. In 1962, for example, the University of Minnesota bumped its yearly undergraduate tuition by 12.7 percent, but this amounted only to a $27 increase. Thus, raising tuition was a way for a school to prop up its revenue base without jeopardizing enrollments.[2] But this pricing flexibility also had a downside: it meant that there were few incentives for colleges to restrain their operating costs. Consequently, academic decisions about embarking in new directions, offering specialty courses with low enrollments, or sponsoring community outreach projects were made mostly on academic, social, and political grounds. Curricular changes and innovations were initiated by faculty members who were seldom cautioned to consider the cost implications of their recommendations. Not that costs were irrelevant in those days; it was rather that the pressure to restrain costs was eased by the ability of colleges to raise their fees without harming enrollment or provoking public complaints.[3]

In this context, it is not surprising that the university decision-making process itself became cost-insensitive. Whereas the outside world of business was always under great financial pressure to make decisions quickly and efficiently, the absence of an analogous cost pressure in academia allowed a more leisurely, broad-based decision-making process to evolve. Decisions and recommendations that in business would be made promptly by a manager or small working group were at universities often delegated to large, democratically balanced committees. Over the decades, this practice of participatory governance became an important part of the university culture. At public universities especially, with their undertones of taxpayer democracy, the expectation grew that all interested parties—faculty, alumni, students, staff—should be consulted on substantive matters. Whereas the business world valued decisiveness, strategic skills, and problem-solving ability in its leaders, the academic world placed a premium on openness, willingness to listen, and consensus building. A future chapter will explore the academic rationale for this governance model, the heart of which is the belief that the free exchange of ideas requires that interested constituencies be consulted and empowered to weigh in on decisions. In fact, it is accepted dogma in academia that importing the hierarchical management structure of business would be not only inappropriate but a threat to academic freedom. The point, however, is that participatory governance in academia developed because it could be afforded. Freed from worries about earnings growth, profitability, and shareholder satisfaction, and operating in an environment with growing demand, ample state support, and the ability to raise prices, public universities and colleges could easily absorb the inefficiencies and higher costs of shared governance. Today, however, that environment has changed, and the financial flexibility enjoyed by universities in prior decades has largely vanished. It is thus unsurprising that shared governance has come under stress. As university administrators try to avoid layoffs, maintain salaries, and cope with neglected physical plants, and as the public grows increasingly intolerant of tuition increases, disagreements over governance practices often become the point of contention between university professors and their administrative leaders.

The loss of financial flexibility in public higher education was brought on primarily by a confluence of demographic and social changes that put increasing pressure on state treasuries and reduced the ability of lawmakers to make large discretionary appropriations.[4] Partly this pressure came from growing societal needs—for health care, road and infrastructure maintenance, K–12 education, public employee pensions, and federal entitlements—but it also came from the growing scale of public higher education itself. In 1960, for example, there were seven four-year state colleges and universities in Ohio; by 1990, the number had grown to thirteen, with total enrollments of about 400,000 students.[5] The 1960s were years of extraordinary growth in higher education, with enrollments in the nation's colleges doubling from four to eight million students. (By 2000, enrollments had grown to fifteen million.) This increase was fueled mostly by an increase in the college-going rate and not by absolute population growth.[6]

As the pressure on state treasuries grew, lawmakers became increasingly concerned that public universities were making up for appropriation shortfalls by hiking tuition charges. As we saw in the previous chapter, it became common practice for legislatures and controlling authorities to regulate tuition charges, partly to enhance access to higher education and partly to put the brakes on campus expenditures. But this strategy provided no positive incentives for campuses to become more productive. There were no carrots; there was little a faculty member, department chair, dean, vice president, or president could do either to increase the revenue received from the state or to grow tuition income by raising prices.

Nevertheless, public universities still had to live within their means, and as state budgets tightened word often came down from the campus budget office that the state appropriation either had been cut or was lower than expected and academic units should therefore quickly reduce expenditures. But cutting expenditures in this way does not enhance efficiency. Unexpected budget cuts translate quickly into canceled courses, reduced services, dingier offices, elimination of conference travel, abandoned searches for new professors, and reduced library subscriptions. This is a point to which I will frequently return. From the perspective of a university president, forced expenditure reduction is not a strategic decision intended to improve the institution by focusing resources; rather, it is a damaging action that harms the institution and makes life worse for the university's students, faculty, and staff. Furthermore, to diffuse their impact, university administrators tend to distribute nonstrategic budget cuts across the board so that the pain will be spread uniformly. Even under the best of circumstances, in a consensus-oriented environment it is difficult for a campus administrator to target weak programs for elimination. Rather than face an onslaught of criticism from the disadvantaged, campus leaders usually opt to keep peace by distributing the burden of mandatory retrenchment over the entire enterprise.

And so today public universities find themselves in very different economic environment from that of prior decades. The traditional business model for public higher education worked well only so long as public subsidies held up, state campuses were well maintained, faculty members were paid adequately for their teaching and research, and taxpayers received a solid education at a bargain price. But over the years, as state support has dwindled, public colleges have had no choice but to try to make up the shortfall by shifting the financial burden onto students and their families.

However, in the long run this is a losing strategy that only stays the day of reckoning. In order to maintain enrollments in the face of rising tuition, universities have to spend money they don't have to attract well-to-do students who can afford to pay the higher prices and don't need financial aid, a practice that only further distances needy and middle-class students. Furthermore, the resulting public anger at the growing cost of a college degree translates eventually into punitive legislation and restrictive tuition controls, placing beleaguered state campuses in a stranglehold that starves them of income while simultaneously depriving them of the flexibility to grow revenues. And to make matters worse, demographic changes in the college-age population are softening the demand growth that public universities have historically counted upon to maintain enrollments.[7] Even if state universities were to abandon the needy and the middle class by abrogating their public responsibilities—and let us hope that they do not—there just aren't enough prosperous college-bound Americans in the pipeline to bail them all out of trouble.

A Brief Look Ahead

In this new century, therefore, public universities are weighted down by a morass of social, political, and economic entanglements from which there seems to be no obvious escape. However, in this book I propose an escape route: a systemic reform of the public university financing model. The proposal, outlined in the final chapter, includes a phase-out of government subsidies and a release of universities from restrictive tuition controls. Doing so would empower the market forces of competition, much as they are now empowered to act on private universities.

Under this proposed scenario, public universities would find that raising tuition is no longer a sure-fire way to increase revenue. On the contrary, raising tuition too much could decrease revenue by driving students to colleges that offered better value. Institutional costs would also play a larger role in this new tuition balancing act, because, like revenue, costs fluctuate with enrollment. A college's costs climb as its enrollment grows, and they decline as its enrollment shrinks. However, because many of a school's costs are fixed—plant maintenance, salaries of tenured faculty, utilities, bond debt—it usually spends more by taking on additional students than it saves by shedding the same number. In weighing options to raise tuition, therefore, public colleges would be forced to consider not only the potential decline in enrollment but also the shifting balance point between costs and revenue.

Appendix B shows how the forces of supply and demand lead to a rather complex interaction between a university's revenue structure and its cost structure. This interaction constrains an institution to operate within a narrow band of allowed tuition charges. Outside of this band, the institution cannot pay its bills. Furthermore, we will see there is a natural tendency for the width of this band to narrow over time, progressively reducing the flexibility of the institution to set its tuition arbitrarily. This narrowing places great pressure on a school to rein in its expenditures. However, this cost pressure is of a different sort from that experienced when state appropriation cutbacks force universities to retrench. Under these new marketplace rules, it would not be desirable for a public university to defer maintenance, leave needed personnel vacancies unfilled, or take any steps that make the school less attractive to prospective students. Instead, to remain competitive, the university would be motivated to reduce its unit cost of instruction strategically, while maintaining its campus and preserving the quality of its programs. In short, marketplace forces would compel the university to increase its productivity by becoming more efficient.

Phasing out direct appropriations to public universities (and replacing them with student scholarships) is an important part of my proposal, because appropriations weaken marketplace forces. Government subsidies reduce the pressure for universities to compete; a subsidy not only gives an automatic price advantage to schools that private-sector competitors do not enjoy but also lowers the price sensitivity of student demand. In appendix B, I will illustrate how a subsidy insulates schools from marketplace pressures to control expenditures.[8]

A second key part of my proposal would free public universities from government-imposed tuition restrictions. To the extent that college tuitions are fixed by an outside agency, the forces of supply and demand are undermined. Furthermore, the expenditure reductions imposed on campuses by below-market tuition pricing are not the beneficial kinds that enhance productivity; on the contrary, they simply drive campuses into a mode of generalized retrenchment that undermines value by eating away at infrastructure.

Finally, I will take up the sensitive topic of shared governance. The public university culture of participatory democracy has struggled to adapt to the changed environment in which public universities now find themselves. As noted by James J. Duderstadt, former president of the University of Michigan, "The academic tradition of extensive consultation, debate, and consensus building before any substantive decision is made or action taken will be one of our greatest challenges, since this process is simply incapable of keeping pace with the profound changes swirling about higher education."[9] As the screws have tightened on the nation's public universities, the academic culture has understandably become entrenched and defensive. Each round of budget cuts endured over the years has taught campus constituencies how to use the governance system to stave off unwelcome change and circumvent the negative impacts of budget cuts. Later we will look at ways to moderate these counterproductive forces. But for now it is appropriate to look in some detail at how the forces of supply and demand lead me to my recommendations.

A Constellation of Submarkets

The basic idea underlying market balance in higher education is summarized in figure 1, which shows a familiar supply-demand curve, as might appear in a first-year economics textbook. In the figure, both curves plot the number of enrolled college students as a function of their tuition charges. The downward-sloping demand curve reflects the obvious fact that as tuition falls, more students will desire or be able to attend college. The upward-sloping supply curve says that the willingness of colleges to enroll students depends on the tuition paid. If the tuition is too low, colleges cannot afford to admit students, because their tuition revenues would not cover their costs. However, at higher tuition levels, schools have a financial incentive to expand enrollments, and if the tuition is high enough, they will build more dormitories, open more classrooms, and do whatever else is necessary to accommodate the influx. The intersection of the curves is the classic equilibrium price point. In a perfect market, supply and demand are in harmony, with both buyers (students) and suppliers (colleges) comfortable with the tuition level paid.

That is the theory, anyway. In actuality, this description of the higher education marketplace is rife with problems. The first is the fact that these supply-demand curves are purely imaginary, in the sense that we cannot conduct a controlled experiment to plot them over their full ranges. Normally, the best one can do is to determine small variations around an equilibrium price point, which amounts to knowing only the slope of the supply and demand curves at that point. In principle, one could construct a curve that *resembled* a demand curve by surveying all the colleges and universities in the country and plotting a graph of their enrollments as a function of their tuition charges. I am not aware of anyone who has actually done this, but such a graph would undoubtedly be a downward sloping curve illustrating that as tuition dropped, college

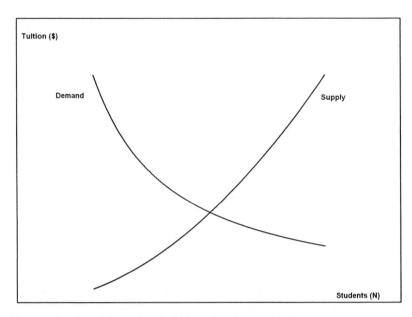

Figure 1. Supply and demand in the higher education marketplace

enrollments climbed. The area under such a curve would be the total enrollments in the higher education system, with each point on the curve
showing how many students were enrolled at each tuition level. But this
graph would not really be illustrating student demand. What our hypothetical curve actually would show is a range of equilibrium price points
throughout a spectrum of different educational submarkets. For example, at the low-priced end of the curve, the schools represented would be
mostly community colleges, whereas at the high-priced end they would
be elite private universities and liberal arts colleges. Furthermore, external influences on supply and demand would vary greatly along the
curve. On the low-tuition end, Pell grants, tax credits, and student loans
would no doubt be important drivers of enrollment demand, whereas
on the other end, interest rates on municipal bonds and social prestige
might be important.

Furthermore, many of the nation's colleges have selective admissions
and turn away applicants who would willingly pay their charged tuition,
thus making their enrollments an underestimate of actual demand. Selective colleges deliberately set their tuition charges below their market
price point so they can match enrollments to their classroom and dormitory capacities. And even within any narrow segment of the curve,

one would undoubtedly find colleges with very different educational products (e.g., music conservatories or business schools) whose tuition charges happened to coincide. Ultimately, about all one could learn from such a graph is that there are more college students of modest means in the country than there are rich students, and of course we knew that anyway. The point is that in a diverse industry like higher education the notion of a single marketplace is a fiction. Higher education is in fact a constellation of submarkets, and the laws of supply and demand operate more or less independently within each submarket.

The Broad Brush of Government Regulation

This fact has important public policy implications. It means that attempts to influence university enrollments and pricing by imposing legislative controls on the marketplace are likely to be undermined by the law of unintended consequences. Legislation paints with a broad brush, and what works for one segment of a diverse market may have the opposite effect on another segment. For example, as noted in the previous chapter, many states annually impose percentage limits, or caps, on tuition increases for state schools, the goal being to "make college more afford-able" for taxpayers. Generally these caps apply uniformly throughout a state system, even though the colleges within that system may operate in different competitive environments.

At my own university, such state-imposed tuition caps have had exactly the reverse of their desired goal. Because these caps required Miami University to peg its tuition below the actual market value, they reduced the revenue collected from affluent students who normally paid full tuition. The resulting revenue shortfall forced the university to scale back its need-based scholarships, thereby raising the out-of-pocket costs for students of modest means. The legislation failed to accomplish its goal because it was based on assumptions about supply and demand that did not apply to Miami's particular submarket. One-size-fits-all solutions seldom work across complex markets.

Market-manipulating exercises are also difficult to pull off successfully because one seldom knows a market's true price sensitivity, which in our case is the impact of tuition on student demand. Assumptions about price sensitivity can miss the mark, one reason being the common tendency to confuse causation with correlation. This is a rather subtle point, but it can be illustrated through the following analogy. Suppose a social scientist plots a graph that relates family income to annual visits to art galleries and finds that the data lie along a smooth curve. Despite this strong connection between personal wealth and interest in the arts, it would be foolish to propose building more art galleries in order to increase the nation's wealth. The reason is that the relationship reflects an associative and not a causal connection. (Furthermore, whatever causal component exists, however small, would undoubtedly run the other direction: personal wealth surely drives art gallery visits, not the other way around.)[10]

Similarly, in higher education, it is known that low-income students tend to enroll in colleges that have low tuition charges, and the familiar explanation is that this is the only option that poor students can afford. But this explanation does not account for government grants, loans, and scholarships available to low-income students, all of which weaken the link between tuition level and educational demand. And second, the explanation ignores the fact that there may also be nonmonetary factors that draw low-income students to low-tuition colleges: geographical proximity of an urban campus to home, ample parking for commuters, availability of evening classes, a practical, job-skills curriculum, remedial programs to redress educational deficiencies, and so forth. These other considerations may well make inexpensive colleges attractive to low-income students who, on the basis of finances alone, could afford to attend more costly institutions.

In other words, as in the art gallery example, the two variables (tuition and college enrollment) have an associative component. Efforts to expand low-income enrollment by holding down college tuition may not grow enrollment as much as desired, because the assumption about the price sensitivity of demand is inaccurate. In higher education especially, tampering with one market variable can throw the others out of kilter. For example, hoping to make college more affordable, task forces, commissions, and higher-education interest groups often propose to expand federal loan and grant programs and to eliminate merit-based scholarships in favor of need-based scholarships. However well intentioned, such proposals can be sabotaged by unanticipated consequences.[11] For example, if a selective college converts its merit scholarships to need-based scholarships, it may lose fee-paying upper-income students from its applicant pool and simultaneously gain more low-income applicants. With fewer upper-income students, the school then loses the revenue flexibility it needs to discount its tuition for needy students. The result can be a net decrease in financial aid for the low-income students whom the school had wanted to help. Such seeming paradoxes can pop up unexpectedly in complex markets.

The key lesson, therefore, is that in higher education good public policy must not only allow for the wide diversity of academic institutions but also recognize the precarious balance of demographic, social, and economic forces that keeps the marketplace stable. This fact raises two fundamental questions: Can government intervention in the industry really control costs and enhance college affordability? And if so, what sort of intervention will accomplish these goals? The answers depend on understanding how supply, demand, and competition affect individual campuses, a topic to which we will now turn.

Supply and Demand at the Local Level

Figure 2 shows a simplified demand curve for a hypothetical public university campus.[12] The figure plots the number of students who are willing to enroll at the university as a function of the tuition they must pay. (Note that the axes are reversed from Figure 1 to reflect the idea that tuition is the independent variable in the example.) To make the numbers seem plausible, we will assume that the "cutoff point" for demand (i.e., the tuition level above which no students choose to enroll) is $20,000 and that 40,000 students would enroll if the tuition were zero.

At the left end of the curve, the number of enrolled students is a maximum (40,000) because everybody receives a free ride. At the right end of the curve, enrollments are zero because the school charges such high tuition that no students will pay it. The downward slope of the curve is a measure of the price sensitivity of demand. In general, if a school's applicant pool consists primarily of low-income students, then this slope will be steep, indicating that increases in tuition can rapidly choke off enrollments. For-profit schools, such as the University of Phoenix, typically enroll students who are very sensitive to price changes, as do community colleges and urban nonselective four-year public colleges. (To keep the explanation simple, I will ignore the impact on the curve of grants, low-interest loans, and other financial aid, all of which reduce the price sensitivity of demand.) Well-to-do students, those who might attend an expensive private college, would exhibit a flatter demand curve. To them tuition is just not all that important, and while price has some influence on their enrollment decisions, there are likely greater considerations.

In practice, an enrollment demand curve says as much about the col-

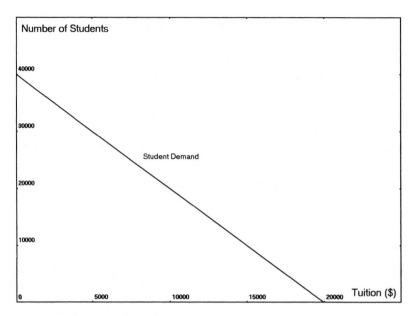

Figure 2. Single campus demand curve

lege and the overall academic environment as about students' ability to pay tuition. As a consequence, colleges can take actions to change the profile of student demand. Adding a popular major to the curriculum can increase demand, for example, as can building a new basketball arena or choosing to schedule classes in the evenings or weekends. These kinds of investments will tend to flatten a school's demand curve, because at each tuition level students are getting more for their money and will thus be more likely to enroll. Clearly, different actions affect demand in different ways. For example, if a college steps up its marketing and recruiting but makes no other changes in its operations, it might increase demand at all price points by, say, 10 percent. For this case, the slope of the demand curve becomes steeper, but the right-end cutoff point doesn't change. The demand has increased because marketing has increased the school's exposure to potential applicants, but students are not receiving more value for their tuition dollars. This is not a particularly desirable outcome from either the student's or the school's viewpoint. Generally, a college prefers a flat demand curve, because it then can raise its tuition without significantly diminishing enrollments.

For selective universities, both public and private, the shape of demand curves is determined mostly by competition from other schools.

For example, if Northwestern University increases its scholarship offers to engineering students, then that will suppress the demand at the University of Illinois, which recruits engineering majors from the same cohort of applicants. The penalties can be great for any selective university whose tuition charges rise above those of its competitors, and, conversely, the enrollment rewards can be great for those that are able to charge less than their competitors (while still maintaining quality). Thus, competitive forces not only exert strong price constraints but provide powerful incentives to increase value.

Two additional points: First, no two students have exactly the same sensitivity to tuition levels. One can always break down a university's average demand profile into subprofiles for different cohorts of applicants. For example, a college can partition its applicants according to their income levels, recognizing that low-income applicants will have a greater price sensitivity than upper-income applicants. This kind of partitioning exercise can be a powerful tool for colleges to optimize the use of their financial aid dollars.

And second, one should not assume, as lawmakers sometimes do, that if allowed to do so public colleges would inevitably raise their tuition charges in order to make more money. This assumption is incorrect for several reasons: it oversimplifies the relationship between tuition rates and tuition revenue, a topic I will take up shortly; it neglects cost considerations (specifically, a college's average per-student cost of instruction); and it presumes that nonmonetary considerations are irrelevant. Because these issues are so central to the policy debate over public university financing, it is worth considering them in some detail. I will discuss the first point here and refer interested readers to appendix B for a more detailed treatment of the other points.

The Relationship between Tuition Rates and Tuition Revenue

Let us consider again the hypothetical public university whose student demand was shown previously in figure 2. Figure 3 illustrates how that university's total collected tuition revenue varies with its tuition charges. The left-side vertical axis shows total tuition revenue collected by the university, while the right-side vertical axis shows the number of enrolled students, up to our assumed maximum of 40,000. The horizontal axis shows tuition charges that range from zero up to the cutoff price of $20,000.

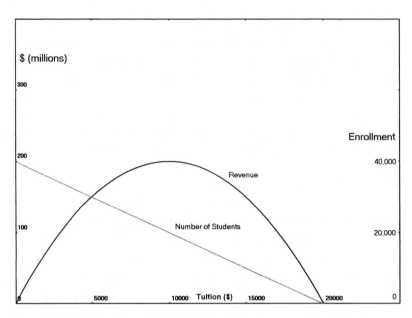

Figure 3. Tuition dependence of revenue and enrollment

The figure shows that as tuition increases, the total collected tuition revenue rises from zero, goes through a broad peak, and then falls to zero at the cutoff price.[13] The general features of this curve are easy to understand. At the left edge of the curve, the university collects no revenue because it charges no tuition. At the right edge, the university collects no revenue because it has no students. For this example, the maximum possible revenue that the university can collect is $200 million, and it occurs when the tuition is $10,000, resulting in 20,000 enrolled students.[14]

There are several other observations that can be made about this figure. First, no matter what assumptions are made about demand, it is a mathematical necessity that there always will be some point along the tuition axis that results in maximum revenue. Where that point is, however, and the actual amount of revenue collected are dependent on the particular shape of the demand curve. Additionally, notice that there are always two values of tuition that generate the same revenue, one on each side of the peak. (Of course, if tuition is priced exactly at the peak, then these two tuition charges converge into one.) On the high side of the peak, enrollments are lower for a given revenue level. Here, a university needs fewer faculty and support staff and fewer dormitories, and it has lower expenses. Furthermore, the university can see its net revenue increase if it lowers tuition, thereby expanding enrollments. In contrast, on the low side of the peak, the school will increase net revenue if it raises tuition. Because higher tuition will drive down enrollments, the school's costs will also diminish. Seeing revenues increase while costs drop is, naturally, music to the ears of a university's fiscal officer.

All of these scenarios are based on the idealized assumption that our hypothetical university has a perfectly elastic enrollment capacity and that it can adjust its capacity to accommodate every student who will pay tuition. In real life, of course, this is a practical impossibility for a host of reasons, one being the enrollment ceiling caused by the capacity limitations of classrooms, dormitories, parking garages, etc., and another being the large fixed costs (e.g., salaries, bond debt) that mean enrollment must not fall too low. Thus even though figure 3 illustrates an interesting economic principle, practically speaking, universities can accommodate only limited enrollment variations.

The schools that come closest to the hypothetical university of figure 3 are the nonselective "open admissions" institutions that constitute the majority of public universities. Such schools see their enrollments fluctuate up and down in response to economic cycles, tuition charges, and other external influences. Such schools are to be juxtaposed to selective universities (public and private), such as my own, that have a surplus of applicants. Selective institutions fill up their classes to capacity and then turn away the excess applicants. Because such schools have predetermined, stable enrollments, raising tuition always generates more revenue. On the other hand, raising tuition also suppresses the number of applicants and thereby lowers the average academic quality of the entering students. Raising tuition too much, of course, eventually turns a selective institution into a nonselective institution. Small, thinly endowed liberal arts colleges are increasingly following this path, as circumstances force them to raise tuition in order to remain solvent.

If a university makes investments that decrease the price sensitivity of demand, then it is readily shown that the revenue peak of figure 3 shifts to the right and its height increases. Therefore, one of the easiest ways for a college to grow revenue is to invest in the accoutrements that increase its attractiveness to high-income, price-insensitive students. If the gain in collected revenue exceeds the cost of the investment, as it generally does, then the school props up its revenue base while simultaneously enhancing its competitive standing. The purpose of such investments is often misunderstood by public officials and higher education activists, who complain about public universities' spending money on "frills." Such frills can actually be a sound strategy for universities forced by declining state support to seek out compensating sources of tuition revenue. Of course, there is a social downside to this strategy, because investments aimed at high-income students also contribute to the growing cost of college for low- and middle-income students. Still, the example shows how public universities can exploit marketplace forces to bolster their operating revenues.

It nearly goes without saying that any university should know which side of its revenue peak it is operating on. If on the low-tuition side of the peak, raising tuition will increase revenues, and if on the far side, lowering tuition will do so. That said, it is not as easy as one might imagine for a public university to know its tuition-revenue relationship. Private colleges can more easily obtain this information, because they commonly discount their published tuition by providing scholarships to applicants. At some private colleges, the discount rate can be as much as 50 percent, which means that a student's average out-of-pocket cost is only half the published tuition. By monitoring the "yield" of applicants (the fraction of accepted students who actually enroll) as a function of their net discounted tuition, schools can empirically determine the price sensitivity of their applicant pool. With few exceptions, public universities do not have this tool at their disposal, because they typically charge a flat rate tuition to all students, with comparatively minimal discounting.[15]

How Enrollments Affect Campus Costs

It is an error to suppose that if allowed by their states to do so, public universities would invariably raise their tuition charges to maximize revenues.[16] Legislators, in particular, often worry that if given free rein public universities would jack up their tuition levels indefinitely. But such a conclusion ignores the importance of costs. Since universities are nonprofit entities, what really matters is their ability to generate sufficient revenues to cover the expenses of their operations. Raising tuition may actually be a bad idea, if expenses were to go up more than the additional collected revenue. Expenses, like tuition revenues, are also dependent on enrollments, and as a result there are likely to be regions of the revenue curve of figure 3 where a university cannot afford to admit students even though revenues may be high. This situation is akin to that of an automobile manufacturer who grows revenue and market share by heavily discounting cars but ends up losing money because it cannot make the cars at the price it sells them for. The balancing act between expenses (costs) and revenues (income) is discussed in detail in appendix B.

The Market Pressure to Control Costs

It is universally acknowledged that the forces of competition exert great pressure on businesses to become more efficient and productive. If public universities are no longer shielded from their competitive environment by state subsidies, then these forces will come to act on them as well. But how public campuses respond to these unfamiliar forces is crucially important, lest they aggravate the very problems they are trying to solve. Public universities are all too familiar with the practice of curtailing expenditures by retrenching—laying off employees, deferring maintenance, enlarging class sizes, and imposing across-the-board cuts on departmental operating budgets. But these kinds of cost-cutting measures are not appropriate as a response to competitive imperatives, because they reduce the attractiveness of the institution to students. A university can probably get away with this sort of cost-cutting for a year or two, but eventually word will get out that the buildings need to be painted, that classes are larger, that professors are spending less time advising students, that lines are longer in the health center, and so forth. And once that happens, demand will start to fall off and the admissions office will receive fewer applications. Of course, falling demand for its services translates into a drop in revenues, thus setting in motion a potentially disastrous chain reaction: every decline in revenue forces another round of retrenchment, which then drives the revenue down further, which then forces even more retrenchment, and on and on. For a private college or university, the cycle eventually ends in bankruptcy. However, since a public university cannot go bankrupt, its final destination is to become a decayed vestige of its former self and a refuge of last resort for students. Sustained on life support by its state subsidy, the universities that go down this path will become higher education's version of failed inner-city schools.

Ironically, academic communities will resignedly accept retrenchment and generalized deterioration. If the faculty, especially, believe there are no other options, they will accept across-the-board reductions in operating budgets, salary freezes, replacing permanent faculty with temporary instructors, scaling back janitorial services, and postponing building renovations. In one sense, these are the easiest cuts to implement, even though they gradually grind the school into the ground.

But there are other options, and these are the cost-reduction measures that are hardest to implement. Within this second category of options, the university continues to put professors in the classrooms, hold down class sizes, keep the lawns mowed, and serve appetizing meals in the dining halls. These other options preserve the schools' strengths, because these are the qualities that attract the students whose tuition dollars the university depends on for survival. So instead of retrenching, the university implements cuts that make it more productive. It eliminates weak or unpopular academic majors, stops offering underenrolled courses, and closes down underutilized facilities. The university focuses its energies. It curtails service activities that fall outside its mission, scales back committee sizes to stretch faculty and staff time, purges itself of noncritical administrators, eliminates underperforming sports teams, enforces performance standards for faculty and other employees, and eliminates layers of bureaucracy.

Unfortunately, over the years, the culture at universities, especially public universities, has become especially adept at resisting this second category of cost reduction. In this sense, perhaps, public universities have become their own worst enemies—staunchly resisting precisely the kinds of changes that are needed to ensure their own survival. Part II of this book examines this perverse culture in detail—how it came to exist, what perpetuates it, and how it might be changed without throwing the baby out with the bathwater.

Why Public Universities Cannot Restrain Costs

In the previous chapter I noted that the gradual transition from subsidy dependence to tuition dependence for public universities has awakened the forces of supply and demand. We saw that competition for students exerts a pressure on campuses to restrain tuition charges, to increase value and productivity, to rein in expenditures, and to become leaner and more efficient—a pressure that was largely absent when a state appropriation was the dominant source of a university's income. Yet despite these marketplace forces, for three decades public universities have been able to raise their tuition charges significantly faster than inflation, while simultaneously letting their costs eke upward. How have they been able to do this? And why, despite ever-growing tuition revenues, do they always seem so short of money?

I have already alluded to part of the explanation. Campuses allow themselves to deteriorate slowly rather than make the difficult and unpopular choices that will stretch their budgets and boost their productivity. Of course, this is not a strategic nor even likely a conscious decision. It is, rather, an expedient choice that preserves campus harmony and respects the insistence of academic constituencies on having a decision-making voice. But as a consequence, each year public universities become a little more de-pleted. They are like the frog in the pot that doesn't realize it is being boiled alive because the water is heated very slowly. When the truth fi-nally dawns, the deed will already be done. However, campus resistance to change is only part of the explanation. More fundamentally, public colleges have been shielded from the beneficial forces of competition by outside influences, specifically government subsidies, tuition controls, and other regulatory mandates. As we will see, these external influences act in different ways but ultimately lead to the same result. We also will see that universities have been able to stay the day of reckoning because the competitive pressures on them have been alleviated by ever-growing student demand, but that the clock is ticking.

The Impact of Government Subsidy on Cost Containment

Public universities receive their state support through a variety of mech-anisms. In Ohio, for example, the state appropriation to campuses comes in two basic forms: a biennial capital appropriation for construction and renovation and an annual "State Share of Instruction" that helps under-write campus operating expenditures.[1] The State Share of Instruction is allocated to each campus according to a complex formula that is mostly based on enrollment; general studies first-year students generate smaller subsidies than, say, senior chemistry majors. There are also incentive pro-visions in the subsidy designed to enhance access for needy and at-risk students, to reward schools with high graduation rates, and so forth.

The higher education budget is set by the Ohio General Assembly ev-ery two years. As each budget season approaches, there is a flurry of ac-tivity as lobbyists (each Ohio public university employs at least one full-time lobbyist), college presidents, and higher education groups make the case for an increased appropriation. Data are presented showing how higher education creates jobs and boosts the state economy, how faculty salaries lag behind those in other states, and how campus physical plants are deteriorating. Often, flashy initiatives for research and teaching are proposed, in the hope of capturing lawmakers' imaginations and loos-ening their wallets.

Budget season is also the occasion for legislators to express their dis-satisfaction with the state's universities. Typically, the complaints focus on rising costs, excessive tuition increases, waste and inefficiency, and perceived lack of accountability. Occasionally do-nothing tenured faculty, foreign teaching assistants with thick accents, and leftist professors also come under fire, as do college social policies (e.g., health benefits for gay partners) that some lawmakers find objectionable. Eventually, however, the ritual grinds to a close and the Ohio General Assembly decides on a total dollar allocation, earmarks some funds for special statewide projects, sets constraints on uses of the money, and imposes a cap on allowed tuition increases. After the dust settles and all the numbers are crunched, the state's universities typically receive a subsidy adjustment that fluctuates around zero, plus or minus a few percentage points. Over the decades, the minuses have frequently outweighed the pluses.

Every state has its own procedures, but in the end public universities receive a payment from their legislatures that ideally permits them to hold down their tuition increase. This payment, and its presumed favorable impact on college affordability, underlies the fundamental promise of public higher education. But does this payment really hold down tuition? The history of the past few decades suggests that it does not. Let us look at what a subsidy payment to a public university actually accomplishes.

First, consider how a typical public university prepares its budget for the upcoming academic year. As always, the budgeting process begins with a list of anticipated expenditures. The president would like to give salary raises and wage increases to her employees and also make some improvements in selected academic programs. She knows that electricity and natural gas rates are expected to rise, as is the cost of health benefits. New roofs needed for some buildings, replacement computers for the payroll office, laboratory equipment for new engineering professors, and salary lines for several new fund-raising professionals are also on the list. If the state's economy has not expanded that year, so that tax revenues are flat, then the president cannot count on any significant increase in state appropriation to the university. She therefore has to think long and hard about how to pay for all the items on her list. The director of admissions is worried about meeting the enrollment target for next year's freshman class and is dead set against raising tuition above the inflation rate. Furthermore, the vice president for development observes that increases in alumni gift giving cannot be counted on because of the weak economy.

Realistically, the president and her executive team have little choice but to pay for most of these new items by carving money out of her existing budget. But where to carve? Learning that enrollment in a summer program for high school science teachers has been falling, she decides to cancel the program. The philosophy department didn't give tenure to an assistant professor, and since a recent program review gave low marks to the department, she elects not to refill the position. Given that the university has been subsidizing the campus public radio station, she decides to recoup the money by asking the station to step up its listener pledge drive and to cancel an amateurishly produced local program. Eventually, she is able to sweep up most but not all of the needed dollars. She asks the payroll office to make do with its old computers for another year.

Elements of the university community are furious at the president for her actions. The philosophy faculty, incensed about their lost faculty position, introduce a resolution in the faculty senate condemning the president for "not being sensitive to the crucial role of the humanities in the undergraduate curriculum." Radio station listeners write in to complain about losing their favorite program. The president of the school board and the local state representative are upset about the canceled science-teacher program. The president is resigned to weathering these criticisms, in part because she understands that reallocation decisions invariably generate pushback, but mostly because she knows the steps are needed in order to make her university better. She believes the new investments are necessary to maintain her school's competitive standing, while the losses from reallocation will not materially harm that standing. This is how the beneficial forces of supply and demand work in academia. Progress is made in tiny steps, as old branches are pruned to make way for new growth. Each step requires courage and diplomacy on the part of the school's leaders, but in the end there is no other way to improve the institution. The pressure of the marketplace to contain costs while maintaining quality is both relentless and uncompromising.

But now let us construct a different scenario. We will suppose everything is the same in our example except that the state's economy is healthy, leading the president to believe that the legislature will substantially increase its university subsidy during the upcoming budget cycle. This fact changes the whole ball game. Now the pressure to reallocate funds internally is eased. The president will not have to incur the wrath of her campus, because the state can pay for the items on her list. Her job has become much easier: the radio station gets to keep its local program, the philosophy department refills its assistant professor slot, and the president is still is able to give pay raises to the faculty and staff. These new subsidy dollars augment the increase in revenue that she garners by also bumping tuition in proportion to the inflation rate.

But no pruning has taken place. In this scenario, the old growth stays around forever because there is no financial imperative to remove it. With every new infusion of state money, the school just ratchets up its cost base. All the new money is immediately absorbed into the school's budget, and most becomes part of the continuing expenses that must be paid again in the next budget cycle, and every cycle thereafter. Over the years, costs keep rising, the university's bureaucracy grows, the mediocre programs survive, and the campus leadership becomes risk averse and unwilling to make unpopular decisions. Ironically, everybody on campus rejoices when the state announces a significant subsidy increase for higher education. Only years later will they realize that there was a worm in the apple.

Now let us go back to the other extreme and suppose that the economic news from the state legislature is bad, leading the governor to announce that a cut in funding to higher education is in the offing. At this point, the president is really caught between a rock and a hard place. Her list of hoped-for improvements has become a pipe dream. She can ignore the advice of her admissions director and raise tuition above the inflation rate, but doing so would risk an enrollment shortfall the following year. There isn't time to scale back programs selectively. At this point the president has little choice but to freeze salaries, cancel searches, and reduce operating budgets across the university. The subsidy cutback has bludgeoned the campus into economic submission. Of necessity, the president has reduced the cost of running the enterprise, but with an ax and not a scalpel.

Having grown dependent on its government appropriation, the university has acute withdrawal symptoms. Life goes on, but the quality of that life is reduced. Weak and strong programs suffer alike, and a morose despair settles over the campus. From the president's perspective, the only bright spot is that nobody blames her for the cutbacks. By not singling out any specific areas for retrenchment, she has effectively redirected campus anger at the governor and legislature. Because hope springs eternal, the president resolves to redouble her lobbying efforts in the coming year and persuade the state to restore the lost revenue. It probably does not occur to her that another option is to begin weaning her school from the state appropriation over which she has so little control and whose unpredictable fluctuations have created so many problems for her.

Before leaving this topic, let us consider one last scenario. Let us assume, once again, that an increase in state support for the new year will be forthcoming. But in this final scenario, the president decides to pass all of the new money back to students, in the form of a dollar-for-dollar tuition reduction. With lower tuition, she knows that student demand will increase and that this increase will be reflected in a larger entering freshman class. But she also knows that if she returns the money to students, she will not have it to fund any of her desired improvements. From a revenue perspective, the subsidy increase is a wash and the pressure is back on. The president will have to pay for her improvements by reallocating money internally. Is she likely to inflict this pain on herself? Of course not. A president's first loyalty is to her university and its employees. Any president would be foolish to give away "free" state money, and from the point of view of her colleagues, doing so would be an abrogation of her responsibilities.

However, let us suppose that the state, instead of giving the money to the university, had put it in the hands of students in the first place. Then the president would have no choice. Unable to bring the money to her campus directly, she would have to do everything possible to bring it in indirectly; her success would depend on how well she could attract those newly cash-laden students. In other words, if she and her campus colleagues were ever to see that infusion of new state money, they would have to work for it. This basic concept is at the core of the recommendations of this book's final chapter.

How Government-Imposed Tuition Controls Harm Public Universities

In chapter 1, I observed that state governments commonly impose restrictions on the tuitions charged by public universities, either by mandating tuition rates explicitly or by placing caps on the increases that campuses can charge, as in Ohio. As noted, lawmakers argue that tuition controls are needed to protect the public from the escalating cost of a public college degree, while university officials see them as disruptive to sound fiscal management and a barrier to maintaining quality. Now that the necessary economic foundation has been laid, let us turn again to this topic and analyze these two points of view.

To do so, we'll consider another hypothetical example, in this case the financial impact of a state-imposed cap on a campus tuition that is 3 percent below what the campus would otherwise like to charge—a roughly typical situation. To be consistent with earlier examples, suppose our hypothetical public university has an enrollment of 20,000 undergraduates and a yearly tuition of $10,000. In order to develop the example, we also need to make three assumptions: First, we assume that the university has nonselective admissions (as do most public universities), so that its enrollments will vary up or down in accord with student applications. Second, we assume that a 1 percent decrease in tuition results in a 1 percent increase in enrollments, in other words a "straight-line" demand curve. And finally, we assume that two-thirds of the university's total educational revenue comes from tuition and one-third from state subsidy, a ratio that is typical for many public universities. The total revenue the university receives from each enrolled student is therefore ($10,000 tuition) + ($5000 subsidy) = $15,000, and if its budget is balanced, its per-student average cost is also $15,000.[2]

With the imposition of the cap, the tuition collected from each enrolled student will drop by 3 percent, or $300. This figure translates into a $6 million revenue decrease for the entire student body of 20,000 undergraduates. Further, the 3 percent decline in tuition leads to a 3 percent increase in enrollments, which is 600 students. To educate these additional students, the university's expenditures will increase by a net amount of ($15,000/student) × (600 students) = $9 million, while the additional tuition revenue collected is ($9,700/student) × (600 students) = $5.82 million. The additional students thus create a revenue shortfall of $3.18 million.[3] To accommodate the tuition cap, the university will have to cut its costs by $9.18 million: $3.18 million to handle the additional enrollments and $6 million to absorb the lost tuition revenue. This amount is 3.06 percent of the university's total educational budget of ($15,000/student) × (20,000 students) = $300 million. However, since at least 50 percent of a university's budget consists of fixed costs, the discretionary part of its budget must be reduced by at least 6.12 percent.

An episodic one-year cut of 6.12 percent in discretionary spending would have widespread impact on the institution. Most likely it would result in salary freezes, unfilled vacancies, cuts to operating budgets, and so forth. In order to weather the reduction, the university president may decide to draw down the school's fiscal reserves. However, if the reserves absorb the shortfall, the university buys time but also weakens its financial underpinnings and its ability to handle future cuts. Nevertheless, one-time expenditure reductions in the range of 3–5 percent fall in the category of "belt-tightening" and not financial emergency. In and of itself, a one-year tuition cap does not do irreversible damage to an institution, which is what makes these caps seem so attractive to lawmakers.

In the short term, students see an immediate benefit through reduced tuition bills, while the universities are only forced to take a little fat out of their operations.

But when such caps are imposed year after year, for a decade or longer, their cumulative impact becomes very significant. And that is exactly what has been happening in public higher education. Like a perverse backward law of compound interest, tuition controls do their work inconspicuously, chipping away year after year at the financial base of their targets and over the long term weakening the entire structure more than anyone might have imagined.

And what about the impact of tuition controls on students? Have caps and similar government interventions held down the price of a college degree? Only in the short term, because, once started, tuition controls perpetuate themselves indefinitely. The reason is that when an institution is required to set its prices below what it needs to cover expenditures, it creates a backlog of unmet needs. Every year this backlog grows, widening the gap between what the university must charge to maintain services and what it is actually permitted to charge. As this pricing pressure builds up, legislators and controlling boards become reluctant ever to take the lid off, fearing huge tuition increases as campuses try to make up for lost ground. So in this sense, yes, tuition controls keep universities from raising prices.

But in the long term, tuition controls, like other forms of price-fixing, do not serve the interests of the public. Tuition controls, in combination with government subsidies, weaken the competitive pressures for universities to become efficient and productive. And absent this pressure, institutional costs rise unnecessarily, thus forcing universities to increase tuition to cover costs that never should have been incurred in the first place. Of course, if state governments *never* permitted their campuses to raise tuition charges, then tuition would forever remain low. But whereas students might be paying a lower price because of the controls, they would also be receiving less value for their money. This is an important point. A small Toyota coupe may be priced far lower than a large Lexus sedan, but it provides equal or better value to owners. In public higher education, however, artificially suppressing prices also suppresses value. It is simply not possible for public universities to avoid losing muscle when their budgets are repeatedly hammered by years of subsidy cutbacks and tuition controls. The evidence is run-down buildings, classes taught by part-time teachers, a growing bureaucracy, and a defensive and change-resistant campus culture.

The lesson here is that we cannot have it both ways. The public wants a high-quality, affordable public college education, but the current financing mechanism cannot pay for it. And in this context, efforts to rein in prices through government regulation only drive the system further into disrepair. That, unfortunately, is the bottom line, and there is no escape other than to alter the underlying financing mechanism itself.

How Rising Demand Reduces Competitive Forces

Let us return to the question of why market forces have been so ineffective at reining in public college costs and tuition charges. As I have just shown, government subsidies have weakened the cost discipline normally imposed by competition, resulting in an increased pressure for colleges to raise tuition. Furthermore, state-mandated tuition controls have been only partly effective at resisting this pressure, and then only by retrenching the institutions and eroding their infrastructure.

But a generally rising national demand for higher education has also been a significant factor in exempting public colleges from competitive forces. As we will see, however, this rising demand does not mean that increasing numbers of students are wanting to attend college. Rather, it means that students and their families have been willing to pay ever higher prices for that privilege. Although total enrollment in higher education grew from 11.2 million in 1975 to 17.5 million in 2005, an increase of 56 percent, enrollment at public four-year institutions increased only 37 percent over the same period.[4] Although this is still a significant per-

Table 1. Enrollment in public four-year colleges, 1970–2005

Year	Enrollment	Autumn Freshmen	Baccalaureate Degrees
1970	4.23M	754K	520K
1975	5.00M	772K	635K
1980	5.13M	765K	624K
1985	5.21M	717K	652K
1990	5.85M	727K	700K
1995	5.81M	732K	777K
2000	6.06M	842K	811K
2005	6.84M	954K	932K

Source: National Center for Education Statistics, Digest of Education Statistics Tables and Figures: 2006, table 184; 2007, tables 180, 266.

centage, over these years the number of four-year public campuses also increased by 19 percent, from 537 to 639.[5] Table 1 shows public four-year college enrollment trends over a thirty-four-year period, together with numbers of autumn-term freshmen and baccalaureate degrees awarded.

Table 1 indicates that the increase in total public four-year college enrollment averaged only 1.76 percent per year between 1970 and 2005 and that much of this increase occurred in the first and last five years of the period. In fact, there is a twenty-year span, between 1975 and 1995, during which average enrollments climbed less than 1 percent per year, and one five-year span in which they declined. Freshman enrollments increased only about 0.76 percent per year over the full period, and when one allows for the increase in the number of campuses during this time, freshman enrollments per campus showed essentially no change. Overall enrollment increases per campus came to fewer than 100 students per year.[6] Over the full thirty-five-year span, the numbers of baccalaureate degrees roughly tracked overall enrollment, but the numbers of entering freshmen did not. Up to year 2000, there was a decrease in the number of new freshmen enrolling in four-year public colleges; this decrease confirms that the proportion of traditional eighteen-to-twenty-two-year-olds in public campus student bodies has declined.

The data make it clear that application pressure driven by demographic changes in the numbers of public college students has not accounted for the rise in public college tuitions. Instead, the rising family income of students, the expansion of grant and loan programs, and the growing perceived value of a college degree have decreased the price sensitivity of demand, which means that, on average, students have to date been willing to pay the higher tuitions demanded by four-year public colleges rather than curtail their aspirations. Averages, of course, tend to obscure important information. Studies have also shown that each year, growing tuition charges now turn away about 250,000 students who otherwise would choose to attend college.[7] As noted previously, when flat demographic projections (in the college-age population and participation rates) are combined with the stagnant income growth of middle-class taxpayers, public campuses will soon have no choice but to confront the cost-containment dictates of the marketplace; in the long run, the public and legislative pressure to rein in tuition increases cannot be ignored.

The University Prime Directive

Thou shalt always seek better students. To some degree this has always been the guiding credo for institutions of higher learning. Other things being equal, colleges and universities always prefer to admit strong students over weak students. However, in decades past, state schools sought good students primarily for prestige, because their presence enabled them to recruit better faculty (who enjoy teaching smart, motivated students), and for a host of other intangible reasons. Because revenues primarily came from a state appropriation that was blind to students' SAT scores and high school class rankings, public campuses had no particular *financial* incentive to enroll good students.

Today, however, with tuition having displaced state appropriation as the major instructional revenue source, public colleges have plenty of financial incentives. Good students are less expensive to teach. They do not need remedial courses to make up for educational deficiencies. On average, they commit fewer campus crimes and have fewer disciplinary problems. Their graduation rates are higher, and after graduation they tend to get better-paying jobs. Ultimately, they become wealthier alumni, who in turn are more generous to their alma maters at annual giving

Table 2. Income dependence of SAT scores

Family Income	SAT Critical Reading	SAT Mathematics	SAT Writing
Less than $20,000/year	434	456	430
$20,000–$40,000/year	462	473	453
$40,000–$60,000/year	488	496	477
$60,000–$80,000/year	502	510	490
$80,000–$100,000/year	514	525	504
$100,000–$120,000/year	522	534	512
$120,000–$140,000/year	526	537	517
$140,000–$160,000/year	533	546	525
$160,000–$200,000/year	535	548	529
More than $200,000/year	554	570	552

Source: College Board, College-Bound Seniors National Report, 2008, table 11.

time. But the biggest financial incentive of all is that good students generally have more money than weak students and are thus able to pay full tuition. Table 2 shows the relationship between family income and SAT scores for 2008 college-bound high school seniors.

Students from the lowest income bracket, as shown in table 2, have average SAT scores that place them roughly in the bottom quarter of all college-bound students, whereas students from the highest income bracket are in the top third. There are corroborating studies that show, for instance, the positive correlation of family income with high school grade-point averages.[1] Thus, to the extent that academic performance is a proxy for wealth, college admission directors' quest for better students translates into a quest for upper-income students. As they watch their state dollars dwindle, campus administrators understand well the revenue potential of students who don't need scholarships and can afford sizable tuition payments. As much as public university leaders may be philosophically committed to serving students from all socioeconomic backgrounds, when push comes to shove they have very little choice but to try to bring in students who can prop up an inadequate revenue base.

Increasingly, colleges—public and private—are targeting full-fee-paying students, whether they are strong academic achievers or not. When colleges award "merit" scholarships to applicants who are not particularly meritorious, or when they invest in posh dormitories, putting greens, and fitness centers, they are catering to an upper-income market that is accustomed to luxury and special treatment and is willing to pay for it.[2] The ability to grow tuition revenue is determined by how ably colleges respond to their market environment. Responses involve careful tuition pricing, development of recruitment strategies, and investments in infrastructure.[3] Earlier I noted that the higher education industry is a constellation of submarkets, each of which operates within its own competitive environment. Princeton University and the University of Phoenix, for example, may be at opposite ends of the educational spectrum, but both compete for students and both are shaped by the nature of their marketplace.

Understanding how competitive forces vary across the continuum of educational submarkets is thus a prerequisite to addressing higher education's shortcomings. Let us take a look at some of the principal submarkets, organized roughly according to the selectivity of the schools' admissions offices.

For-Profit Universities

For-profit schools will enroll virtually anybody who can speak minimal English and has a high school (or roughly equivalent) degree. Although their websites always have an "admissions" link for prospective students, for-profit schools are actually in the business of selling their services to customers. Being "admitted" to the University of Phoenix or a similar school is a bit like being admitted to a barbershop to get a haircut. For-profit universities often employ sophisticated marketing strategies to draw in students. Their websites do everything possible to extract the name and contact information of viewers. They describe themselves with the trappings of traditional universities, but their "campuses" are often just leased office buildings near freeways. The curriculum of for-profit schools is unashamedly pragmatic and aimed at working adults. For example, at the six-campus American InterContinental University (the school has a facility in London), where "your background means more to us than just a transcript," the curriculum is "focused on helping students acquire industry-current knowledge and skills as they pursue, build and advance their careers in many of today's most in-demand fields."[4]

The business plan of for-profit universities is brilliantly strategic. On the revenue side of their balance sheets, they take maximal advantage of government grants, employer reimbursement programs, and state and federal scholarships and loan programs. Their financial aid offices assist students in obtaining third-party financial aid, but the schools put up no dollars themselves. Their operating strategies are aimed at preserving flexibility and holding down costs. These strategies include

1. maximizing the ability to expand and contract enrollment
2. minimizing fixed costs
3. maximizing the ability of management to make rapid changes
4. marketing aggressively and strategically to potential customers
5. minimizing regulatory and constituency pressures

In accord with these principles, for-profit schools do not have tenured or tenure-track professors; they generally draw their instructors from a local labor pool of working professionals. Their faculty have no research or service expectations, and curricular decisions are made by management. The schools have no libraries, dormitories, sports programs, glee clubs, or student organizations. There are no alumni associations, student health centers, or student unions, all of which run up costs. For-profit schools do not cross-subsidize their program offerings. Whereas nonprofit colleges will underwrite, for example, a small-enrollment classics department using excess revenue from a heavily enrolled psychology department, in the for-profit sector all programs are expected to make money.

In all of higher education, for-profit schools are the most strongly influenced by raw competition and market pressures. If a school cannot justify its tuition and fees to its working- and lower-middle-class adult students, then it will have no students. Since these schools are located in metropolitan areas, there are always plenty of community and technical colleges and regional public campuses happy to pick off their students. For-profit alumni have no school loyalty, and the schools cannot count on prestige or academic reputation to buttress their enrollments. For-profit universities operate in a dog-eat-dog environment where only the fittest survive. As one might expect, all of their efforts are focused on maximizing revenue at the lowest possible cost.[5]

Nonselective Public Universities

Cleveland State University typifies the many urban public campuses that serve the educational needs of their local communities. Founded in 1964, Cleveland State enrolled about 9,800 undergraduates in 2008, 90 percent of whom also held full- or part-time jobs and about half of whom enrolled as part-time students. The school's 2008 minimum admissions requirements included a high school GPA of 2.3 and an ACT score of 16, which is the eighteenth percentile.[6] The school has ninety thousand alumni, most of whom live in northeast Ohio, and a 2008 endowment of $26.4 million, whose annual payout amounts only to about $135 per undergraduate student.[7] Historically, the school's primary revenue source has been its public subsidy, but declining state support has forced Cleveland State to raise its tuition and fees to $7,920 per year (in 2008). In 2000, the state appropriation for the university was $72.8 million, but by 2005 that figure had dropped to $63.3 million, or about $4,000 per student. The rapidly growing tuition burden has posed particular challenges for Cleveland State's students, one-third of whom live in areas whose median family income is below twenty thousand dollars.[8]

Typically, universities like Cleveland State draw students from their immediate locales. Many of these students are working adults from modest backgrounds who have financial, academic, family, and work-related constraints that make it impossible for them to comparison shop for their education. As President Michael Schwartz observed in 2002 testimony to the (Ohio) House Select Committee on Higher Education, "It is fair to say that without Cleveland State University, higher education would be well off the radar screen" for most of the area's low-income residents.[9]

Because state schools in this category tend to be single-source suppliers for their geographic area, competition from other four-year colleges is not a major issue for their admissions office. In fact, in some ways such schools resemble monopolies that can exploit the price advantage of their public funding to fend off private competitors. Despite the absence of competition from peer institutions, however, nonselective state schools are still subject to the laws of supply and demand. With inexpensive community colleges and technical schools nipping at their heels, and with selective public and private colleges siphoning off their top applicants, nonselective universities face their own brand of competitive pressures. These pressures are aggravated by the critical need to maintain enrollment. Because they admit nearly all comers, they have no safety cushion against economic downturns or other circumstances that might drive down enrollments. Furthermore, given their demographic market, nonselective public colleges face great price sensitivity in their student body. Applicants facing high tuition and fees are much more likely to abandon or downscale their college plans than are the more affluent

applicants at selective colleges. Nonselective urban universities generally live a hand-to-mouth existence. Beset by state cutbacks, saddled by
faculty and employee unions, and unable to raise tuition without losing
students, their prospects look increasingly bleak.

Of course, not all nonselective public campuses are in dire straits.
However, this category of colleges is particularly vulnerable to the social
and economic forces acting on state budgets. Lacking pricing power and
having few other revenue sources, they are literally at the mercy of their
state government. In one sense they are the neglected children of the
nation's higher education system.

Selective Public Universities

This is a broad category that ranges from tiny but prestigious College of
William and Mary in Williamsburg, Virginia (enrollment 7,700 students[10]),
to huge, comprehensive research universities like the University of Texas
at Austin (enrollment 50,170[11]). It includes all of the so-called flagship
public universities. Selective public universities have annual budgets that
range from about $200 million to well over $2 billion. Although such
schools mostly draw their undergraduates from their home state, they
face appreciable competition from other four-year colleges. These schools
have well-developed alumni giving programs and often conduct hundreds of millions of dollars of research, both of which buttress their revenue. Their visibility and prominence in their home state means that they
are continually in the spotlight of their legislature and statewide media.

The largest universities in this category verge on being ungovernable.
Their presidents or chancellors are expected to ride herd over huge hospital complexes, wide-ranging outreach and community service programs, a labyrinth of research centers and facilities, tens of thousands of
employees, more than one hundred academic departments, and numerous accrediting organizations, alumni groups, and booster clubs. Throw
into the pot endless rounds of receptions, dinners, workshops, and community meetings, and it is no surprise that many of their presidents bail
out or burn out in four or five years.

As state appropriations have lagged, schools in this category have given
increasing attention to student recruitment. Many have emphasized their
undergraduate honors programs in an effort to lure high-ability students
from private colleges or universities. High-ability students are seen as an
important drawing card for other tuition-paying students, as well as a way

to boost a school's prestige. Despite their enormous operating budgets, many large public universities are in economic straits. The University of Massachusetts at Amherst typifies an increasingly common pattern of deteriorating physical plants. A 2007 report examined the campus's 6.5 million square feet of building space, spread over 140 academic and administrative buildings, and found many with leaking roofs, broken heating systems, and outdated classrooms. The price tag for rehabilitating this space is $1.8 billion, on top of $1.3 billion the university has already spent in the past seven years on capital projects.[12] The *Boston Globe* reports, "The daunting price tag for future building costs highlights the gravity of the state's lack of investment in public higher education, say university officials and a key lawmaker." According to State Senator Robert O'Leary, "Public higher education has been badly underfinanced for a decade."[13] One could cite similar examples from nearly all fifty states.

Private Colleges and Universities

Private colleges and universities are the largest category of four-year institutions in the United States, and they span the range from the elite universities and colleges discussed in the next section to tiny liberal arts colleges. All of these schools operate in an intensely competitive environment. For them, market competition dominates their tuition charges, their curricula, their student services, their faculty salaries, and virtually all aspects of their operations.

Private college applicants generally have other places to turn. Thus, if a school fails to invest in a new student recreation center, maintain its dormitories, or recruit top-notch teachers, then it stands to lose students to schools that have made those investments. Unlike the place-bound students at many public campuses, most students at selective private colleges can vote with their feet. Tuition discounting—the so-called high-tuition/high-aid model—is a way for private institutions to exploit their market strengths to meet admissions goals. In this practice, colleges offer large scholarships to desired price-sensitive applicants. These might include students from poor families or those with especially sought-after abilities, talents, and background. By contrast, applicants without financial need or special academic qualifications may be asked to pay the full price.

From an economic viewpoint, this admissions practice is a form of auction, whereby private colleges annually engage in bidding wars for students. High-school seniors put themselves on the auction block by sending out many applications, often ten or more. The colleges evaluate each student's credentials and bid for the ones they want. Highly coveted applicants have a higher market value and thus command larger bids. This auctionlike process has allowed the best private colleges and universities to assemble well-rounded student bodies that reflect the socioeconomic, racial, geographic, and intellectual diversity of the nation's population. Furthermore, as in any auction, the process is generally fair to the participants, because the decision to accept or reject a school's offer rests in the students' hands. Those who end up paying the full tab do so willingly, because that is the best deal they could strike among their college preferences. In practice, the high-tuition/high-aid model works well only if a school's market position is strong enough to ensure that some students will pay the full, undiscounted price. The college can then use some of this revenue to attract other students who are unwilling or unable to pay the full tab.

Schools at the bottom end of the private college spectrum operate on the edge of insolvency.[14] Lacking substantial endowments, they are hurt most by rising tuition charges and competition from public universities. Briarcliff College in White Plains, New York, which closed its doors in 1977, is a typical example of a small, underendowed college forced to seek bankruptcy. Other schools have been acquired by other colleges, such as the Western College for Women, which was acquired by Miami University in 1974. More recently, tiny Sierra Nevada College, facing bankruptcy, kept its doors open by partnering with two for-profit colleges, Knowledge Universe Learning Group LLC and Cardean Learning Group LLC.[15]

Elite Private Universities and Colleges

One of the first things visitors notice when they stroll across Princeton University's manicured lawns is that even the ivy is named after alumni. Virtually every gate, sidewalk, garden, fountain, and outdoor sculpture has a donor plaque affixed to it. And, of course, so does nearly every building, classroom, laboratory, and lecture hall. At the upper strata of the nation's private universities and colleges, a school's physical campus is a vital cog in a sophisticated moneymaking machine. Stripped to its financial essence, the difference between a Princeton University and, say, a Cleveland State University is alumni giving. In fact, gifts from graduates are what have created the great private universities of America.

Princeton sets the standard of alumni gift giving for all other colleges and universities. Behind every one of Princeton's 7,242 students (in 2006–7) are endowed funds of $1.8 million, or over $13 billion in total. In 2007, the yearly return on that endowment was about $80,000 *per student,* which dwarfed Princeton's not-insignificant undergraduate tuition charge that year of $33,000. At Princeton, gifts and endowment income fund half of the university's total operating budget, while tuition and student fees provide only 22 percent.[16] Where does all that money go? It goes for Nobel laureates and Pulitzer Prize winners, laboratory equipment, and huge research centers (such as the Princeton Plasma Physics Laboratory). It goes for sustaining the school's world-class libraries and an array of student services that other universities can only dream of. And nearly 15 percent of it funds scholarships, making the ability to pay an irrelevancy for accepted students. But as fundraisers note on the university's website, presumably with a straight face, "Some important areas remain significantly underfunded." It is a fact of life that university expenditures always grow to absorb the available money. So even Harvard University, with its $37 billion endowment (2008), the largest in the world, has plenty of unmet needs. The principle is the same everywhere. At rich and poor schools alike, aspirations always grow faster than budgets.

At the elite end of the higher education continuum, competition for students has no financial implications; an admissions staff that turns away nine out of ten applicants knows it will always fill the school's freshman class. In principle, Harvard could triple its undergraduate tuition to $100,000+ and still have enough student demand left over to meet its enrollment targets. But Harvard would never do that. In fact, it is more likely that Harvard may someday eliminate its undergraduate tuition entirely. For the top selective colleges, the SAT scores students bring with them to college are more important than their dollars. These schools have to compete fiercely for top students, but, as in the America's Cup race, the competition is not driven by financial imperatives, because all the players can afford to play. But if a school's goal is to cherry-pick the best and brightest students from across the nation, then removing tuition as a barrier to enrollment is obviously one path toward that goal.

Still, as desirable as a large endowment may be to college fiscal officials, overdependence on gift money can lead to bad habits. Like the state subsidy of public universities, gift income is decoupled from performance. Thus, the more money that alumni gifts provide, the fewer financial incentives exist to minimize layers of administration, eliminate weak programs, reallocate internal resources, and rein in out-of-control salaries. That is not to say that well-endowed private universities are bastions of waste and inefficiency. However, universities supported by endowment income live with the same handicap as that of adult children living off inherited trust funds: the money gives them the freedom to pursue their interests, but it also can sap them of the energy and drive that come from being lean and hungry.

The broad spectrum of American higher education poses great challenges to policy makers. Currently, the best and wealthiest students tend to enroll at the best and wealthiest colleges. Furthermore, the country's higher education system is adept at identifying extraordinary ability: a young math prodigy from an unknown high school in rural Arkansas, or from an impoverished school in Detroit's inner city, will seldom escape the attention of the country's Harvards and MITs. But the mass of Americans get no such special treatment, and legions of them receive mediocre educations from underfunded, poorly performing state colleges. From a public policy perspective, then, where should government support of higher education be focused? If one believes, as most people do, that the appropriate role of government is to help people who cannot help themselves, then the answer may seem clear: taxpayer dollars should be targeted at those who really need the money.

But the counterargument is also persuasive. Building on weakness almost never accomplishes as much as building on strength. Is it really sensible for taxpayers to put their dollars into run-down, bureaucratic, poorly run public campuses, just because those are the colleges that needy students attend? Or is there another option? This is the seminal question to which we will return in subsequent chapters.

Part II

The Academic Culture of Freedom and Waste

The Faculty Are the University

Cat-Herding in the Academy

> Being a university president is like being the groundskeeper of a
> huge cemetery: there are thousands of people beneath you but
> nobody is listening.

This is the joke that tends to come up when public university
presidents vent their frustration at trying to steer organizations
that want to head toward all compass points simultaneously. A
vocal alumni group lobbies to expand the football stadium, but
the faculty senate would rather abolish intercollegiate athletics.
State legislators criticize lackadaisical professors for teaching but
a few hours a week, while those criticized protest to their deans
about onerous teaching loads. A new student dining hall is an
assault on nearby restaurant owners; a celebrated increase in minority student enrollment proves that the university is lowering
academic standards; an alumni magazine article about the business school shows a lack of appreciation for the liberal arts; an
initiative to boost faculty research signifies a weakened commitment to undergraduate teaching.

Modern public universities have become the organizational embodiment of Newton's Third Law, where every action prompts an equal and opposite reaction. And as forces from all directions whipsaw deans, vice presidents, provosts, and presidents, it can seem that change in the academy comes about not by planning and foresight but by an uncoordinated drifting of the center of mass; that academic leaders with a grand vision for their school will ultimately be stymied because nobody wants to follow their lead; and that, in the end, they will discover that "their success or failure may be due more to the vagaries of luck and history than their own dedication and skill."[1]

In one sense universities are at the cutting edge of society. Great social movements have traced their origins to college lecture halls, and academic research laboratories have spawned entire new industries and fields of human inquiry. It is not exaggerating to claim that the world's universities and colleges have been the root drivers of civilization's advance. And yet in another sense there are few other social institutions more steadfastly committed to preserving the status quo. In fact, it frequently appears that the university's cumbersome governance system, with its maze of committees, protracted debates, and labyrinthine procedures, is deliberately intended to slow down innovation and resist change. University presidents who speak publicly of increasing productivity or improving efficiency are viewed by faculty members as dangerous boat-rockers. In academia, to be told that one has a "bottom-line" approach or a "businesslike" attitude is to receive an admonishment.

Understanding the Faculty

There is always some underlying tension between a university's faculty and its administrative leaders. At the benign end of the continuum the tension is manifest in professors' desire to audit and comment on administrative actions and policies, mostly in the spirit of constructive criticism. At the other end it can be virulently nasty, as in the outraged (and tenured) associate professor of biology whom I heard in a public forum accuse her affable and mild-mannered dean of being a "jack-booted Nazi." The tension between a university's faculty and its administration often grows out of the suspicion among the former that the latter do not adequately appreciate that "the faculty are the university." Many a new dean, who just weeks earlier had been teaching classes, publishing papers, and advising students, has noted with bemusement that his credibility with former colleagues diminished the instant he moved into his new office. And even though relationships with faculty colleagues may remain cordial, they are inevitably clouded by the suspicion that the newly anointed administrator has lost an important faculty insight. In extreme cases, it is almost as if one has defected to the enemy camp.

This perceptual shift lies at the heart of the difficult and sometimes problematic relationship between faculty and administration. Why do the faculty believe that they *are* the university, and why do they feel their unique domain is so frail that it must be constantly protected against administrative incursion? The answer goes back to the earliest days of the European academy, when universities were not cohesive administrative structures but rather loose consortia of scholars and teachers who negotiated individual agreements with students. In those days, the faculty literally were the university, and the classrooms, residential flats, pubs, and hostelries were not so much an organized infrastructure as a means to meet the basic necessities of life of the students and their tutors. As the centuries passed, the university infrastructure grew larger and better organized, and it was inevitable that members of the professoriate would eventually begin to worry that their stature and role had diminished. Today, large universities are cities, where nonacademic employees greatly outnumber the teaching faculty and the number of peripheral activities has become so large that it seems often to dwarf the core functions of instruction and scholarship.

It is important to keep in mind, the faculty believe, correctly, that the scientific breakthroughs, the seminal books, articles, and inventions, and the passing on of knowledge to future generations—in short, all of the accomplishments that justify the university's existence—are not the work of presidents, deans, and business managers. In this sense, the faculty belief that they *are* the university is not unreasoned, nor is their conviction that all other aspects of the academic establishment should be in service to their very special role. Contributing to this view is the nature of advanced scholarship itself. Progress in almost any academic discipline requires intense concentration, long spans of uninterrupted time, freedom from distractions, and above all the freedom to pursue knowledge for its own sake. Furthermore, the specialized nature of academic scholarship means that, realistically, only the practitioners themselves and their close peers are qualified to pass judgment on the work that is done. Thus, a department head may have only a general notion of what the members of her own department are studying, and the higher one moves up the administrative ranks, the more superficial one's understanding becomes. How could one possibly expect a dean whose academic background is, say, nineteenth-century German history, to understand the work of the polymer chemists or elementary particle theoreticians who also belong to the dean's faculty?

This is not to say that there is no such thing as an academic pecking order. In fact, most professors are acutely aware of the reputation and capabilities of their colleagues. If each professor in a mathematics department were asked to rank order his or her department colleagues on a scale of most talented to least talented, it is highly likely the lists would show a remarkable consistency. However, the academic hierarchy is quite distinct from the administrative hierarchy, and in relation to the administration, university faculty members consider themselves more as free agents than as employees. They see their profession almost as a kind of academic priesthood to which they have risen through years of training, sacrifice, and hard work. The prerogatives that come with being a member of this priesthood include the right to come to work at times of their own choosing, to structure their classes and lectures as they see fit, to research whatever topics strike their interest, and generally to act in accord only with the dictates of their sense of professionalism and the minimal requirements that classes be met, office hours held, and exams graded.

Those outside academia are often shocked at the lack of accountability and tolerance for abuse of this system, which seems so out of step with the generally accepted practices of the larger society. In fact, even within the university itself, the nonacademic staff often resent what they perceive as an unfair double standard. From the point of view of a university janitor, who wears a uniform, punches a time clock, and is allowed a thirty-minute lunch break, the freedom enjoyed by professors can seem the embodiment of an institutionalized caste system that is almost intolerably discriminatory. Yet it is the nature of advanced scholarship that its practitioners really do need a high degree of independence in order to do their work. Critics of this independence frequently overlook the fact that many university and college professors are self-motivated workaholics (they were, after all, often A students in school and college) who drive themselves harder than any corporate nine-to-fiver can appreciate. There is nothing easy or forgiving about the academic profession for those who aspire to excel in their career.

But is also true that, human nature being what it is, there is a small percentage of professors who take advantage of academia's permissiveness. Every department head can point to faculty members who are slackers, who haven't had an original idea in years, and who put forth the bare minimum effort in their classes. Although the professoriate is quite good at policing itself with respect to academic misconduct, immoral behavior, and blatant illegal acts, it often turns a blind eye to plain old-fashioned laziness and incompetence. Nobody, it seems, has yet figured out how to rein in the abuses of freedom without eliminating freedom itself, and from a faculty member's perspective, the abuses are the price that must be paid if the larger value is to be protected. But the people who actually pay that price—namely students, parents, and taxpayers—often come to a different conclusion.

Understanding University Administrators

To understand the tension between a university's faculty and its administration, it is also necessary to understand the perspective of those who keep the machinery moving. To a degree the conflicting perspectives reflect the difference between theory and practice. Whereas faculty members like to view themselves in the context of abstract ideals and ancient academic traditions, administrators tend to see them in more prosaic terms. Faculty members are employees of the institution; they are paid a salary to perform a job; they consume university resources, and they have an impact on the balance sheet. A few excel, some do their job very well, most do their job adequately, and a few are chronic problems whose presence in the organization is mostly unproductive. The latter group consumes a disproportionate share of the administration's attention.

To administrators, the faculty desire to pursue knowledge for its own sake must be tempered by the laws of supply and demand, as well as myriad other considerations. A responsible dean will not authorize a new faculty position in an area for which there is little student demand, or in a branch of science that has little growth potential or in which external grant support is unlikely. A responsible dean will assess departmental requests for budget increases by looking at the department's track record. Has the senior leadership in the department mentored its junior faculty? Has the department head dealt with problems forthrightly? Have the department's dossiers for promotion and tenure been objective and well reasoned? Would a proposed new appointment be consistent with the larger strategic plans of the college?

There is an inevitable tension between these two perspectives, what some have called a "history of distrust and animosity" between faculty and administrators.[2] It is not that one group is right and the other wrong; in fact, both views are necessary to the university's long-term ability to fulfill its mission. But out of these disparate viewpoints grow predictable disagreements, especially over the use of resources. While it overstates the point to claim that professors have a budget-be-damned attitude about their work, and while it overstates the point to say that administrators are mere bean counters who would unthinkingly subordinate academic priorities to the balance sheet, each group probably leans in the direction of its stereotype.

Buy Now, Pay Later

Consider, for example, the ever-controversial issue of faculty tenure.[3] Yale University recently announced a revamping of its tenure guidelines.[4] According to the new guidelines, "Consideration for promotion to tenure will be detached from resource considerations."[5] The university will accomplish this detachment by guaranteeing that money will always be available to provide lifetime employment for any newly hired junior professor. (Tenure at Yale is typically awarded nine years after employment.) This new policy has clear academic benefits: it reduces the stress for nervous fledgling professors, who need not fear now that their department will be unable to afford them nine years down the road, and it makes a Yale job offer more attractive to top faculty candidates by assuring them that the university is seriously interested in promoting its internal candidates to senior positions.

But it is also the kind of policy that can give night sweats to chief financial officers. In effect, the new policy states that Yale's decisions to give lifetime employment guarantees to its professors, now and into the future, each decision representing a commitment of many millions of university dollars, will be made without consideration of whether the institution can actually afford to spend the money, or whether the department actually needs a new tenured professor, or whether the academic specialty of the candidate for tenure is still at the forefront of the discipline. At Yale, the people responsible for the most costly decisions universities ever make will now have no responsibility to come up with the future dollars to pay for their decisions. Presumably, Yale's administration and trustees, buttressed by the school's high tuition and multibillion-dollar endowment, are confident they can afford the new policy. And they probably can. Even so, the example illustrates how the tug-of-war between the academic and management sides of colleges and universities can weaken the cost discipline that is the hallmark of most well-run organizations.

Of course, sometimes the initiative for excessive deferred spending originates in the administration, as when a president hoping to leave a legacy of achievement embarks on a major campus-building program funded with long-term debt that can be passed on to a successor. But wherever it begins, buy-now-pay-later commitments, whether in the form of pension guarantees, debt service on bonds, or, as in this example, lifetime personnel appointments, have a way of building up over time and eroding an organization's financial base. This erosion has already taken place at many American public universities and colleges, where trustees, presidents, and financial officers increasingly find themselves hamstrung by decisions made by their predecessors. The weighty burden of prior commitments can not only sabotage a school's current operating budget but also make it nearly impossible for a school in financial straits to dig itself out of its financial hole.

The take-away message of this chapter, therefore, is that the academic culture is a powerful force, noble and pure in its goals, that seeks always to elevate the intellectual richness of the academic community and thereby enhance the environment for scholarship and learning. But to the extent this cultural pressure consistently prevails over the need for restraint and fiscal conservatism, the results are fast-rising costs and increasingly shaky financial underpinnings. In the next chapter, we will see how another aspect of the academic culture works to impede productivity and efficiency gains and hampers the ability of universities, particularly public universities, to accommodate changing circumstances.

The Cargo Cult College

The Triumph of Form over Substance

What I love about my academic field, physics, is that it is grounded in common sense—an assertion that may surprise those who have bought into the mystique of lofty abstraction that we physicists work to cultivate. Physics strips the fluff from the fancy talk, the philosophical overtones, the textured nuances, the noble sentiments and heart-stirring rhetoric. To a physicist, truth is a nuts-and-bolts subject about data.

The most commonsensical physicist of them all was Richard Feynman, who died in 1988. Feynman was born in Brooklyn and died in Palo Alto, and between these end points he worked on the atomic bomb, cracked safes, deciphered Mayan hieroglyphics, proved that frozen O-rings caused the *Challenger* space shuttle to explode, figured out why ants walk in single-file lines, and discovered something called quantum electrodynamics, for which he received the Nobel Prize. In 1974, Feynman gave the commencement address to the graduating seniors at the California Institute of Technology, where he had taught for many years. His essay was called "Cargo Cult Science," and despite the fact that it was hurriedly written and rife with clunky sentences, among scientists it is a classic.

Feynman was worried about the triumph of form over substance. For example, if a science teacher has her students memorize the names of constellations, then she is not teaching them about stars but about people. Her lesson may have the trappings of science, but it is not science. The title of Feynman's essay refers to cults in remote Melanesian islands that sprang up after nineteenth-century merchant ships docked at the islands and then departed. Anxious to bring back the ships and their cargoes of Western bounty, the islands' native peoples mimicked the motions of the departed dockhands and harbor masters. When the ships didn't return, the cults eventually died out. Cargo cults sprang up again at the end of World War II, when the Allied forces abandoned Pacific island landing strips and the military cargo planes disappeared into the sky. In hopes of bringing the cargo-laden aircraft back out of the clouds, the islanders fabricated headsets and flags and runways and went through the motions of operating imaginary airfields. When the huge planes never came back, the cults, like those of the previous century, faded away.

But it is not only native south Pacific islanders who practice ineffective rituals. Cargo-cult thinking is pervasive in modern times, especially in American colleges and universities. Universities are bastions of process and ritual. Department heads hold faculty meetings and appoint committees. Deans write reports and send e-mails and hold conference calls. Faculty senate leaders convene public forums and take votes and offer amendments and record these actions in minutes, which are themselves voted upon and amended. Vice presidents forge strategic plans, and presidents give speeches, write editorials, and lead ceremonies. All of these administrative actions are intended to make the gears turn smoothly and thereby perpetuate a high quality of teaching and scholarship. However, this abundance of academic procedures does not necessarily ensure that anything tangible will be accomplished. Lengthy committee meetings that result only in neatly formatted minutes reflect cargo-cult behavior. Focus groups that fail to focus, reports that recommend the status quo, and complex issues debated in endless unproductive circles are all examples of cargo-cult behavior. Any university president can recall many instances in which the academic mountain has labored mightily but ended up giving birth to a mouse.

Case Study: The Battle against Grade Inflation

A few years ago, I gave a speech to the Miami University community about grade inflation and academic standards. I noted that grade point averages had been drifting upward for thirty-five years and that students reported studying only half as much as their professors expected. I observed that many of our best students had complained about the lack of challenge in their courses. I drew a connection between grade inflation and declining academic standards, and I challenged the faculty to think about their expectations for students and the rigor of the undergraduate curriculum. Let us pull together, I said, to solve this problem.[1]

In the ensuing two years, the faculty thought deeply about student expectations. Committees examined philosophies of grading and issued reports about new teaching paradigms. The faculty reaffirmed its commitment to a learning-centered environment, to engaging with other learners, and to helping students connect with their prior experiences. They sought to place the context for grade inflation in the larger fabric of society and the evolution of American culture. For two years, the university community rallied the troops, fired the heavy artillery, and gave it their best shot. They got down to brass tacks, stepped up to the plate, and left no stone unturned. They put their heads together, their feet to the fire, their shoulders to the wheel, their noses to the grindstone, and their ducks in a row. They pushed the envelope, pulled out the stops, tied up loose ends, and thought outside the box.

All to no avail. Not only did the planes never return, but they never even circled the airfield. Over the two-year period, grade inflation at my university got worse. That so many smart people could contemplate a problem for two years—a problem whose seriousness was acknowledged by all, that threatened to sabotage the rigorous education that was the core goal of the institution—and still make absolutely no progress reveals a fundamental reality of academia.

On the One Hand, on the Other Hand

University communities are designed to analyze issues, to understand contexts, to explore nuances and conceptual underpinnings, to consider all perspectives and points of view, and to identify weak arguments and misguided reasoning. But what universities are not designed to do is fix their own problems. It is not that individual professors are indecisive and incapable of coming to conclusions—in fact, quite the contrary. It is rather that the academic community is *collectively* indecisive. There are few mechanisms whereby, all the shades of gray having been parsed and contemplated, somebody can step in, make a decision, and expect that the community will lay the debate to rest and follow along willingly.[2]

In principle, grade inflation should be easy to fix. At least a half dozen solutions quickly come to mind: (1) require each department to grade on the curve, giving, say, 15 percent of the students As, 25 percent Bs, and so forth; (2) provide financial rewards to departments that rein in their grades; (3) make course rigor part of promotion and tenure requirements; (4) call on the carpet professors who give overly generous grades in their classes; (5) deny salary raises to deans and department heads who permit lax grading in their college and departments; (6) report students' rank in class on their transcripts, along with their course grades.

There are several reasons that none of these solutions surfaced in the two years of campus deliberations. The first is that the topic exposed wide philosophical differences within the faculty about grades and academic rigor. In the school of education, which enrolled students who frequently had weak academic credentials but awarded them nearly all As, high grades were seen as a reward for "mastering the material." If all students in a class mastered the material, then all should receive an A and the professor should be duly proud of the class's achievements. Professors in the economics department, by contrast, would have been hard pressed to give Milton Friedman an A. They viewed the Cs and Ds they doled out in abundance as evidence of the difficulty and high standards of their discipline. In economics there could be no such thing as mastering the material.

But philosophical differences were only part of the puzzle. Would lower grades on student transcripts hurt graduates as they applied for jobs? Would medical and law schools reject our graduates? Would lower grades be fair to students who would have received a higher grade had they taken the course the previous year? Would lower grades lead to poor student course evaluations that could harm a young faculty member's chances for tenure? And on and on. All reasonable questions, these, and they point to the core nature of academic inquiry. Universities are in the business of scratching the surface to see what lies beneath. This is almost a compulsion. Should the math department award the corner offices in its new building to the most senior members of the faculty? Hold on a minute. What about awarding the offices to the department's best teachers? But then who would decide who the best teachers are? And what are the criteria, and besides, wouldn't that be sending a message that the department valued teaching more than research? And wouldn't that conflict with the department's promotion standards, which deem teaching and research to be weighted equally?

People outside academia can pull out their hair over the tendency of college professors to wallow in ambiguity. Most folks just want to see results and have a very limited tolerance for on-the-one-hand-but-on-the-other-hand discourse. But this method of inquiry is one of the great strengths of academic scholarship. It is through boring into issues deeply, exploring ramifications, and looking at different points of view that discoveries large and small are made. Universities are peopled with laser beams, not floodlights, with scholars who devote their lives to the mating habits of insects or the color of light from distant stars. Such people, as quirky as they may seem, help advance civilization, but it isn't in their nature to make seat-of-the-pants decisions. Nor would it be appropriate for them to do so.

Faculty Autonomy and the Sanctity of the Classroom

But there is yet another reason that my grade inflation experiment flopped. Underneath the two years' worth of rhetoric and committee meetings and analysis was an underlying issue about academic culture. In the end, to solve the grade inflation problem, some outside authority would have been empowered to check up on faculty members, look at the grades awarded in their classes, pass judgment on those grades, and most likely require them to start grading differently. Nobody said so explicitly, but faculty apprehension about loss of control was a subtext that infused the entire grade inflation discussion. An important part of the academic culture is the sanctity of the classroom, the rationale for which is the preservation of academic freedom and the unfettered exchange of ideas. This is such a core part of the academic culture that professors will go to great lengths to protect the principle, and if doing so means that a few of them give all As or all Fs to their students, then, frankly, that is their own damn business and anybody with other ideas should just butt out.

Naturally, very few college teachers really want to give all As or all Fs to their students. But nearly all university and college faculty members become prickly when their independence is challenged. In some circumstances, they will tolerate directives from their faculty colleagues, but only a clueless department head or dean or provost would insist that tenured professors show up for work at 9:00 a.m., five days a week, or complain to a senior professor that teaching classes dressed like Che Guevara after a long night in the cantina doesn't present the professional image that the school seeks.

The desire of faculty members not to be subordinate to a supervisory authority goes hand in hand with the drawn-out and frequently unproductive practices of academia. It is nearly the antithesis of efficient business practice to permit any large group of employees to work in an uncoordinated and undirected manner, or to ignore or even challenge without repercussions the goals and priorities of the institution's leaders. That universities and colleges willingly accept this organizational inefficiency in the name of academic freedom often frustrates education reformers, who see academia's many inefficiencies simply as an outgrowth of a professoriate that has been allowed to become spoiled and self-indulgent.

The Many Goals of Academic Governance

But this judgment is as simplistic as the judgment of those who see Pacific island cargo cults as merely the foolish practices of primitive and ignorant islanders. In both cases, ineffective rituals and practices have arisen out of service to larger values. Specifically, they are shaped by the prevailing culture in order to meet the needs of their practitioners. In academia, lengthy collaborative processes serve many functions beyond their overt goals. A departmental curriculum committee, for example, provides a means for faculty members to visit with colleagues and break the tedium of grading examinations, reading manuscripts in a library carrel, or laboring over a research proposal. University-wide committees are opportunities for professors to network and meet people outside their home department. They can provide an important mechanism for untenured professors to demonstrate their spirit of collegiality and make an impression on those who will one day pass judgment on their future. Aspiring deans and department heads use committees as training grounds for demonstrating and honing their administrative skills.

For some professors, service to the university is a way to gain the respect of colleagues. It is frequently observed, for example, that campus legislative bodies, such as faculty or university senates, can be magnets for faculty members who have lost interest in their scholarship. Participating in such bodies provides a way for otherwise undistinguished professors to assert their value to their colleagues. What all this means is that the administrative practices and rituals of academia are to some extent ends in themselves. While it may be desirable for a faculty senate to pass legislation that, for example, clarifies a grievance procedure for students who receive failing grades, it is also satisfies ancillary goals for the senate merely to meet regularly, conduct debate, hold votes, and hear committee reports, even if little tangible benefit comes of all this activity.

But at heart, what sustains all of these processes is the underlying principle of faculty autonomy. Faculty autonomy is the most fundamental cultural norm of academia. It means that that a department's professors will turn down a multimillion-dollar gift without a moment's hesitation if they see the donor as trying to influence the department's academic agenda. It means that one never uses the word *management* in connection with faculty members, because the word conveys supervisory powers. One manages cafeteria workers and the maintenance staff, but professors have their needs "administered." In the culture of academia, administrators are expected not to lead but to empower their faculties, by absolving them from the drudgery of filling out forms, paying bills, filing reports, and balancing budgets. At some colleges, department heads serve on a rotating basis, the idea being that all should share in this thankless albeit necessary chore. In earlier decades, colleges even plucked their presidents from the senior faculty, occasionally choosing distinguished scholars who had no administrative experience whatsoever. (This practice, a recipe for disaster, has long been abandoned.) Presidents who retire or step down from their position are inevitably described as "returning to the faculty," much as convicts are returned to society after serving out their sentence.

The Devaluation of Time

But there is a price to be paid for a culture that elevates employee autonomy to a high principle, and that price is the loss of efficiency that comes from devaluing time. The biggest-ticket item on any college or university's budget sheet is faculty compensation, yet faculty time is treated in higher education as if it were a free commodity. Generally speaking, professors come and go as they choose, and if some of them want to spend three hours in a committee meeting with five of their colleagues debating about next semester's colloquium speakers, then that is their prerogative. How they spend the time in their job is seldom questioned and never accounted for.

This sense of entitlement is partly tied to the defense of academic freedom, but it also comes from the belief among academics that what they do is not a job but a calling. Professors feel they are not employees who work primarily to put bread on the table but members of a kind of secular priesthood. They are the chosen ones, charged by society to advance human knowledge and to pass on to the young the accumulated wisdom of the human race. In acquiescence to this noble purpose, society permits them to live in a sheltered enclave where they are screened from the hurly-burly and strife of the outside world and are constrained only by the limits of their intelligence, imagination, and commitment to their discipline.

Although it strikes many as self-serving, this viewpoint is not without merit. There is no doubt our civilization benefits from having a few places where smart people have the freedom to think about the structure of the membranes in a butterfly wing or the early writings of Thomas Jefferson, and there is also no doubt that these practitioners need a measure of freedom and flexibility that would be inappropriate for more directed work. But increasingly, especially for faculty members in some beleaguered public universities, this freedom has unfortunately become, as Kris Kristofferson famously observed, just another word for nothing left to lose. For every Richard Feynman sharing pearls of wisdom with brainy Cal Tech seniors, there are a thousand unknown and underpaid college teachers slogging away in dingy offices and classrooms, trying to make an impact on often ill-prepared students, and worrying about scraping together the down payment for a house and paying medical bills for their children. The Toni Morrisons, Alan Dershowitzes, Milton Friedmans, and Jonas Salks of academia's elite circle have about as much in common with them as LeBron James does with a kid playing pickup ball in an inner-city tenement.

But the dream of a shared purpose is partly what keeps them going, even if the dream may be as fanciful as the gold-filled pot at the rainbow's end. For the faculty members laboring at the broad base of higher education's pyramid—the growing legions of itinerant, part-time, non–tenure-track faculty—the autonomy they enjoy in their work, cloaked in ancient tradition and high academic principle, may be one of the few benefits of their demanding and often unrewarding job. Their autonomy is a membership card, a bond that ties them to the brotherhood of peers at Harvard and Berkeley, to world-famous authors and scientists and historians and economists, to all the men and women who have labored for centuries to move civilization forward. To take away that autonomy would be to sabotage the dream that has motivated their life's work.

Saving the Baby

And so we come to the horns of a dilemma. The culture of colleges and universities perpetuates enduring and important academic values. The culture also meets the needs of individual faculty members. But the culture increasingly fails to meet the economic needs of the institutions. Universities and colleges today face unprecedented problems, problems that require decisiveness, flexibility, and efficiency. However, the ingrained traditions of academia discourage those very traits. The academic culture of analyzing, pondering, and critiquing issues, together with its entrenched defense of professorial autonomy, inhibits institutional flexibility and adaptability.

There is another aspect of higher education's culture that further complicates the picture, and that is the tradition of shared governance. It is not just that professors expect the freedom to do their work and structure their time as they wish. They, along with students, alumni, and virtually everybody else in higher education, also expect to have a say in how things are run. Ironically, colleges and universities, although they are as complex as any organizations on the planet, are run through a decentralized mechanism of participatory democracy in which the voices of the uninformed are often given as much weight as the voices of the knowledgeable.

Not all academicians, including myself, are persuaded that this system is ideal. Harvard economist and former dean of the Harvard faculty, Henry Rosovsky's First Principle for university governance is "Not everything is improved by making it more democratic."[3] That this may partly be wishful thinking, however, is suggested by the words that followed Rosovsky's exposition of his principle: "I shudder as I write this sentence." The next chapter will explore this unique governance tradition in detail, because an understanding of it is a prerequisite to facing the key question of balance: is it really possible to accommodate the present-day needs and realities of American higher education while preserving the essence of a time-honored academic culture that has contributed immeasurably to the well-being of the human race? In other words, is it possible to throw out the bathwater and still save the baby?

7

The Blessing and Curse of Shared Governance

Building Cathedrals[1]

> Faculty participation in governance promotes and encourages diversity of ideas, a sense of shared responsibility, collaboration, collegiality, and institutional excellence, and is essential to the well-being of the University. (University of Michigan Faculty Handbook)

The above statement reflects the traditional belief among the professoriate that faculty governance is an indispensable component of academic freedom and institutional quality in higher education.[2] According to this belief, all members of academic communities, but especially the faculty, share the responsibility for protecting the uninhibited flow of ideas and ensuring that academic priorities are not automatically subordinated to budget and practical considerations. Implicit in this view is the idea of ownership. Students, alumni, staff members, and, especially, faculty members are the true "owners" of the institution. In fact, professors often see themselves not as employees of the organization but as the organization itself, much as the U.S. Supreme Court is taken to be the nine justices and not the building, library, and staff attorneys. Thus, professors clearly differentiate their governance role from that of department heads, center directors, deans, vice presidents, presidents, and other administrative officers; they see administrators as the institution's caretakers, whose responsibility is to keep the school running smoothly and to follow the lead of the faculty on matters academic.

Also implicit in this view is the idea of harmony. An ideal university is a place where members of the community respect each other, celebrate their differences, and welcome each other's views, however unconventional. The members of university communities are building cathedrals, not carrying stones, and they are unified by their shared commitment to a noble societal good. To make this vision work, it is believed necessary that faculty members be given a major voice in decision making, be consulted on all substantive matters, and be the primary source of academic innovation and inspiration. The collective wisdom of the faculty, if not sacrosanct, is at least thought to be more considered than the judgment of administrators, who may be too preoccupied with day-to-day chores and problems to give adequate priority to larger academic values. In this view, the primacy of the faculty underlies the durability of colleges and universities; corporations come and go, but the great universities of the world endure for centuries.

Shaky Foundations

Faculty participation in governance promotes and encourages the rule of mediocrity, perpetuates the status quo, engenders mistrust between the faculty and the administration, and leads to a wasteful use of time and resources that is detrimental to the well-being of the university.

The above statement originates in no faculty handbook, but it captures the sentiments of many critics outside academia's walls. To many elected officials, business leaders, and observers of higher education, panegyrics on the sanctity of faculty governance are disingenuous and self-serving. Underlying the faculty embrace of the concept, critics say, is not so much the advancement of lofty educational goals and a collegial environment as a desire for control—specifically, professors' wishes to insulate themselves from "management," to resist efforts to regulate their activities, and to circumvent the accountability that is the hallmark of professional employment outside academia. To critics, the benefits of shared governance do not compensate for its practical shortcomings. Whereas professors see the concept almost as a high moral imperative, observers outside the academy often see it as a root cause of public dissatisfaction with higher education and a key factor in the rising cost of a college degree.

Costs are high, in the view of critics, because the shared governance model is intrinsically inefficient. When decisions are made only after broad consultation and extensive discussion, and when committees replace individuals as decision makers, then an organization's personnel costs are unavoidably great and the responsiveness of the organization is unavoidably slow. Furthermore, the search for broad consensus makes universities resistant to change. John V. Lombardi, president of the Louisiana State University system, is one of many national academic leaders to have commented on this intrinsic conservatism. Consensus, he believes, "normally results in modest and superficial change," in part because it tends to level out the distribution of resources and in part because it engenders a lowest-common-denominator attitude toward improvement: "Universities that are already high performers benefit from this conservatism. They have a consensus for high performance and high standards the conservative predisposition maintains. Universities that are merely good, have a consensus for good standards, but not for high standards. The conservatism will keep them good, but they rarely will make the considerable and often unpopular effort required to increase their standards to match those of excellent universities."[3]

The Corporate Alternative

Any criticism of university governance inevitably contrasts it with the hierarchical governance model of the business world. The virtues of corporate governance—unity of mission, efficiency, adaptability, and willingness to take risks—are in the view of many precisely the qualities that universities and colleges need to embrace. Furthermore, advocates argue, corporate governance is far more collaborative than many academics acknowledge. Every large business has numerous committees, consults with its employees, and works to engender a sense of ownership and participation in its workforce. The supposed "top-down" management style is not the monolithic dictatorial structure that is sometimes portrayed by academia. Why then would universities and colleges not benefit by embracing the key features of this model?

The answer is that corporate governance is not compatible with the functional complexity of academic institutions. Universities encompass nearly all areas of human knowledge, and administrators cannot make informed decisions about all these disciplines for the simple reason that "complete understanding of the scope and complexity of the enterprise exceeds human cognitive ability."[4] Revising the curriculum, recognizing research opportunities, assessing faculty credentials, modifying academic standards, and evaluating student achievement in areas as diverse, say, as medieval history and organic chemistry require comprehensive understanding that no small group of administrators could ever possess. This need argues for a decentralized decision-making mechanism that entails consultation with those who have specialized knowledge.

Furthermore, universities are socially more complex than most institutions. Not only does the age range of the community span six decades, but the values, priorities, traditions, ways of thinking, communication patterns, and educational styles and philosophies vary enormously among the academic disciplines. Business professors have a unique perspective on their profession that grows out of their training and experience, as do professors of education or, in my case, experimental physics. Shared governance is a mechanism for arbitrating among all the disparate viewpoints, styles, and perspectives and keeping them in balance.

Finally, a university society, despite its intellectual and social diversity, is highly interconnected, so that most decisions have wide-ranging consequences. For example, changes to the academic calendar can affect faculty sabbatical plans, student employment and internship opportunities, long-scheduled athletic events, the registrar's schedule, the bursar's office and fee collection schedules, the timing of financial aid awards, and the plans of conferences, workshops, and summer camps. An important function of shared governance is to minimize adverse unintended consequences. Thus, while the corporate model offers the benefits of versatility and economy, it could not be easily carried over into an academic environment without most likely creating more problems than it would solve.

But the real issue is not a matter of choosing between two alternatives. The issue is whether shared governance is a sacred cow that is so reflexively protected by its advocates that they are blind to its shortcomings, just as its campus critics are intimidated into remaining silent about their concerns. At its core, shared governance is simply a methodology for managing a particular kind of diverse and complex organization, and like any methodology, it can go awry if implemented poorly.

How Shared Governance Fails

Almost every week the *Chronicle of Higher Education* reports a governance meltdown at an institution of higher learning, often resulting in an angry standoff between the faculty and the administration. When these unfortunate events occur, an institution's trustees have little choice but to intervene, in extreme cases dismissing the president or, alternately, siding with the president against the faculty, as did the trustees of Trinity College (now Duke University) in a resolution passed in June 1893:

> Whereas: the Board of Trustees of Trinity College, being impressed with the necessity for harmony and co-operation between the President and the Faculty of the institution, and having learned by experience that a head, invested with full authority is imperatively necessary to the success of the College, therefore: Resolved 1. That the Faculty in its official relations to the College is expected to be under the control and guidance of the President, and that he be governed by their advice only so far as his good judgment may determine. Resolved 2. That this Board pledges itself to renewed zeal in support of the President and the institution.[5]

But the signature of the most common governance failure is not an embarrassing public crisis. Rather, the most common failure is pervasive and incremental dysfunction: the institution or school or department does not solve its problems, or build on academic strengths, or strategically focus resources and capitalize on opportunities. This "soft" failure of governance is insidious, because its root causes cannot be fixed by firing the president or dean or department chair, or negotiating an agreement, or striking a compromise. Rather, its causes are symptomatic of a process that has not worked as intended.

Consider, for example, this story of a small academic department at a public university that for many years had been viewed as a problem area by the institution's central administration.[6] The department's faculty had a reputation for quarreling and filing spurious grievances against each other. The department's curriculum was viewed as undemanding, with a proliferation of easy courses and high grades. These low academic standards were also reflected in the department's graduate program, which had languished for years, unable to attract good students. The faculty had no scholars of national distinction but nevertheless submitted promotion and tenure dossiers that were rife with hyperbole and overstatement. Of particular concern to the university's provost was the fact that the department's rules allowed secretaries and students to vote on faculty tenure decisions. In the provost's opinion, the department lacked senior leadership and had no prospects or desire for self-improvement. The department was not a core discipline with significant student demand and yet was consuming resources at a time when other, highly regarded departments had pressing unmet needs.

The provost had very limited options for dealing with a department of largely tenured professors. The provost could not, for example, follow the lead of her corporate counterparts, whose solution would be simply to close down the department and terminate its unproductive members. While such an action might appear to solve the immediate problem, the provost knew the law of unintended consequences, abetted by plaintiffs' attorneys, would quickly raise its head and wreak long-term havoc. After considerable thought, the provost announced that she planned to merge the department into another, larger and well-respected department. Her proposal involved sweetening the pot for the host department by agreeing to approve several new faculty and staff positions. She felt that with a fresh start the higher standards and stronger leadership of the host department would eventually prevail, resulting in a trimmed-down but higher-quality academic program that would benefit everybody.

This dream was short-lived. The faculty in the first department expressed horror and shock at what they saw as unwarranted administrative interference in their operations. To defend themselves, they mounted a vigorous letter-writing and public relations campaign against the provost. Their case was that the provost knew practically nothing about their discipline, was jumping to unwarranted conclusions, had probably never read any research papers written by department members, and was obviously biased against them, no doubt because of personal animosities. The department produced letters from its alumni testifying that their training had been exemplary and that the faculty had been caring and supportive. In taking its case to the university's faculty senate, the department accused the provost of being high-handed, arrogant, and disrespectful of the faculty voice. If the provost were allowed to get away with this untenable action, would not all academic departments be in jeopardy?

The provost believed that these accusations were unfair and inaccurate. She became frustrated and disappointed not only at the unwillingness of the senate and her other faculty colleagues to support her initiative but also by how quickly and unexpectedly she had found herself on trial. She was surprised that the debate had suddenly changed direction—that the campus discussion was no longer about the wisest course of action for a troubled academic unit but about the alleged shortcomings of her leadership. In the end, beset by criticism seemingly from all directions, the provost had little choice but to back away from her plan. So far as I know, the troubled department is still there, largely intact, continuing to waste resources, continuing to promote inferior faculty members, and doing a disservice both to students and to the university's reputation.

Scenarios like this prompt criticism about the inability of universities to accommodate needed change. To outside observers, it appeared that the faculty's negative reaction to the provost's reasonable proposal was proof positive of the shortcomings of shared governance. But the point that is frequently missed is that while shared governance at that university had indeed failed, the failure had occurred long before the provost had ever announced her plan. It had failed because the quality controls built into that university's governance system had not worked. Over the years, departmental committees had recommended poorly qualified candidates for tenure. Prior deans' and provosts' faculty advisory committees had failed to challenge the weak dossiers, and earlier generations of administrators had rubber-stamped their recommendations. Over the years, new faculty positions in the department had been approved by deans, as had the department's budget requests, course offerings, degree requirements, and rules of departmental governance. In many of these areas, members of the administration had been guided by faculty committees.

In other words, this dysfunctional department was not the real issue. It was a symptom of a more entrenched problem, and that was the long-term failure of the university's administration and faculty alike to discharge their governance obligations responsibly. Although no single decision makes or breaks an institution, the cumulative impact of such decisions is ultimately what determines a university's quality. In this case, the provost, despite her best intentions, was simply not able to undo the damage that had been accumulating for many years. This is the conservatism about which John Lombardi writes. Problems at universities often remain unsolved because decision-making is so decentralized and diffuse that a single leader, no matter how sensible, motivated, and visionary, can contravene the accumulated failures that led to the problems.

But let us suppose that in this example the ground had been meticulously prepared *before* the provost had announced her proposal. Suppose that a formal program review conducted by impartial outside scholars had assessed the weaknesses of the department and that the department had been given ample prior opportunities to fix itself. Suppose that the provost had previously initiated an elaborate formal consultation procedure, with all interested constituencies invited to comment on the department's future, and that an extended period of campus debate on the provost's plan had taken place. In other words, let us imagine that all conceivable avenues of consultation, debate, opinion seeking, and due process had been exhausted. What then? After the dust had settled, months or years later, would the university have been able finally to resolve the problem of its weak department?

Possibly—universities and colleges with strong academic leadership do occasionally merge or shut down weak academic units—but that is certainly not a given. Shared governance ensures that all voices are heard, but it does not ensure closure. Difficult decisions are inherently controversial, and in academia, the tradition of broad community involvement is especially effective at keeping controversy alive. Because decisions about closing programs or reallocating resources or altering priorities ultimately reduce to matters of judgment, these can always be challenged. From the perspective of persons whose ox stands to be gored, there is never enough consultation, never enough objective scrutiny, never enough reasoned discourse. Many a seasoned university administrator, after a valiant effort to redress a serious institutional weakness, has simply thrown up his or her hands in frustration and walked away from the problem.

The Tyranny of the Articulate

When efforts to make significant changes at a college or university founder, as they frequently do, faculty criticism often focuses on alleged wrongful administrator conduct. In academia, officials' decisions to reorganize an academic unit or to eliminate an unneeded degree program are evaluated on a case-by-case basis by faculty members, who generally feel little a priori obligation to support their administration's proposals.

Furthermore, it is not uncommon for professors to level hostile criticism at leaders whose actions they disapprove of.

> Members of the senate have expressed outrage and disappointment at the president's move. Jimmie D. Phaup, a professor of political science, . . . said the president did not understand the concept of shared governance and was ruling like a despot. "Our president missed that part in kindergarten where they talked about sharing," said Mr. Phaup.[7]

However, this freedom to criticize is not a two-way street. The unwritten etiquette of academia is that administrators must be extremely circumspect in passing judgment on faculty behavior. It would be nearly unthinkable, for example, for a dean to criticize publicly a professor's research as shallow and unworthy of serious thought, or to suggest that his lectures were boring and disorganized or that his demeanor set an unworthy example for the young students in his charge. Professors are free to make such criticisms of each other, but any administrator who starts down that path is likely to be loudly and publicly rebuked.

When a college faculty is unhappy with its president (or provost or dean), one almost never hears the complaint that the leader shied away from problems, took too long to make decisions, tolerated low standards, appointed too many large committees, refused to cope with unproductive professors, did not phase out duplicative and weak academic programs, and failed to control expenditures. Instead, faculty complaints tend to focus on allegations about the administrator's unwillingness to share power. Administrators can be characterized by disgruntled faculty members as authoritarian, autocratic, haughty, and arrogant. Those criticized disregard the faculty voice, act unilaterally, do not consult, and have little respect for faculty opinion. They have contempt for shared governance. They are without respect for the traditions of the institution, the values of the institution, the fragility of the institution, and the core beliefs of the institution. They are aloof, high-handed, disrespectful, undemocratic, and poor communicators, and they do not understand what it means to be a leader.

This pattern of criticism generally originates in an unpopular administrative action, often involving closing or merging a program, cutting a budget, or changing the reporting relationship of an academic unit. Once the action has begun, its pros and cons are soon buried under challenges to the process that led to the action, which is viewed as insufficiently collaborative. Quickly, the complaint is generalized to become but the latest step in a long-term pattern of alleged similar behavior, and then the pattern itself is generalized to reflect a core and immutable deficiency in the "management style" of the leader, whose autocratic behavior is harming the institution by marginalizing its faculty.

Thus when Antioch University Chancellor Toni Murdock and her trustees announced in 2007, following years of enrollment declines, an intention to close near-bankrupt Antioch College and dismiss its president, she received a vote of "no confidence" from the college faculty. The faculty complaint did not address the reasons for the decline in enrollment nor the financial management of the campus; rather, it argued that the chancellor did not adequately consult the faculty in coming to her decision. A faculty spokeswoman issued a statement that "the chancellor's precipitous actions have damaged the college to such an extent that her continuation works against the survival of the institution."[8] In academia, alleging a violation of shared governance can be seen as a way to reverse or delay an unwelcome administrative action. In the Antioch case, members of the faculty evidently hoped that they could prevent the closing of their historic college, founded in 1852, by asserting their fervent desire to keep it open, even without a viable plan for dealing with the school's financial realities.[9]

The Governing Board's Response to Faculty Complaints

Faculty charges of administrative incompetence or misdeeds are deeply worrisome to college and university governing boards, which have great difficulty sorting the facts from the fiction. Some college presidents really are autocratic, insensitive, and poor communicators, and no trustees want their school to be headed by a bull in a china shop who tramples over institutional practices. On the other hand, trustees are usually sophisticated enough to realize that generalized assaults on a president or chancellor may reflect mostly a constituency's resistance to needed change and anger over not getting its own way. But even so, when the message is delivered in the form of a no-confidence vote by a faculty senate or in a letter by faculty leaders, such as that delivered recently by the faculty at St. Vincent College, accusing the Pennsylvania institution's president of a "systematic and pervasive disregard for collegiality and shared governance" that has "brought about an unparalleled crisis," trustees understandably feel the need to take action.[10] At some level, trustees may believe that it is irrelevant who is right or wrong but that the dispute itself symbolizes a breakdown of a relationship that is necessary to keep the institution on an even keel. If the president has really lost the confidence of the faculty, then trustees may think that their only option, short of provoking a full-blown confrontation with the school's professors, is to ask the president to step down.

And they may be right, if the criticism is consistent with their personal assessment of the accused, with whom they presumably have a close relationship. In their dealings, have they found the targeted president to be argumentative, reluctant to accept criticism, and impatient? Has the president had difficulty explaining complex subjects and been prone to jump to conclusions? Has the president's use of language been inappropriately blunt and undiplomatic? Yeses to these questions are markers of a problematic personal style that lends credence to faculty concerns.

Moreover, they may be right if they have confidence that those delivering the message are credible. Concerns expressed by respected senior members of the faculty—the institution's top scholars and teachers—or, say, by a delegation of campus deans should always be taken seriously. On the other hand, concerns voiced by a faculty senate or another legislative body may or may not reflect a broader problem. Although there are obviously many exceptions, faculty senates can be magnets for disaffected individuals and those seeking to advance personal or ideological agendas. And while senators in principle speak on behalf of the entire faculty, at most campuses they seldom touch base with their constituencies. In general, university professors go about their business and pay little attention to the doings of the faculty senate or its representatives. I will shortly have more to say about campus legislative bodies.

If the faculty are represented by a union, then trustees should always view criticism of a president in the context of ongoing or upcoming contract negotiations. Aggressive union leaders sometimes try to unite their members and thereby strengthen their negotiating stance by demonizing the institution's leaders. In assessing faculty complaints, trustees should also assess their own responsibility for the president's behavior. Was the president hired to be a change agent who would forcefully address trustee concerns about institutional problems? Change agents inevitably rock the boat, and faculty backlash may be a sign that the president is merely doing what the trustees asked for. It is wishful thinking for trustees to suppose that significant changes in a university or college can take place unencumbered by any strife and discord in the community.

Lastly, trustees should evaluate the specifics that precipitated the criticism and not dwell prematurely on management style. Faculty concerns about inappropriate presidential relationships, lavish spending, conflicts of interest, questionable business dealings, or unethical practices should always receive the most sober attention from governing boards. Concerns about unpopular executive initiatives or decisions, on the other hand, may or may not be a cause for trustee involvement. But no matter where the truth lies, faculty complaints about their college administrations are in many cases really about the sharing of power and the desire of the faculty to protect its autonomy. As we will see, it is hard to overestimate how deep the currents of faculty independence run in academia.

Shared Governance at Public Colleges and Universities

Years ago, I was a finalist for the position of provost at an Ivy League university, a job I very much wanted. After rounds of interviews with the search committee, campus leaders, and groups of students and professors, I concluded my final day's interview schedule by meeting with the university's president. My meeting did not go well. After pleasantries, the gist of the president's remarks went something like this.

> Mr. Garland, you are one of three finalists for this position. The others are an internal candidate and a candidate from a private university. You are the only candidate with a background from a public campus. I have to tell you that in my experience administrators from public universities seldom make successful transitions to the private sector. The reason is that they are unaccustomed to making decisions. Public universities are so weighted down with committees and constituencies that leaders have few opportunities to exercise independent judgment. I am not looking for a politician provost, whose instincts are to keep the peace and work toward consensus. I need a tough-minded decision maker who is eager to make things happen.

It took me years to understand that the president, even if overstating his case, had pretty well sized up the public university environment. The idea of "public" creates expectations about power sharing that do not exist in the private sector. Consider Amherst College, a private liberal arts college headed by an independent twenty-one-person governing board drawn from around the nation. The trustees, seventeen of whom are

Amherst graduates, consist of successful business leaders, journalists, professional people, and academics from other universities and colleges. Only six of the trustees (including the Amherst president) live in Massachusetts. Amherst is frequently ranked as the top liberal arts college in America. It goes quietly about its business of educating students in an amicable and collegial environment characterized by mostly cordial and respectful relationships among the college's faculty, administrative officers, and trustees.

By contrast, the college's larger neighbor down the street, the University of Massachusetts at Amherst, is part of a five-campus statewide system, headed by a president who is appointed by the Massachusetts governor and whose offices are in Boston, two hours distant. The current university governing board has nineteen voting members; seventeen are political appointees, some of whom may have little understanding or knowledge of higher education and at least one of whom is required to be a representative of organized labor. The other two are students who are elected by the students of their campuses and may never have been on any campus but their own. Only three of the trustees live outside the state. In contrast to Amherst College, the University of Massachusetts at Amherst seems to be in near-constant turmoil: "Outraged by last week's shakeup in university leadership, more than 200 University of Massachusetts at Amherst faculty members cast a vote of no confidence yesterday in UMass President Jack M. Wilson and the board of trustees."[11] Over the years, complaints about administrative actions, a legacy of disagreements with the governor and legislature, and a history of retrenchment and budget cutbacks have left many faculty members at the University of Massachusetts feeling embattled and defensive. Faculty complaints often have centered on the assertion that important decisions were made without adequate faculty involvement.

The question of adequate faculty involvement crops up repeatedly in public higher education. From the perspective of many public college professors, their school is a football that is kicked around by governors, legislators, and education reformers. Proposals to restructure their school, impose a new strategic vision, consolidate or eliminate programs, implement cost-saving schemes, expand accountability requirements, and force new workplace rules seem to sprout annually in the political landscape like noxious weeds. Professors often regard such proposals as poorly conceived, politically motivated, inadequately thought out, and, if implemented, hurtful to their campus. Greater faculty participation would, they argue, help ensure that changes and proposals are at the very least well considered and reasonable.

The counterargument is that the demand for greater faculty involvement is mostly a smokescreen and that what professors really want is veto power over any new idea or plan that might potentially threaten their self-interest. For a governor anxious to improve his or her state's higher education system, a university faculty is not so much a potential ally as a conservative and vocal oppositional force. From a lawmaker's perspective, the major challenge can be to implement necessary and desired changes by sidestepping the faculty and preventing it from stalling or emasculating reform initiatives.

Shared governance at the level of academic departments generally works well at both public and private colleges. Faculty-centered committees that deal with curricular matters, searches for new professors, degree requirements, tenure and promotion of junior faculty, and colloquia and seminar speakers, if not paragons of efficiency, nevertheless do their work quietly and amicably. However, at the all-college or all-university level, shared governance on public campuses bears little resemblance to the rosy collegial notion of members of an academic community working arm in arm to share their expertise and judgment in furtherance of the school's mission. Rather, in the public sector, shared governance takes on the coloration of constituency-based politics. At public campuses, the faculty is one of a large number of interest groups that must be always vigilant to defend their territory. For professors, this vigilance often entails circling the wagons against perceived attacks by the administration or outsiders to weaken faculty influence and regulate professors' activities. There is little arm-in-arm collegiality but rather an adversarial sense of continuing negotiation by factions with conflicting agendas.

The sheer size of public universities contributes to the weakening of the shared governance ideal. At the largest public universities, there may be four thousand professors and four or five times that many staff members. Because professors of, say, early childhood education may have nothing in common professionally with professors in the business or engineering or law schools, may work in offices that are separated by a mile or more, and may live and socialize in different suburban neighborhoods, it is nearly impossible for big public universities to foster a strong sense of community and collegiality. I worked at Ohio State University for twenty-six years and never met more than a small fraction of my faculty colleagues. In fact, I would occasionally learn about entire academic departments that I never knew existed.

At the largest public campuses one of the most vocal and influential constituencies is sports fans. As the *New York Times* recently noted, "Simply put, boosters and alumni now act as shareholders, whipped into go-team frenzy to form a new breed of extreme fans as they seek a return on their increased emotional and financial investments in the Program."[12] Intercollegiate athletics at public (and a few private) universities can seem to faculty members, many of whom have little interest in sports, a serious detraction from their school's academic agenda. For faculty members at major public universities, sports-related inconveniences abound, such as the difficulty of driving and parking near their office and laboratory on football Saturdays or the impossibility of reserving hotel rooms for department visitors during major sporting events. But more significant, the obsession of the news media with college sports, juxtaposed to its seeming lack of interest in academics; the preoccupation of local elected officials with obtaining football and basketball tickets; the anti-intellectualism and rowdiness of fervent fans; and the seven-figure salaries earned by major program coaches lead many professors to ask which is the dog and which is the tail. In this milieu, the notion that "the faculty are the university" can seem almost like a mean-spirited joke.[13]

But what most discourages public college professors is the declining financial support of their school by their state government. As professors watch their campus deteriorate, endure budget cutbacks in their department, and go for years with minimal or no salary raises, it is hard for many to avoid feeling like their university is under siege. Compounding this perception is the unsympathetic and increasingly disrespectful language of higher education critics and the unending clamor by elected officials for more accountability. Many senior faculty members have seen their campus degenerate into something quite different from the placid community of scholars where they had hoped to spend their career in the pursuit of knowledge.

The defensive conservatism of professors is thus, unsurprisingly, a natural response to the changed environment of public higher education and their perceived disenfranchisement. A key indicator of faculty frustration is the emergence and growing activism of public university faculty unions, the rationale for which was succinctly noted in an opinion piece in *Advocate Online,* a publication of the National Education Association: "In a period of economic contraction, uncertain funding in higher education, and increased demands for teaching and accountability, the protection and advancement of faculty rights and benefits becomes an imperative. This can rarely be done without the protections of a strong and united faculty union."[14]

In Ohio, nine of the state's thirteen public four-year campuses now have faculty unions, some of which have been openly hostile to their campus administration. In this twenty-first-century public college environment, an environment that spawns grievances, accusations, and angry words, an environment that erodes trust and goodwill and that reduces cooperation among colleagues to negotiation across a bargaining table, shared governance often means little more than the raw struggle for power by frustrated professors and their wistful yearning for an earlier and happier time.[15]

What Price Shared Governance?

Time Is Money

The Washington, D.C.–based company Covington and Burling, LLP, founded in 1919, is one of America's premier law firms, with a roster of blue-chip clients that includes Bank of America, General Electric, Microsoft, IBM, and many other of the household names of American industry. The six hundred–plus attorneys at Covington and Burling partition their working days into six-minute segments, using a sophisticated computer system that not only adds up their minutes but tracks phone calls, conferences, correspondence, memos, e-mails, and faxes and automatically tallies the totals, which are then duly charged to a client's account. The partners at Covington and Burling understand very well that time is money, and one can presume that this concept is also brought home to the company's clients whenever they scrutinize their sizable monthly invoices.

From Covington and Burling it is a short twelve-minute taxi ride to Georgetown University, the venerable Jesuit institution founded at the time of the French Revolution, where more than forty of Covington and Burling's partners and associates received their law training. At Georgetown, there is no effort made to account formally for professors' time. The Georgetown faculty come and go at will, devote as much or as little time to their courses and research as they choose, and do not track the hours spent on committee service, writing letters of recommendation, drafting book manuscripts or articles for professional journals, meeting with colleagues or students, talking on the phone, or composing e-mails. At Georgetown, as at virtually every other university in the country, there is little sense among professors that time is money. Furthermore, one can safely assume that the Georgetown undergraduates who pay for that time, to the tune of $37,536 a year in 2008–9, have only the slightest idea of what their money is going for.

Students probably do not know, for example, that their tuition dollars pay for the monthly meetings of the Georgetown University Faculty Senate, a legislative body nearly as large as the United States Senate, four miles away. The Georgetown body's eighty-one senators (in 2008–9) are drawn from the school's main campus, its medical and law centers (each of which has a caucus that meets regularly), and (ex officio) the central administration. The senate has numerous standing committees, such as the eight-member Academic Freedom and Responsibility Committee, the twenty-two-member Budget and Finance Committee, and the nine-member University Governance Committee. There are, in addition, periodic ad hoc committees, such as the eight-member Ad Hoc Committee on Faculty Career Flexibility, which met for a year in 2006–7 and then issued a final report whose only recommendation was to create a new Faculty Career Flexibility Advisory Committee, to meet for an additional two years.[1] The Georgetown Faculty Senate also appoints members to other university committees and councils, forty-two in all, including the Faculty Club Advisory Committee, the Committee on Investments and Social Responsibility, the Performing Arts Advisory Council, and the University Committee on Rank and Tenure.

Members of the Georgetown University Faculty Senate are, with the exception of a handful of ex officio administrators, elected to three-year terms by their faculty constituencies. As is true elsewhere in academia, faculty senate elections are mostly characterized by voter disinterest. For example, in the spring election of 2006, thirteen main campus candidates at Georgetown vied for ten senate vacancies. Nearly 70 percent of those eligible to vote did not return ballots, and of the ten senators who won election, five were already members.[2] In most campus legislative bodies, it is common to find a core group of professors who stand for reelection repeatedly and may serve for a decade or longer.

On February 12, 2007, the University Faculty Senate held its monthly meeting to consider various items of business. Nearly 60 percent of the senators missed the meeting, but those present heard a report on several minor revisions to the faculty handbook and were notified that the university president had created a new committee "to assist and revise with respect to proposed [future] modifications to the Handbook." Senators were reassured that faculty members would be part of this new Handbook Council and that the council's charge would be brought to the faculty senate in order that senators could comment and debate it.

The senators also heard reports on the operations of the Faculty Ombuds Office and on the status of the university budget, the highlight of which was that the university had ended the 2006 fiscal year with a net operating loss of almost $4 million. After meeting for nearly two hours, the senate adjourned. As the senators walked out the door of their meeting hall, it likely did not occur to any of them to wonder how much impact their meeting had had on the magnitude of the university's deficit or whether the business they had accomplished in the meeting actually justified the thousands of dollars of faculty and administrator time that had been expended for it.

Georgetown University follows a pattern of faculty governance that is typical for American universities, both public and private. But if the rest of America's colleges and universities are marching to the same drumbeat as Georgetown, then what can be said generally about the impact of shared governance on the cost of a college education? To begin to answer this question, we can observe that if time is not valued as an identifiable financial resource, then there is no fiscal incentive to ration it or to make certain it is expended efficiently and productively. When a dollar value is attached to any proposed expenditure, tradeoffs and other options become immediately apparent. Should we take a family vacation to Cancun this year, or would we be better off replacing our old bedroom furniture? Shall we upgrade to Business Class or rent a fancier hotel room at our destination? Organizations and individuals are constantly making these kinds of decisions, because the dollar valuation of options provides a benchmark for making choices. In fact, comparative prices underlie the fundamental concept behind budgeting. A budget is merely a systematic way of assigning priorities and rankings to potential expenditures, using each expenditure's dollar valuation as a unifying bridge. Prices are what make it possible to compare apples to oranges.

But in higher education, faculty and staff labor is not explicitly valued, except as a lump sum in the university budget. Which is better, to have a ten-person curriculum committee or to get by with a five-person curriculum committee and use the saved money to give a scholarship to a talented student? Or to replace an obsolete computer? Or to send a professor to an important professional conference? Or to pass along the savings to students by reducing their tuition charges? Such questions are not raised in academia, because labor is treated as a fixed cost and not as a resource to be judiciously expended. Of course, because faculty and staff members are paid regardless of whether they slave away like dogs or sit gazing out their office window, it may seem that there is no real savings when a committee is reduced from ten to five members. But in aggregate, when the work of the university can be carried out by fewer people, none working any harder or longer than before, then the savings can be appreciable. If, say, seven hundred faculty members can do the same work that formerly took eight hundred, then the savings can be redirected into salary increases, larger operating budgets, or reduced tuition charges. When productivity and efficiency in an organization increase, everybody wins.

But practically speaking, how much money are we talking about? And, equally important, what sacrifices to the academic culture of freedom and autonomy would be required to reap these savings? I believe it is safe to assert that few professors would respond positively to a request that they account for their time in six-minute increments. I will defer the second question to the next section and take up here, using my own university as an example, the question about dollars.

Case History: The Cost of Shared Governance at Miami University

In 2004, Miami University had 193 standing committees above the departmental level.[3] Of these, 64 were associated with the University Senate, and the remainder were college- and school-level committees. There were 1,353 university employees, mostly professors, who served on these committees, which averages out to 7 per committee. In addition, 54 university employees served on the University Senate, 18 served on the Council on Student Affairs, and 13 served on the Graduate Council, which brings the total up to 1,438 members. Search committees for deans and vice presidents and ad hoc committees and councils added 95 more employees to the numbers, bringing the total to 1,533.

In addition, each of the university's 45 academic departments had an average that year of 12 committees, with 5 members per committee, for a total of 2,700 members. Adding this to the earlier number brings the grand total of nonstudent committee members in 2004 up to 4,233. That number does not include purely administrative committees, like the Council of Academic Deans, the President's Executive Committee, or any of the many committees in Business and Finance, University Advancement, Information Technology, Admissions and Financial Aid, the Provost's Office, Intercollegiate Athletics, and so forth.

In 2004, the university spent an average of $87 to pay for one hour of faculty or staff committee time, which means that a six-person committee meeting for two hours cost the university more than a thousand dollars. Per-person University Senate expenses were proportionally higher because of additional administrative support costs. The university ended up spending $112 for every minute the University Senate met, or about $13,400 per meeting. The Senate normally met weekly, with a monthly cost of about $54,000, not counting the meeting costs of the Senate's standing committees or executive committee.

If we assume that each of the university's 4,233 committee members spent an average of one hour per week on their assigned committees— probably an underestimate—then in the course of an academic year, committee service at the university absorbed about 150,000 hours of labor, roughly equivalent to that of 125 full-time faculty members, or about 15 percent of the total faculty. This committee work took about $13 million out of the university's annual budget, not counting the amount spent to provide the meeting rooms, maintenance, staff support, and other overhead expenses. These dollars were essentially invisible; they were not budgeted for, appeared in no ledger book or spreadsheet, were never taken into account by any of the committee members or chairpersons, and were not a factor in the decision to create any of these committees or to structure their agendas. Furthermore, nobody ever inquired whether all the debates, motions approved and denied, decisions made, and other outcomes of this collective effort represented good value for the students and taxpayers who ultimately paid for them.

The question of value is partly a matter of relative efficiency. A committee that meets no longer than necessary, with a clear and focused

agenda, with members who are knowledgeable and thoughtfully chosen, and with a well-prepared chairperson who conducts the meeting in
a crisp, businesslike manner, obviously brings better value to bill payers
than a committee that reflects none of these things.

But in academia, the question of value is muddied by the inten-
tional symbolism of shared governance. For example, when a university
searches for a senior administrator, such as a provost, the search committee may have fifteen or more members, and although these individuals
are undoubtedly highly regarded in the community, many of them have
little or no idea what a provost actually does or what skills are necessary to do the job well. Instead of being selected for their expertise, the
committee members are chosen to portray a symbolic balance. Thus,
there will be representatives from the humanities, sciences, and major
professional programs, in rough proportion to their sizes in the institution. The members will also be parsed by race and gender, in order to
make a statement about the institution's commitment to diversity. The
committee will have faculty members (untenured and tenured), deans or
other senior administrators, clerical staff, undergraduate and graduate
students, and possibly alumni, and if there are branch campuses, they
will also have a voice, as will the major legislative bodies, such as faculty
and student senates.

It can be a major challenge to structure such committees so that no
group feels disenfranchised. When I appointed committees, my staff
and I would draw a large grid on a blackboard, each column labeled for
a constituency group. The name of each proposed committee member
would start a row on the grid, with a check mark in the boxes representing each constituency the person belonged to. Particularly desirable were
candidates who fell into many constituencies, e.g., African American,
female, assistant professor of engineering. At most campuses, multiple-
constituency faculty members can have such heavy committee assignments that their scholarship and teaching are harmed.

It is a common experience for those who appoint search committees to begin with aspirations of creating a small "working" committee
but then to find that complaints from the campus compel them to add
members. The important point is that the stated goal of finding the best
candidate often succumbs to the community pressure for broad participation. These two objectives tend to be in conflict. Not only can large
committees be nearly unworkable from the perspective of organizing
meetings and having productive group discussions, but such committees

are also frequently drawn to lowest-common-denominator candidates whose primary attribute may be the ability to present themselves as outgoing, affable, and nonthreatening to any of the represented constituencies. I will discuss this phenomenon in a later chapter about presidential leadership.

And so the question of value comes down primarily to a matter of perspective. From the perspective of the faculty and other constituent groups in academia, cumbersome and slow governance procedures are necessary to protect the important principles of democratic participation and faculty autonomy. This philosophical commitment to principle is facilitated by higher education's budgeting framework, which conceals the actual costs of governance and conveys the impression that time is freely expandable. But in reality, the cost of shared governance is very high, in terms of both the actual dollar cost and the resulting tradeoffs. At public universities especially, those tradeoffs eventually translate into lagging salaries and deteriorating working conditions. In one sense it is ironic that those most negatively affected are often those who would protect most strongly the system that contributes to their suffering.

But the important question is not whether shared governance in higher education should be sacrificed to the gods of efficiency and cost reduction. The question, rather, is whether shared governance procedures can be modified in a way that enhances efficiency and reduces costs but also preserves the essential principles of faculty freedom and collaboration. If, for example, the work done by the 4,233 committee members at Miami University in 2004 had been done by 3,000 committee members, thus permitting hundreds of professors to spend more time advising students, writing books, drafting research proposals, and preparing for their classes, I believe the overall quality of the committee work would not have declined and might actually have improved. In that event, both the faculty and staff, and the students and taxpayers they serve, would all have benefited.[4]

In chapter 13 I will propose ways to streamline university service activities by providing incentives to reduce committee size and eliminate marginally useful committee activities. The idea will be to implement a simple budgeting tool that quantifies the actual costs of governance. Once the costs are known explicitly, committee service and other types of governance activities can be budgeted for as is any other expenditure, with the value of their contributions juxtaposed against other institutional priorities and needs.

Part III

Renegotiating the Public Compact

The Shape of Things to Come

The Unhappy Family

If it is true that every unhappy family is unhappy in its own way, as Tolstoy famously asserted, then it is equally true that unhappy families are blind to the patterns that perpetuate their discontent. Unhappy families are marked by relationships that do not work but are so intertwined that none of the members can break loose. Unhappy families are blind to the truth about themselves, even though that truth may be obvious to others. The family members blame each other for their problems, refuse to admit their short-comings, lash out at critics, and react hostilely to suggestions for change. Unhappy families remain unhappy because they are fearful of taking risks. In the end, they accept their present state of misery instead of taking responsibility for their destiny and doing things differently.

Public higher education is an unhappy family. The family members are governors and elected officials, trustees, regents and governing boards, college and university presidents and chancellors, professors and administrative staff members. This family's growing dysfunction is obvious to students who face tuition bills they cannot afford; to professors whose jobs become less and less rewarding; to governors unable to revitalize their lagging state economy; to politicians pressured by constituencies to "do something" to rein in college costs; to university presidents whose calls for reform are drowned out by the incessant mooing of sacred cows; and to college finance officers who watch their school's bond rating decline and campus physical plants deteriorate.

Ironically, all the members of this family believe in the noble purpose of public higher education. All members want to provide a high-quality education for their fellow citizens; they all want efficient, well-run, financially stable, and responsive institutions. They all believe in academic freedom, tempered by personal responsibility and respect for others. They all believe that education is the key to prosperity and economic development, and they all share the conviction that the best chance for the continued success of American democracy is a well-educated citizenry.

But like all unhappy families, the members of the higher education family cannot change their behaviors. Elected officials keep pressing for more controls and regulations and accountability, because they have difficulty understanding that these timeworn approaches are actually worsening the problems they are intended to solve. University presidents keep blaming government for their problems; they hire lobbyists and write opinion pieces and testify before legislative committees, always imploring lawmakers to step in and fix their problems by giving them more money. Professors and other faculty members keep turning a deaf ear to their critics. They reject public criticism of their traditions and practices as unfounded and ignorant. They say politicians do not adequately value academic freedom and that college administrators are too heavy-handed and autocratic. They see themselves as the defenders of the faith but their problems as somebody else's to solve.

Step One: Challenging Assumptions

As with all dysfunctional families, the medicine is easy to prescribe but difficult to swallow. The first step of any cure is for the family members to admit that the problems will not disappear unless the underlying behaviors are changed. This first step is difficult, because it means challenging long-held assumptions. It means that legislators must give up their assumptions that more laws and controls and mandates will create efficient and affordable public colleges. It means accepting the lesson of history that there are limits to what a blunt instrument wielded from the statehouse can accomplish. The first step means that professors must come to accept that their interests will not be advanced by their reflexive defense of wasteful and unproductive academic practices. It means that university and college presidents must give up hoping that adequate public money will be forthcoming to fix their school; that the taxpayers will bail them out of their financial troubles if only they voice their needs more persuasively; that public frustration with their university can be assuaged if they respond with incremental, business-as-usual changes.

But mostly, the first step is to let go of the notion that it is possible to go backward in time and to acknowledge that the era of inexpensive taxpayer-supported college educations for all Americans is now past and will not return. It is to realize that, barring fundamental structural changes, the future of public higher education now holds only the promise of higher tuitions, lagging faculty salaries, deteriorating campuses, more government controls and regulations, an increasingly demoralized professoriate, and a campus atmosphere marked by polarized, fractious constituencies. It is to accept the fact that the disease is worsening, and that while the infection may have taken hold so far mostly at small regional public campuses, it will eventually spread to and overwhelm the Virginias, Berkeleys, Ohio States, and other flagship public universities.

Step Two: Recognizing Destructive Patterns

The second step of the cure is to see the repetitive patterns of dysfunctional behavior that perpetuate the problems. University presidents, as they tour their state capitol asking for more state support, must come to realize that they are reciting from a decades-old script that has not worked for years and will not work in the future. Elected officials who complain about waste and inefficiency at their state universities must come to understand that they are tilting at the same windmills as their predecessors. Faculty union leaders who stage unproductive confrontations with their administrative counterparts or faculty senates that reflexively oppose reform initiatives must realize they are following a time-worn playbook that is only locking their campus into a slow state of decline.

The second step of the cure also means recognizing that dysfunctional behaviors are intertwined—that every time a state imposes an unwelcome new regulation on its campuses, it creates a counter-response of institutional and faculty resistance that provokes only another round of regulations. Recognizing destructive patterns means learning to look through a wide-angle lens, to step back from the immediacy of this year's operating budget, this year's government appropriation, tuition charges, and salary raises. Viewed from a distance, are faculty salaries keeping up with the competition or are they falling behind? Is the backlog of deferred building maintenance getting shorter or longer? Is tuition becoming more or less affordable?

Diagnosing the health of the patient is a particular problem in public higher education, because the fortunes of public campuses are so dependent on the short-term and often unpredictable outcomes of the legislative process. If the state removes a tuition freeze or increases a public subsidy by a few percentage points, it is only natural for university leaders to breath a sigh of relief. If the opposite, there is a feeling of despair. Public colleges are so buffeted by the short-term vagaries of external circumstances that it is difficult for academic leaders to avoid becoming myopic. How do salary raises, freshman applications, state appropriations, and so forth compare to last year's numbers? If the numbers are up, then things appear to be getting better. If down, worse. But drawing such conclusions is like assessing the direction of the economy by looking at daily fluctuations in the S&P 500 index. Until all the players come to understand that, despite occasional moments of optimism, public higher education is in a gradual long-term decline, there will be no strong incentive to do things differently.

Step Three: Accepting Responsibility

The third step of the cure is for the members of the higher education family to stop pointing fingers at each other and to accept their share of responsibility for perpetuating the problems—not *creating* the problems but perpetuating them. This is an important distinction. The problems were created by larger economic and social forces over which the participants have no control, but how they respond to the problems is very much under their control. Step three requires more than just looking inward. It requires policy makers and academic leaders to visualize how they seem to others; for college presidents to imagine, for example, how whiny their complaints must sound to legislators who have to deal with massive unemployment in their inner cities, the health care needs of their state's elderly, the deteriorating roads connecting their cities, and the pleas for help from middle-class taxpayers whose jobs have been outsourced overseas.

It means tenured faculty-senate leaders should think about how wasteful and picayune their protracted debates and arguments over process must seem to campus administrators who are trying to find the money to avoid laying off university employees. And it means elected officials should imagine how just how hypocritical their claimed commitment to higher education must appear when, year after year, they never translate that commitment into increased financial support.

Seeing oneself through others' eyes is important because it facilitates dialogue and breaks down barriers; it tempers immoderate actions and words; it reduces the temptation to brand others as the enemy; it makes it clear that problems are more complicated than they appeared at first blush and that solutions will require compromise and working together.

Step Four: The Light at the End of the Tunnel

The fourth and final step is the return of optimism, to see that if old patterns give way to a spirit of cooperation and compromise and a willingness to experiment and take risks, the family can be saved. But the hope and optimism come with a price. For professors, it means accepting a degree of unaccustomed accountability for their activities. For university administrators, it means streamlining their ranks and reemphasizing academic goals. For legislators and governors, the price entails giving up some control over their state's public campuses and asking them to accept more responsibility for their own future. It means acknowledging that if the old strategies cannot make the campuses stay afloat, then it may be better to throw them into the lake and let them flounder around until they learn to swim on their own.

These will be difficult and controversial adjustments. For university faculty and administrators who have seen that the hand of government seems always to harm their universities, or for elected officials who have learned through experience that public colleges will do everything possible to resist structural changes and innovation, it is hard to accept the notion that sacrifices and letting go can actually be for the good. But is it better to accept a predictable but unhappy present and the certainty of an even grimmer future or to take a risk now that entails some uncertainty but opens the possibility of brighter days ahead? Like the alcoholic who has to hit bottom before turning his life around, many public universities in America are drifting toward the state where they have little left to lose. This year may be tolerable, and so may next year, and even the year after. But what about ten or twenty years from now? If each year brings another thousand tiny cuts, then what kind of state universities will we be sending our children and grandchildren to? What will have happened to the American dream of opportunity for all?

Prelude and Variations

The remaining chapters focus on my recommendations for arresting public higher education's downward slide. These recommendations are based on two premises. The first is that the decline of this important national resource cannot be reversed by our simply tinkering around the edges of the problems or hoping for the return of a state of affairs that is no longer possible. Instead, my premise is that public higher education's problems can be solved only if the system itself undergoes some fundamental changes. Of course, in the public arena systemic change of nearly anything—the tax code, health care, public schools, social security—is difficult to accomplish. Opposition from vested interests, the tug-of-war among constituencies, the reluctance to redistribute power, and the sheer inertia of political and social institutions all contribute to preserving the status quo. So in general the major challenge is not to convince people that a better world is possible but to show them how to get to that better world from here. And so in making these recommendations I have tried to give attention to transitions. My proposals require all parties to make some changes and accommodations, but they do not create winners and losers. Instead, they require a spirit of cooperation among elected officials, university and college leaders, and faculty members, combined with a realization that no good can come from a perpetuation of the status quo.

There are three major themes in the following chapters. The first pertains to the crucial role of leadership. Realistically, no substantive change in public higher education can come about unless those empowered to make changes—governing boards, system heads, and university presidents and chancellors—are committed to doing so. But the mechanisms for choosing higher education's leaders tend to attract people who know how to play the game but do not have the instincts for changing the rules of the game. So in the following chapters I propose that governors and governing boards revise their hiring and appointing practices and also expand and codify their performance expectations for those chosen. Because college and university presidents and chancellors obviously are crucial to reforming public higher education, I give particular attention to their role.

The second major theme is necessary changes in the academic culture, the pluses and minuses of which have been discussed at length, both my me and many other authors. Changing the culture is important because over the decades it has evolved into a culture of defensiveness. Although dressed in academic principle, many academic traditions and practices, particularly at public universities, have morphed into unhealthy strategies for resisting innovation. The culture must change also because it has become a barrier to legislative risk-taking. It is simply not reasonable to expect elected officials to grant greater autonomy to public universities unless those universities give something back in return, and in this case that something is a good-faith effort to respond to politicians' concerns about universities' lack of accountability, waste and inefficiency, and disregard of public needs. In one sense, changing the campus culture is the biggest hurdle of all, but only partly because of the difficulty of persuading campuses of the need. The larger difficulty is to define the goal. American higher education sets the world standard for academic freedom and excellence, and the campus culture of permissiveness and faculty autonomy is part and parcel of that strength. The objective, therefore, is to steer a reform path that does not jeopardize these important values but diminishes their ancillary unhealthy consequences.

The third theme pertains to the need for reforming the business plan of higher education. As I develop this theme, my working assumptions are that the current financing model of public higher education flies in the face of American economic reality, that financial incentives are more effective at creating systemic change than are legislation and wishful thinking, and that the laws of supply and demand, if allowed to operate, can be powerful tools for advancing and protecting the public interest.

Leadership Begins with the Trustees

The Buck Stops on the Governor's Desk

Public higher education cannot be turned around unless the right kinds of leaders are calling the shots. Public higher education in the twenty-first century calls for individuals who are problem solvers, who are not wedded to old and ineffective solutions, and who have balanced judgment and the knowledge and skills to make changes. But as we will see, the mechanisms for choosing public higher education's leaders—the trustees, regents, presidents, chancellors, vice presidents and deans—often fail to select people like this. Because they paint with the broadest brush, governing boards play an especially crucial role in the leadership continuum. Trustees and regents are at the interface between a state's government and its public campuses. They thus have responsibilities both to protect and advance the public interest and to monitor and preserve the health of the campuses.

Superficially this dual role would seem to present few conflicts, because the public interest is clearly advanced by the existence of healthy, vital educational institutions. But scratching the surface brings out a multiplicity of tradeoffs: the public wants inexpensive, affordable colleges, but the colleges want more money, new buildings, and competitive salaries for their employees. The public wants accountability and stringent reins over the uses of taxpayer dollars, but the campuses want fewer restrictions and greater flexibility in the uses of these dollars. Furthermore, governing boards are expected to deal with complex and controversial social issues—affirmative action, race-based admissions, gay rights, classroom bias, academic freedom and free speech—and to reconcile the frequently different perspectives on these issues coming from the campuses and the statehouse.

Generally speaking, governing boards fall into two broad categories— the statewide or systemwide boards that oversee many campuses and the campus-specific boards that oversee single institutions. Many states— including New York and Florida—have a single governing board for all the public universities in the state. There are many variations on this theme. California, for example, clusters its public campuses into three statewide systems that reflect different educational missions and has a governing board for each system. A few states, Ohio being one, have both campus-specific governing boards and a statewide board that provides coordination among all the campuses and serves as higher education's primary interface with the state legislature. There is also wide state-to-state variation in governing board responsibilities. Obviously, the state-wide or systemwide boards are more involved with larger policy matters than are the campus-specific boards, which focus more on implementing state policy and providing oversight for their particular campuses.

All of these approaches have pluses and minuses, and it is difficult to say which one works best. Generally speaking, however, institutional quality goes hand in hand with campus autonomy. It is no accident, for example, that the State of California, which grants considerable freedom to each of the campuses within the University of California system, has produced several world-renowned institutions, while New York, which has a highly centralized system managed by a large bureaucracy, has no public universities of similar distinction. States that mandate uniform systemwide tuition rates, faculty compensation scales, personnel regula-tions, line-item budgeting, building and construction requirements, and admissions criteria for their public universities create a leveling effect that makes it difficult for one campus to elevate itself above the others.

There are also state-to-state differences in the ways trustees and re-gents are selected. Most states give appointing authority to their gover-nor, although a few states, e.g., Colorado and Michigan, have trustees who run for office and are elected to their positions. It is difficult to find any university president or chancellor who will speak positively about an elected governing board. Such boards tend to attract single-issue crusaders, are often fractious and politicized, and tend to have at least a few members who lack relevant qualifications for their position.[1] For a university that aspires to excellence, an elected governing board can be a major if not an insurmountable obstacle. But in most states, governors appoint public university trustees or regents, or at least have a strong hand in selecting them.

In Ohio, for example, the governor appoints nine voting trustees for each public four-year university (fifteen for Ohio State University), each of whom serves a nine-year term.[2] (There are also two student nonvoting trustees, who serve for two years.) With thirteen public universities, that means a total of 123 voting-level appointments, or nearly fourteen appointments each year. By law, each trustee must be a current resident of Ohio. Of course, the Ohio governor also makes many other appointments. In addition to the state's four-year universities, there are twenty-three Ohio public community colleges, a nine-member Ohio Board of Regents, and dozens of nonacademic Ohio commissions, all headed by governing boards. Because of this large number, the Ohio governor, like his or her counterparts in other states, assigns staff members to coordinate and oversee these appointments. Many of Ohio's nonacademic commissions require members with specific expertise. For example, the five members of the Public Utilities Commission of Ohio (PUCO) oversee a four-hundred-person agency, and commission members must understand the regulatory requirements, rate structures, safety, zoning, and legal issues for the electric power, natural gas, coal, and water utilities in the state. Because the PUCO is no place for amateurs, the governor makes his appointments from a list of prescreened candidates produced by the Public Utilities Commission Nominating Council. This council proposes candidates who have the knowledge and experience that a PUCO membership calls for.

But in making trustee appointments to Ohio's public universities, the governor is guided by no such advisory panel. Instead, potential trustees are screened in great part on the basis of nonprofessional considerations. Are candidates members of the same political party as the governor? Are they major campaign contributors? Will they bring gender balance, racial balance, and geographical balance to a university's board? Although in their brainstorming sessions governors and their aides try to select competent individuals, they are often relying on hearsay, limited personal interactions, and a cursory examination of credentials. Furthermore, their choices are seldom based on the actual needs of the institutions, which are frequently not consulted or kept in the dark during the selection process.

Furthermore, because a trusteeship is viewed as a prestigious position, especially at selective, flagship universities, governors can be tempted to use trustee appointments to reward loyalty, recognize prior accomplishments, or recruit allies among influential state residents. Sometimes, trustee appointments are made as a capitulation to lobbying efforts by alumni, sports fans, or others who want to join a board in order to advance personal agendas. During my years in Ohio, I have seen governors appoint their friends, campaign contributors, family members, spouses of business colleagues, and former coworkers to trustee positions. These people generally were well-meaning and took their responsibilities seriously, but many did not have the experience, insight, or expertise that the position really called for. A report by the *Chronicle of Higher Education* found that fewer than 15 percent of surveyed college and university trustees felt well prepared for their responsibilities, and nearly half felt "not at all" or only "slightly" prepared.[3]

Systemwide Trustees and Campus-Specific Trustees

Expertise is somewhat less important for systemwide boards than for those overseeing individual campuses, because the issues tend to be more generic, political, and social in nature. However, in today's higher education environment, trustees of individual campuses wrestle with a multitude of specialized, complex questions: How relevant are Sarbanes-Oxley principles to the governing structure of the university's foundation? Is it desirable for the university to invest its temporary cash float in hedge funds? Do tenure requirements in the engineering college provide adequate due process to candidates? Is the indirect cost rate on federal grants harming campus researchers? What is the liability exposure of failing to comply with OSHA requirements in the nuclear reactor laboratory? Are the school's cash reserves adequate? Are the IT backup systems robust enough to survive a natural disaster? The list is never ending.

Single-campus trustees are also expected to assess the quality of leadership of their school. The students and alumni may adore the personable and outgoing chancellor, but is she facing up to the personnel problems in her inner cabinet? Does she adequately understand the nuances of the university's balance sheet? Is the athletic director able to stand up to the out-of-control basketball coach? Does the finance vice president have an adequate handle on continuing commitments in the E&G fund? These are the kinds of questions that call for mature judgment developed through years of experience—the kind of experience that one sees on private university governing boards but that often is lacking on public university boards.

Because of their broad mission to serve the public, state universities have lay governing boards that reflect the principles of constituency-based democracy. But the notion that student board members are needed to "represent" somehow the interests of the student body, or that a southern Illinois trustee is needed to speak for the people of southern Illinois, underestimates and misinterprets the work that governing boards actually do. A governing board should not be a ceremonial group whose primary purpose is to send a reassuring message about democratic inclusiveness. But to the extent that it is, instead of really tackling the challenges facing their institutions, trustees will participate in meetings that are steeped in bland formality. Trustees will watch presentations about the good works the university is doing; they will hear reports and "updates" from administrative officers, faculty, and student leaders. When board action is called for, the nuances and implications of administrative decisions will be compressed into brief formal motions, read by a secretary and approved with little substantive discussion.

Thus, trustees may approve construction of, say, a twenty-million-dollar child-care center primarily on the basis of a president's recommendations and pleas from university employees who are parents of small children. But approving such an expenditure is unwise unless the board first verifies how much annual subsidy from the general fund will be needed for the facility to break even, what the unit costs per child are when the debt service payments are factored into the expenses, whether the administration has an adequate plan for complying with state licensing requirements, and whether the proposed business plan is really doable or based on pie-in-the-sky assumptions about participation rates and fee schedules. How could a twenty-year-old education major, a local dentist, a football fan, a wealthy widow, or others without any pertinent experience be expected to raise such questions and evaluate the answers? To the extent that trustees are appointed without adequate regard for their professional backgrounds and credentials, public universities are shortchanged of the oversight they need.

Bad Trustee Choices

There are certain types of individuals who make particularly poor choices for trustees and who can do damage to a college or university. Generally these are single-issue people: sports fans wanting to restructure the football program and influence coach selection; social activists; partisan advocates for any group or cause; crusaders who want to do away with tenure, root out liberals (or conservatives) from the faculty, advance religious agendas, do away with affirmative action, ban smoking, ban T-shirts from Latin American sweatshops, ban investments in countries headed by dictatorships, or redesign the mission of the institution to their own liking. Trustees who see themselves as the mouthpiece of constituencies—parents' groups, alumni associations, or labor unions, for example—are poor choices, as are people who do business with the school, such as developers, heads of construction firms, and providers of academic goods and services.

Good Trustee Choices

What kind of credentials *are* desirable? In general, public higher education needs trustees and regents who are thoughtful, open-minded, and inquisitive, who have balanced judgment and good interpersonal skills, who come without prior agendas and are able to frame issues in context and assess objectively the merits of proposals. Public higher education needs trustees who come to their job knowing they have a lot to learn, are eager to learn, and are willing to put in the hours the position requires. In addition, campus-specific boards need trustees who have certain skills and experience. All such boards need sophisticated budget and finance experts who can read balance sheets, understand accounting and auditing principles, and evaluate financial models and projections, and who know how to assess cash flow, reserves, investment strategies, and other important parameters of an institution's financial health. Financial oversight is the core responsibility of a campus governing board, and with hundreds of millions, or even billions, of dollars at stake, there is no substitute for trustees who have a high level of financial competency.

Second, campus-specific boards need members who have run a large, complex organization, preferably as president or chief executive officer. These trustees will have faced regulatory constraints, will have negotiated with employee organizations, and will know firsthand the challenges of working within a complex bureaucracy. They also will know what it means to lead an organization—the problems of delegating, managing time, motivating a workforce, conveying a vision, planning strategies, and when to stand on principle and when to capitulate to expediency. They will know how to differentiate genuine leadership from popularity, and they will know when they are being sold a bill of goods.

Third, universities need trustees who have prior experience serving on governing boards, in either the for-profit or nonprofit sector. Such persons will understand the dangers of micromanagement and inappropriate board involvement in administrative territory. They will know the importance of maintaining confidences, of defending the president from critics, and of building trusting relationships with members of the administration.

Fourth, all institutional boards would benefit from having one member with an academic background, preferably as a former or current provost or president, and preferably from a more highly ranked institution. This trustee can help the board strip the fluff out of academic strategic plans, can decode the peculiarities of the academic culture, and will know about tenure and promotion criteria and how to assess academic quality. A trustee from academia can also help his or her trustee colleagues build credibility with the school's faculty.

Lastly, the majority of campus trustees should be graduates of the school they are overseeing. Alumni will understand the mission and traditions of the institution, will appreciate its values, and will have an historical framework for the policies and priorities of the current administration. But mostly, alumni trustees will care deeply about their school and will want to protect it from harm. They will see their alma mater in the larger context of the value that it brings to society and to the thousands of men and women whose lives it has changed for the better. That kind of personal identification is important if the board is to personify the broad, humane values of the institution and if it wants to be viewed positively by the school's alumni, students, and faculty.

Beyond these broad criteria, there are other criteria for trustee selection that depend on circumstances. It may be that a university tied in knots by a fractious employee union would benefit from having a good labor attorney on the board; a university with strained relations with the local community may want a trustee who is a well-known resident with good political connections; a school gearing up for a major fund-raising drive may desire a wealthy donor involved with the alumni association. If the school's president is nearing retirement, then the board might benefit from an executive who has recent experience negotiating and recruiting senior talent. Or possibly the school just needs a hometown trustee with the time to represent the board at receptions, dinners, and ceremonial occasions.

Political Considerations

In one sense it is ironic that out of all these desired traits, some based on knowledge and experience, some based on intrinsic character qualities, those least relevant to actually doing the work of the university are the social and political considerations of party support and affiliation and de-mographic, geographic, racial and gender balance. Yet these factors may well receive the bulk of attention from a governor's staff. In a practical sense, it could hardly be otherwise; when the volume of gubernatorial appointments is added to all the other items on staffers' plates, there just isn't time for them to conduct a comprehensive analysis of a candidate's professional qualifications. Furthermore, as a practical matter, it would obviously be unwise for a governor to ignore political and social criteria in making appointments to public commissions and boards. The pub-lic always gauges such boards by the yardstick of social inclusiveness, and no governor wants to alienate voters and attract criticism by seem-ing to downplay such considerations. So the issue becomes a question of balance—of identifying trustees with appropriate professional back-grounds but who also satisfy desired social and political criteria. Fortu-nately, it is possible to have one's cake and eat it too, provided applicants are prescreened for their professional qualifications before political and social considerations are factored into the final selection. Realistically, such a prescreening requires some sort of external, nonpartisan advisory group.

An independent advisory group could also bring helpful perspec-tive to trustee appointments. There is so much rhetoric swirling in the public domain about public higher education's perceived deficiencies— "unbridled" tuition increases, lazy tenured professors, politicized class-rooms, out-of-control costs, and so on—that governors feel a particu-lar obligation to appoint trustees who will carry out their agenda for improvement. This is a perfectly appropriate desire, but it must be executed carefully. Long history has shown that there is no quick fix to higher education's problems, and if governors are committed to making positive changes, then their trustee appointments must meet a high standard of sophistication, knowledge, and interpersonal skills. Careful, objective screening would minimize the chances that a newly appointed trustee will charge into the minefield, creating division on the board, angering faculty, and provoking sullen resistance from the institution's administration.

A Process for Trustee Selection

There are many ways to skin a cat, but to be effective, a formal process for trustee selection should be rooted in several general principles. First, the process itself calls for consultation, particularly with respect to the development of desired trustee criteria. The announcement that a formal trustee-selection process is being developed is an opportunity for governors to send a message to their state universities that they support higher education and that they consider competent board leadership an important part of the equation for improvement. If consulted, universities will be inclined to welcome such an initiative and less likely to brand it as just another bureaucratic intrusion from the state.

An independent advisory body is an essential part of a credible screening process. To ensure objectivity, this body should be made up of people who are very familiar with the nature of trustee leadership and the many demands on university governing boards. The group might include former university presidents, trustees and board chairpersons, business leaders, and elected officials, people drawn from inside and outside the state. The group should include nobody who has a vested interest, partisan bias, or agenda to advance. The advisory body could be provided by a commercial consulting firm or a panel recommended by a national association such as the Association of Governing Boards or the American Council on Education, or it could be made up of individuals based on recommendations to the governor by state and higher education leaders. The important point is that the group be seen as independent, nonpartisan, and well qualified.

The charge given to this group is central to its effectiveness and value. Here is an example of the kinds of instructions such a group might receive:

1. The group's deliberations are private, and all recommendations will be made in confidence to the governor. A representative from the governor's office will act as liaison and attend the group's meetings.

2. The group will advise the governor on specific campus needs for trustee representation (such as the need for a trustee with budget experience). To gain this information, the group will consult with the campus president or chancellor and board chair for their advice and opinions and also use these meetings to gauge the effectiveness, strengths, and shortcomings of the existing board.[4]

3. The group will review the curriculum vitae of proposed trustee candidates only with respect to appropriate professional qualifications. If requested, the group will also conduct due diligence with candidates to determine that they are free of scandals, criminal convictions, conflicts of interest, or other considerations that would render them unsuitable for appointment.

4. The group will suggest names of suitable trustee candidates, as well as review the qualifications of individuals proposed to them.

An important caveat: while it is important that opinions and recommendations from each university's administration be solicited, it is equally important that campus advice not automatically be deferred to. Like their corporate counterparts, university CEOs often hope (at least subconsciously) that their governing boards will be docile and undemanding, will not challenge or dispute their recommendations, and will not insist on extra documentation and explanation for their proposals. In my own case, I remember joking with my senior staff that the most successful board meetings were those that spectators found to be particularly boring and tedious. Every university president hopes his or her judgment will be deferred to and initiatives enthusiastically embraced. But, of course, this is not the kind of oversight one receives from smart, inquisitive, and experienced board members, and neither is it the kind of oversight that the public is entitled to.

And, truthfully, it is not the kind of oversight that university leaders should want either. Looking back over my years as a university president, I am struck by how many of my achievements could be directly attributed to the good advice and direction from my trustees, even if they were sometimes telling me things I didn't want to hear. And so while campus opinions about potential trustee qualifications and needs should be solicited, governors, their aides, and advisory groups should also be aware of the tendency for campuses to recommend against candidates whom they suspect may be demanding and challenging. Occasionally, of course, those attributes may be exactly what is called for. The trick, as is always the case with personnel appointments, is to strike the appropriate balance between a multiplicity of conflicting needs and interests.

One final comment about workload. While theoretically it may be desirable for governors to formalize a mechanism for reviewing the qualifications of trustees, it is also desirable that they avoid adding to state bureaucracies by creating costly and cumbersome procedures. In states that have dozens of two-year and four-year colleges and universities, the practicalities may make a comprehensive formal mechanism undesirable. However, one way to lighten the workload is to focus on those institutions that merit special attention. A state's flagship research university should always be at the top of the list, while other campuses could be added or subtracted, depending on circumstances. Public campuses whose enrollments are either falling or surging, whose finances are in shaky condition, or that have undergone strife, turmoil, or leadership problems obviously merit great care in trustee appointments. But whatever mechanism is chosen, the general principle is that when the health of a state's higher education system is at stake, the buck stops on the governor's desk. No matter how creative governors' reform initiatives may be, no matter how heartfelt their claims of being the "education governor" may be, when push comes to shove, nothing trumps the ability to put top-notch people in positions of leadership. Ultimately, that authority is the strongest tool governors have for improving the education of the citizens who elected them to office. Given the importance of higher education to those citizens, careful trustee selection should be high on any governor's to-do list.

The Role of Governing Boards in the New Era

A Little Knowledge Is a Dangerous Thing

It is surprising how little the trustees of public universities often know about the workings of the institutions they oversee. Most trustees can speak in broad-brush language about the success of the latest fund-raising drive, about how the president seems to be doing with the alumni, about newly completed buildings, and about the latest campus strategic plan. But this kind of knowledge is only skin deep. What does the university spend on average to educate a student? Which majors generate the most revenue, and which are the most costly? How do promotion and tenure standards vary among the different departments? What are the school's weakest programs, and how is the provost working to strengthen them? Is faculty grant and contract support holding up in the life sciences? What are laboratory startup costs for new chemistry professors? Are network expenditures growing too fast? Posed to trustees, these kinds of questions often draw puzzled looks, and yet they are the kinds that can provide important clues to a school's overall health.

Trustees, of course, are overseers, not managers, and it would not be right for them to trespass into the territory of their campus administration. But sound oversight carries with it a responsibility to be well informed, and, unfortunately, there is no other path to knowledge than rolling up one's sleeves and digging deep. Lay trustees may not be experts in higher education, but they need to know enough to ask perceptive and probing questions of those who are. The stresses on public universities in these times call for a higher level of trustee knowledge and involvement than was necessary in more placid times.

There are two reasons university board members, especially in the public sector, often do not know much about their campuses, and neither is their fault. The first grows out of the nature of their appointments. Governors frequently appoint university trustees without consulting the campuses, and they may choose persons who are unfamiliar to university officials or who appear to have minimal credentials. Rather than share information with unknowns, campus leaders follow the safer strategy of feeding their trustees a diet of good-news presentations and filtered information that touches only superficially on campus problems. The desire of management to keep appointed trustees at arm's length is especially strong if the governor is perceived as being disinterested or unsupportive of higher education, or having a problematic reform agenda. Too much information in the wrong hands, presidents believe, is simply asking for trouble. But trustees who are not well informed may not spot the early warning symptoms of campus problems and therefore may not have much helpful advice for the administration.

The second reason is the general perception that a public university trusteeship is largely an honorary appointment, high in prestige but low in real responsibility. As a result, newly appointed board members may not realize how much effort will really be asked of them. Some work very hard, of course, especially during presidential searches or in times of campus crisis, but by and large many if not most university trustees expect to spend only a few pleasant days a year on their duties. However, with state universities and colleges reeling from budget cuts and chronic complaints about high tuition, strong oversight is needed. University presidents must be able to work with their governing board to solve problems, make changes, and forge a campus strategy that accommodates an ever-shifting environment. What is needed is a working partnership between campus administrators and trustees, where trustees are seen as close allies of the administration and not as a potentially worrisome group to be managed. But for this partnership to develop, it is important that trustees begin delving deeper into the workings of their campus and investing a greater amount of time and effort in carrying out their duties. Steering trustee expectations toward greater involvement is obviously a chore for governors or whoever is charged with making trustee appointments.

A Case for Compensating Public University Trustees

Trustees of universities, like their counterparts at virtually all nonprofit organizations, are not paid for their services. By comparison, directors of public corporations receive an annual retainer that can be tens of thousands of dollars or more, plus stock grants or options, plus additional payments for attending and chairing committee meetings. In exchange for these payments, corporate directors are in principle, if not always in practice, held to a high standard of performance and accountability. They are expected to study carefully the documentation provided them before meetings, to make attendance at meetings a high priority, and to help and advise their CEO about corporate problems. There is nothing ceremonial about a corporate directorship. For the best-run companies, it is sober and demanding work that requires a serious commitment of time and talent. This is the kind of commitment that public universities need if they are to survive and prosper in this new era.

Realistically, it is not reasonable to expect this level of involvement from a volunteer lay board. During my years as Miami University's president, I was favored to have many board members who worked hard and diligently to discharge their responsibilities. For my university and for me, they were a godsend. But there were a few board members who skipped meetings, came unprepared, expressed off-the-wall opinions, didn't study issues, and let their mind wander when complex topics were discussed. I believe public universities would be well served by an embrace of the corporate model of governing boards. Trustees should be paid for their services, not as an honorarium or "thank you" for their efforts but as compensation for the value they bring to their institution. This compensation need not be exorbitant, but it should be enough to send a message that a serious commitment is expected, that there is important business to be conducted, that many millions of dollars are at stake, and that the institution's administrators understand that trustee time is valuable. This last point is particularly important. As previously discussed, much of the inefficiency in higher education comes about because faculty and employee time is not valued as a costly resource that should be expended judiciously. Changing this attitude will be difficult so long as it is perpetuated at the board level.

With compensation also comes accountability. Therefore, the chairman of the board should prepare a confidential annual report to the appointing authority, usually a governor, about the board's performance. The attendance record of each trustee at board functions and committee meetings should be provided, as well as a synopsis of each board member's contribution. Governors would then be in a position to assess the quality of their choices and, in principle, to question or replace appointees who had not discharged their responsibilities seriously.

There are obviously pluses and minuses to this proposal. One minus, from a governor's perspective, is that the decision to compensate trustees will attract critics who could claim that the state is wasting money by paying for services that previously it got for free. Furthermore, governors would now be obligated to justify their appointments on objective grounds. It is one thing for governors to appoint friends, colleagues, campaign supporters, and family members to positions that carry only honorary significance. Once money changes hands, however, ethics laws, potential conflicts of interests, and possible political repercussions come into play. Under the new system, a governor would have to justify appointments on the basis of the candidates' professional qualifications.

But, of course, that is the idea. When money is involved, people are inclined to take responsibilities seriously and insist on a measure of accountability. If governors really care about the quality of oversight at their state's public universities, then compensating trustees gives them the tools to monitor that oversight and insist on a high level of performance. So long as trusteeships are viewed merely as patronage appointments, there is no mechanism for enforcing those goals nor any tangible incentive to appoint appropriately qualified people to these crucial positions.

Presidential Oversight

Most university board members would agree that assessing their president's or chancellor's job performance is one of their top responsibilities, and clearly it goes hand in hand with hiring the person in the first place. (The next chapter discusses presidential recruiting.) Often, governing boards have a small committee charged with evaluating presidential performance. A typical process is to ask the president to submit a written statement highlighting the prior year's achievements, as well as a list of long-term and short-term goals. This document is then reviewed by the entire board and also serves as the basis for personal discussions between the president and board chairman. At this meeting, the president receives a "report card" from the trustees, usually in connection with the next year's salary adjustment, along with suggestions for improvement and redirection of effort.

This is generally a good, tried-and-tested process, but it does not guarantee that trustees will focus on all the pertinent aspects of the president's performance. Here are a few sometimes neglected items that should appear on the discussion list.

1. *Personal relationship with the board.* Do trustees feel that the president truly confides in them and shares information and problems at a sufficiently detailed level? Does the president give the board advance warning of bad news? Does the president accept criticism well or seem defensive? Does the president talk frequently enough to the board chair? Trustees should not hesitate to speak frankly to the president if they have concerns in any of these areas.

2. *Balance between internal and external activities.* Some presidents spend most of their time in public and quasi-social activities—hosting receptions and dinners, attending alumni events, speaking at Rotary clubs, interacting with student groups—and relatively little time in their office solving problems, planning strategies, and implementing changes. Other presidents are so focused on management issues that they seldom stray out of their office and may seem nearly invisible to campus constituencies. Obviously, neither extreme is desirable, and trustees should assess whether their president is striking the right balance. To some extent, the issue is a trade-off between getting the message out and improving the product, and trustees have to decide which is more relevant to their school's needs.

3. *Corporate directorships.* A 2005 survey by the *Chronicle of Higher Education* showed that 90 percent of college presidents serve on outside boards.[1] Nearly a third (32.7 percent) of those polled served on at least one for-profit board, and more than a third (35.9 percent) served on four or more charity boards. Typically, nonprofit board duties are rather minimal, frequently entailing only one or two meetings a year.

But corporate directorships can meet more frequently, once a month being not uncommon. The commitment required by corporate directorships is often defended by the contacts and influential people the president meets, as well as by the presumed beneficial virtue of a president's occasionally straying from the ivory tower and immersing himself or herself in the real world of corporate life. For the most part, this rationale is patent nonsense. Presidents like to serve on corporate boards in part because the work is interesting and a welcome break from the routine of their jobs. But mostly, corporate directorships are a moneymaker that significantly augments a president's income. John L. Hennessy, president of Stanford, holds the record, having taken in $43 million in five years from his board duties at Cisco Systems, Google, and Atheros Communications.[2]

The downside of directorships, whether for-profit or nonprofit, is that they divert a president's attention from running the institution. Realistically, a corporate board meeting is at least a full day's commitment (depending on travel time), and committee meetings use up even more time. Most presidents serve on only one or two boards, and often these are regional or local companies. But some presidents serve on multiple boards. For example, Shirley Ann Jackson, president of Rensselaer Polytechnic Institute, in 2007 served as a member of the Board of Directors of the NYSE Euronext, chaired the New York Stock Exchange Regulation Board, served on the board of regents of the Smithsonian Institution, and was a director of IBM Corporation, FedEx Corporation, Marathon Oil Corporation, Medtronic, and Public Service Enterprise Group Incorporated.[3] Universities that allow their president to serve on multiple boards are in essence being led by a part-timer. Public universities, especially, need a full-time commitment, and it is incumbent on trustees to monitor carefully the extracurricular activities of their president. If board members believe they cannot prohibit their president from serving on outside boards entirely, which is my preference, then they should carefully limit those kinds of activities.

4. *Budget savvy.* Trustees should evaluate whether the president really knows where the school's money goes. This may seem an obvious point, but most university presidents do not come from a financial or business background and may have surprisingly little interest or understanding of their school's finances. It is bad practice for presidents to delegate too many important financial decisions to a chief financial officer, no matter how competent that person may be. Thus, if a president announces at a

board meeting that, e.g., the school is facing a deficit in the general fund of $20 million but is unable to speak knowledgeably about cash flow, reserves, continuing and one-time expenditures, debt service, revenue projections, and all the other factors that are germane to the deficit, then the trustees have grounds to worry. When presidents are seen as big spenders—buying university aircraft, building opulent sports facilities, expanding the president's staff, etc.—that can be a signal of a lack of fiscal discipline that at the extreme can weaken or even wreck a school's financial underpinnings.

5. *Presidential decisiveness.* It is easy for trustees to spot a president who acts impulsively and is disinclined to consult and take advice. Faculty complaints of "autocratic" or undemocratic presidential behavior will quickly come to the board's attention, and trustees will surely see signs of this trait in their personal relationships with the president. However, if presidents veer too far in the other direction, there may be few overt warning symptoms. In the short term, campuses tolerate or even welcome indecisive leaders, because the status quo is almost always the most comfortable course of action. One signature of presidential indecisiveness is a proclivity to spin off large commissions, committees, and study groups. In academia, it is easy to drape such groups in the cloak of shared governance and consensus seeking, when in fact the actual motivation may be a failure of nerve or an unwillingness to face critics. Too many large, democratically balanced groups, whose members have obviously been chosen to represent multiple constituencies, can be a symptom of lack of presidential courage.

There are, of course, legitimate reasons for creating presidential commissions and committees. Key criteria for evaluating them are the importance of the issue under deliberation, its potential for controversy, the likelihood that a committee will be able bring the issue to timely closure, and, most important, whether the topic really calls for a breadth of multiple perspectives. Although it can be difficult for a governing board to evaluate whether their president has found the right balance point, it is important that they try to do so. Public universities need decisive leaders to shape their agendas. Neither weak-kneed milquetoasts nor iron-fisted despots will get the job done.

6. *Presidential fatigue.* Running a public university is a relentless, seven-day-a-week job that over time can deplete the spirit of even the most energetic leader. Trustees should assess the toll the position is taking on their president, and if it appears that the cumulative impact of an unremitting

and demanding schedule is too great, then trustees should insist that the president slow down, back off, take a vacation, or go on sabbatical for a semester. Trustees should also assess the job's impact on the president's spouse. Traditional first ladies, especially, can have a full calendar of social events, volunteer board assignments, and other university-related activities. Smiling graciously and attentively at one's husband while he delivers a dull speech at an event in which she has no interest is part of the role, but over time the fatigue and boredom can build into a sense of resentment and of being taken for granted. Although in the past there has been less of a public expectation for the husbands of female presidents to be fully involved in the life of the university, gender roles are changing, and it is very much in the interests of the university for governing boards to monitor and support all presidential spouses and to make certain their responsibilities are carefully defined and the burdens of the role are not becoming oppressive.[4]

Fund-Raising and Development

Governing boards of public universities increasingly see the path to self-sufficiency for their institutions coming from alumni, corporate, and foundation gifts. Presidents are frequently hired on the basis of their perceived fund-raising skills, and to have initiated and completed a successful campaign is always the gold star on a presidential job-hopper's résumé. It is not surprising, therefore, that trustees almost always take a great interest in their institution's development efforts. The problem is that, since public universities are rather new at this game, public trustees may have unrealistic expectations both about what is possible and about the beneficial impact that gifts can have on their institution.

With respect to the first point, the majority of public universities do not have significant gift potential in their alumni base. Nonselective or minimally selective public universities tend not to have many well-heeled graduates in the age range appropriate for making large donations. Furthermore, in the public sector, the culture and tradition of alumni giving is not strong. While public college alumni may write a check for a hundred dollars at annual giving time, they are generally inclined to see the financial support of their alma mater as the responsibility of the taxpayers.

The depth of the donor pool is greater at large public flagship universities, especially if they have a medical school, a law school, and other professional colleges. In this group it is increasingly common to hear of gifts of a hundred million dollars or more and of campaign goals that exceed a billion dollars. Trustees should keep in mind, however, that there is often less to these well-trumpeted figures than meets the eye. First, big-ticket fund-raising campaigns can go on for seven years or more, so that on a yearly basis the dollars raised are much smaller than the grand total might suggest. Furthermore, large gifts are usually spread out over many years, sometimes ten or more, which means that the present cash value of, say, a $50 million gift may be only a fraction of the announced amount. Furthermore, there are nearly always strings attached to large gifts. They must be used to endow chairs, build buildings, create scholarship programs, and so forth. While these are worthy benefits, such gifts cannot erase a deficit nor dig a struggling institution out of a financial hole.

In fact, paradoxically, large gifts can exacerbate a school's financial problems, because of the gift's matching requirements. If a university accepts a $20 million lead gift for a performing arts center that costs $60 million to build and has maintenance and operating expenses of $5 million a year, the university has to come up with the extra money, even if it cannot afford it. It is also important for trustees to keep in mind that for every gift dollar raised, the actual money available to the school is only about four to five pennies a year. In other words, a million-dollar gift to endowment pays out less than $50 thousand a year. A million-dollar gift for a new wing on a building has about the same equivalent value, because the school could borrow the million dollars and pay it back for $50 thousand per year. What all this means is that even a large flagship university that successfully completes a $2 billion campaign will not appreciably have improved its bottom line. The impact on a smaller public university that achieves, say, a $50 million campaign goal will be even less.

None of this is to suggest that public governing boards should discount the importance of fund-raising. Rather, I am suggesting that trustees keep it in proper perspective. Fund-raising can enhance the long-term future of the institution, but in the near term it cannot prop up a school's shaky budget base. Furthermore, there are significant costs associated with successful development programs. Fund-raising is an expensive, people-intensive activity that requires major up-front expenditures. Before deciding how aggressively to build and pay for this kind of infrastructure, trustees have to decide realistically whether their school can afford to make the investment.

Admissions and Financial Aid

As public universities become increasingly dependent on tuition dollars for survival, trustees need an in-depth understanding of their school's admissions and financial aid practices. It is not enough for trustees merely to receive a report each year on the admissions statistics for the entering freshman class. Historical trends of application numbers, campus visits, e-mail inquiries and other expressions of interest, and confirmation ("yield") rates are important indicators of a university's competitive standing and drawing power (although the proliferation of online applications has made trends difficult to interpret).

Trustees should be aware of the geographical, socioeconomic status, gender, and racial distribution of both applicants and enrolled students and should look carefully at shifting patterns in these categories. They should know who their university's top competitors are and whether the "win rate" for each competitor is changing. Sometimes, declining applications and acceptances point to problems in a school's recruiting and marketing efforts. Trustees should ascertain whether inquiries are being answered promptly, whether admissions officers are maintaining good relationships with high school guidance counselors, whether campus tour guides are being trained well, and so forth. Applicants to selective universities have very high expectations for individual attention, and any school that doesn't respond to this expectation will see declines in the number or academic quality of its student body.

Sometimes, shifting enrollment and application patterns suggest that the competitive environment has changed. At my own institution, for example, we historically had enrolled about two-thirds of the applicants who also had been recruited by Ohio State University. One year we noticed that our win percentage was dropping, suggesting that Ohio State was becoming more successful at recruiting the students we wanted. A bit of research revealed that Ohio State had revamped its honors programs and had upped its scholarship offers to high-ability applicants. In response, we made adjustments to our own programs and were able to restore the balance. These kinds of strategic actions can be important in meeting enrollment goals, and trustees need to know that their school is collecting the necessary information and responding appropriately.

With the rapid growth of public college tuition, a school's financial aid practices also play an important part in maintaining enrollments.

The days in which schools simply divvied up their scholarship dollars into need-based and merit-based pools are long gone. Today, financial aid is an important strategic tool for meeting enrollment targets, and the allocation of those dollars requires a nuanced understanding of their impact on recipients. Is it better to give a $10 thousand scholarship to a poor, inner-city straight-A student or to give a $1 thousand scholarship to each of ten B students from middle-income families? What size scholarship will it take to recruit successfully a talented young violinist into the freshman class? How price sensitive are Hispanic applicants from first-generation immigrant families? Financial aid practices implement important institutional priorities, and trustees need to make sure those practices are in harmony with those priorities.

Public Relations and Communications

Consider the following types of vehicles: Dodge pickup truck, Chrysler minivan, Jeep SUV, high-performance BMW coupe, and large Mercedes sedan. Now, match each vehicle with each of the following universities: Michigan State University, Texas A&M, University of Colorado at Boulder, Yale University, California Institute of Technology. Chances are your matchup looked like this:

Dodge pickup truck—Texas A&M
Chrysler minivan—Michigan State University
Jeep SUV—University of Colorado at Boulder
BMW coupe—California Institute of Technology
Mercedes sedan—Yale University

The exercise illustrates how every university has a unique image that shapes public perception of it—a perception that can strongly influence student applications, lawmaker attitudes toward tuition levels, faculty recruiting efforts, and public support. An important trustee responsibility, therefore, is to monitor their school's public persona to make sure the image is consistent, desirable, and accurate. Does the school's winning basketball program convey a message about teamwork and good sportsmanship, or does it suggest lawlessness and scandal? Does the university's Web site emphasize faculty research at the expense of undergraduate teaching? Do photographs in brochures show huge, imposing buildings or small clusters of smiling faces? Are students pictured tossing

Frisbees, studying in the library, or racing down ski slopes? Public perceptions are shaped by thousands of such small icons.

Universities are so decentralized that it is difficult for them to package a coherent, consistent message about themselves. The business school, college of fine arts, and engineering college may have conflicting views of the ways to portray their programs. A proliferation of logo designs, stationery letterheads, and business cards can further muddy the waters. Does the university want to present itself as steeped in tradition, with a long history of excellence? Or does it want to portray itself as youthful, dynamic, and cutting edge? These are the kinds of issues where trustee advice can be particularly helpful. With their feet both on and off campus, trustees can spot image problems and inconsistencies more easily than the school's administrators can.

Trustee involvement in public relations is particularly important as public universities learn to adapt to their twenty-first-century environment. Monitoring the campus image is one aspect of that job, but another is to help their school respond effectively to immediate events and to explain changed practices. Significant change is always disruptive, and trustees can play a key role in moderating and defusing complaints and concerns. Responding thoughtfully to critics and complainers, presenting new policies as well reasoned and strategic, and laying to rest unwarranted fears are important trustee functions.

Trustees can also monitor large, visible expenditures and pull the plug on untimely ones that would send an undesirable public message. Examples might be remodeling the president's home, buying a new university airplane, or building a major sports arena. Such expenditures often strike the public as extravagant and unnecessary, especially when budgets are tight and state economies are languishing. University leaders shoot themselves in the foot if they appear to be spendthrifts at the same time they are asking their state to increase their appropriation and ease up on regulatory constraints. Trustees are well positioned to help prevent these kinds of blunders.

Budget Oversight

Monitoring their institution's financial wherewithal and approving its annual budget is arguably the most important responsibility of university and college trustees. Although the procedure varies from school to school, budget approval generally follows a standardized process that rolls up the university budget into several large expenditure categories and then presents the categories to the trustees for consideration.

As the first step in the process, board members are shown spreadsheets that contain revenue projections—tuition income, state appropriation, earnings from dormitories, ticket sales, various ancillary operations, and so forth. Then, once the projected revenues are shown, there are additional spreadsheets that highlight expenditure categories, the most important being faculty and staff salaries, equipment and operating budgets, debt service, renovation, and new construction. After reviewing this information, along with reports of year-end cash balances and size of reserve accounts, trustees vote on a budget that balances revenues and expenditures. If their state allows it, they can control their revenues to some extent by adjusting tuition and fee charges. Otherwise, they are stuck with whatever revenue their legislature allows and have to accommodate this number by bringing expenditures into balance. I have discussed previously at length how declining state support and tuition controls have greatly squeezed public universities, resulting in depressed salaries, deferred maintenance, and minimal operating budgets, and, in some years, in layoffs, program closings, reduced course offerings, and other retrenchment measures.

What all this means in practice is that the fiscal oversight of governing boards is primarily aimed at ensuring the existence of a balanced budget and ascertaining that appropriate fiscal controls are in place. While these are important responsibilities, they are business-as-usual measures that have mostly ensured that public universities' slow decline is methodical and systematic. Specifically, this procedure does not address the inability of public universities to monitor costs adequately and exercise cost discipline. To tackle the problem of cost control, governing boards need to look beyond their administration's standard financial statements and press for additional processes. The core issue is that the year-to-year financial and accounting framework for monitoring overall financial viability does not provide the information that administrators need to prepare, implement, and monitor their budgets.

What further information is needed? At the global level, trustees should ask their administration to prepare a long-range financial plan that projects the total revenues and expenditures of the institution over at least a five- and preferably a ten-year period. On the revenue side, the plan should include best-guess estimates of state appropriations, tuition and fees, income from auxiliary enterprises, gift income, and research grants and contracts. On the expenditure side, it should include projected changes in salaries, benefits, energy costs, debt service, and financial aid. In order to make these projections, it will be necessary to predict future interest rates and changes in the Consumer Price Index. Since there are uncertainties associated with all of these variables, the projections should include worst-case and best-case scenarios.

The benefit of a long-range financial plan is that it gives an early warning of future trouble, as it did for my own institution (as discussed in the preface). A five- or ten-year perspective makes long-term patterns immediately visible. Should the university shut down a department, school, or college? Can it sustain its football program, its nursing program, its European campus? Is it necessary to rethink the school's mission in order to grow enrollments? These are trustee-level decisions that can be greatly informed by long-range financial planning.

At the local level of, say, a department or college, the prerequisite to controlling costs is first to understand what the costs are. Unfortunately, university accounting systems generally do not present financial information in a format that is useful to department heads, deans, and other decision makers. For example, years ago, when I was the chairman of the physics department at Ohio State, I would receive a monthly statement about the status of my department's budget. The statement had numerous budget categories. In the personnel category, for instance, separate listings were given for nine-month faculty members, twelve-month faculty members, senior administrative and professional staff, unclassified personnel, visitors, classified civil service employees, student workers, temporary lecturers, and graduate teaching and research assistants. There were also numerous entries within the general category of operating budgets: equipment, materials and supplies, postage, telephone, travel, maintenance contracts, etc. For each of these categories, one column on the spreadsheets showed monthly expenditures, another column showed year-to-date expenditures, and another showed the remaining balance in each category. Fold into the mix carry-forward funds or deficits from the previous year, different account subcategory codes, encumbrances, transfers, and overhead and indirect costs, and the result was a maze of numbers that would glaze over the eyes of any but the most committed bean-counter. All these numbers may have brought solace to the accounting gods in some distant office in the university's central administration, but they did not help me decide, for instance, whether our undergraduate instructional laboratories had been spending too much money.

Account balances, which is what university financial systems generally provide, give little guidance for understanding and controlling costs, and they do not facilitate good budgeting practices. When I was a department chairman, what really interested me was whether the dollars allocated to each faculty research group in my department was justified by its performance; whether faculty members were spending too much time in committee meetings or traveling to conferences; whether the per-student cost was too high in small-enrollment graduate courses; whether it made sense for highly paid full professors to make their own travel arrangements.

This is not the place to expound on new budgeting methods. Rather, the point is to stress that if university trustees are serious about controlling costs, they need to evaluate their institution's infrastructure for monitoring those costs and also the information provided to those who prepare and monitor budgets. Effective budgeting requires stepping outside the familiar accounting mindset to look more generally at the school's information systems and institutional research capabilities.

This is a topic to which I will return at length, in connection with changing the university culture to facilitate change. Most institutions of higher learning, public and private, do not collect and organize the information they need to become more efficient. As we will see, the reason is not so much a failure to understand the problem as an academic culture that makes it hard to collect and quantify information about performance.

Recruiting Presidential Leadership

We are seeking individuals who are: magnificent communicators
and passionate for the vision and mission of the University; demonstrated leaders who can define the next level of excellence and propel
the University toward that vision; decision makers who can balance
decisiveness and consensus building.

> *A. T. Kearney management consultants,*
> *letter advertising presidential vacancy for the*
> *University of Denver, February 24, 2005*

Unmet Expectations

The University of Toledo is a respectable and attractive urban
university that has served the regional educational needs of
northwest Ohio for more than 130 years. In 1999, following the
retirement of a longtime president, the trustees selected Vik J.
Kapoor, the school's dean of engineering and an authority on mi-
croelectronics, to be the school's fourteenth president. Kapoor
pledged to be a change agent who would shake the school out of
its doldrums by reorganizing the administration, recruiting talented new faculty and administrators, and turning the university

into a major center of academic research. The trustees were persuaded that Kapoor was just the man to lead the university into the twenty-first century, and they looked forward to the day when the world would see their school as the "crown jewel of Ohio."

Today, the university's Web site makes no mention of Kapoor's presidency. By the time the trustees removed him from office, seventeen months into his term, the University of Toledo lay in disarray. Nearly a fifth of its faculty had gone, and many of the senior administrators had either departed or been fired, including vice presidents, deans, and top professional staff. Important centers, offices, and programs had been abruptly closed. Today, faculty members recall the brief Kapoor era as an academic reign of terror, during which the school seemed as if it were being precipitously dismantled.[1]

Each year, a surprising number of academic presidencies end in failure. Scarcely a week goes by that a college or university president isn't fired over lavish spending, mismanaging funds, botching a sports scandal, offending members of a racial minority, alienating the faculty or alumni, or simply flubbing the job in one of a hundred ways. And for every president who is fired, a half-dozen jump ship after only a few years, because they could see things turning sour, didn't like the work, discovered they were badly matched to the school, or merely saw job-hopping as a way to boost their income. Some presidents are more skilled at landing their job than they are at doing their job.

But even if most presidents don't crash and burn, leaving their dispirited campus in disarray, and even if most don't bail out prematurely, the majority will eventually fail to deliver on initial trustee and campus expectations. A quick review of national rankings reveals that over, say, a decade, the vast majority of colleges and universities never make it to the next level. Even if we set aside embarrassing presidential flameouts, the odds are that a third-tier university at the beginning of a new president's tenure will still be a third-tier university when the president departs. In this global sense, at least, most university and college presidents are disappointments to their campus.

In nearly all cases, university presidents are hired as the result of a lengthy process that typically involves professional search consultants, a large search committee of campus and community leaders, a comprehensive position description, and a determined governing board. In nearly all cases, references are carefully checked and candidates are screened through numerous interviews. Yet despite the best efforts of all these committed people, some of whom may devote the better part of a year to the task, down the road it may become discouragingly apparent that the anointed leader had been a poor choice for the institution.

However, a poor choice does not necessarily mean an unpopular choice. This is an important but often overlooked distinction. Presidential success is often measured in the public arena by the yardstick of popularity. Presidents who are genial and outgoing, have good interpersonal skills and a sense of humor, and make themselves visible and accessible often generate high marks from students, alumni, faculty, and editorial writers. Popular presidents have staying power, because everybody likes them. But the kind of academic leadership that significantly improves an institution calls for a very different set of skills. Those skills are keen judgment, problem-solving ability, sophistication, insight, courage, and a tough skin. Effective leadership also calls for knowledge, strong communication skills, intelligence, and a commitment to improvement. Effective leaders put the larger interests of their institution first, even if it means siding with the minority and making themselves a magnet for criticism. Strong leaders are not afraid to disrupt the status quo. Weak leaders perpetuate the status quo in order to avoid conflict.

Too many universities and colleges have weak leaders, but not because the presidential search process failed. On the contrary, the search process most likely did inadvertently what it was constituted to do, and that is to weed out candidates who had the qualities that the institution really needed. This is a bizarre, contradictory aspect of academia that may be one of the biggest challenges facing governing boards. Unless trustees can solve the problem of identifying and recruiting leaders who have the right mix of experience and instinct, then they have little hope of positioning their institution for the practical realities of the new century.

The Yin and Yang of University Presidents

What is it, exactly, that university presidents do? Presidents wine and dine wealthy donors, put out fires, lead the cheering squad, charm the media, give rousing speeches, thrive on rubbery chicken, inspire the faculty to new heights, get tough with unions, lobby governors, and solve intractable problems. Presidents also draft strategic plans, balance budgets, fire coaches, suffer fools gladly, drink sparingly, and lead squeaky-clean personal lives. Presidents instill pride in students, alumni, and sports fans. They are 100 percent devoted to their job, love intercollegiate athletics, revere the arts, and are accessible to all. Presidents are scrupulously honest and refreshingly humble, not to mention charitable and caring, except when they need to be strong and uncompromising, in which case they are as tenacious as bull terriers.[2]

University presidents have split personalities. There is the "good cop" personality, whose job is to woo the school's constituencies—making speeches, hosting dinners and receptions, walking visibly around campus, staging photo ops, charming the media, and being as friendly and approachable as possible to students and staff members. The good cop president likes to appoint large committees, tries to skirt conflict, and speaks of noble goals, inclusiveness, and success. The good cop president wants to be well liked, believing that popularity goes hand in hand with high morale and a strong sense of campus community. Good cop presidents carefully monitor their reserves of political capital and focus their energies on growing those reserves. They gauge their job performance in terms of the ebb and flow of their approval ratings.

But university presidents also have to play "bad cop." Bad cop presidents are problem solvers and boat rockers. They know that improvement comes from disrupting the status quo and thereby making people uncomfortable. Bad cop presidents are willing to set limits, discourage bad ideas, push for higher standards, and raise performance expectations. Bad cop presidents are tough. They do not fear criticism, do not eschew controversy, and do not skirt decisions or offload them onto committees. Bad cop presidents would rather be respected than well liked, and they gauge their job performance in terms of budget and enrollment growth, improvement in national rankings, focused resource allocation, and successfully completed initiatives.

What makes the job of university president difficult is that the "good cop" and "bad cop" personalities coexist in one person, even though they are fundamentally in conflict. One cannot set limits by saying yes, or build popularity by saying no, or be decisive by asking committees to make decisions, or change the status quo by keeping people comfortable. Yet in a successful presidency each role must exist in harmony with the other. The best college and university presidents carefully balance their good cop and bad cop personalities by judiciously choosing their battles. They attend carefully to the ceremonial and symbolic aspects of their job—schmoozing with alumni and politicians, writing thank-you notes, giving glass-half-full speeches, and hobnobbing with faculty and students. In the privacy of their office and in meetings with their executive staff, however, they are smart and strategic problem solvers who can be as tough as nails. The best presidents always have a mean streak hiding behind their nice-guy public persona.

When university presidents fail in their job, it is usually because their two personalities are out of balance. Good cop presidents keep building their political capital but never spend any of it, and bad cop presidents don't have the political capital to spend. Good cop presidents can languish in their job for decades, while their school drifts sideways. Bad cop presidents, as in the University of Toledo case, tend to flare out like supernovas, leaving their successors to pick up the fragments.

As we will see, the traditional academic search process is especially effective at finding good cops. Higher education is peppered with genial, benign leaders who keep their ship afloat and their constituencies happy, and in prior decades this leadership mode was a natural consequence of the stability of the educational landscape. For much of the twentieth century, the nation's colleges and universities neither needed nor welcomed change agents. But today we are not in a business-as-usual environment. The problems of higher education, especially in the public sector, are forcing wrenching adjustments onto the nation's colleges and universities. Declining revenues, unsympathetic legislatures, a distraught public, and a potpourri of disruptive social forces call for more forceful presidential leadership. What is now needed are higher education leaders who understand how important it is to make changes and who have the insight, skills, and courage to do so. As one might expect, such individuals are rare birds, thus placing an especially heavy burden on the governing boards charged with finding them.

Reaching for the Brass Ring

In the entry hall of Lewis Place, the historic home of Miami University's twenty-one presidents, hangs a large oil portrait of Robert Hamilton Bishop, the university's first president, who was appointed in 1824 and presided over his small, pastoral college for seventeen years. President Bishop, cloaked in academic regalia, is seated in his library, surrounded by leather-bound volumes, and is quietly reading a book of logic, the title conspicuously visible in the painting. It nearly goes without saying that this charming conception of a university president's life bears little resemblance to the realities of the modern job, and it probably didn't bear much resemblance two centuries ago. Yet the painting illustrates an important point, which is that university and college presidents are viewed in the public eye through a blurred lens.

In an earlier era, college presidents were idealized as quiet, reflective scholars who presided over their flocks—many, like President Bishop, did in fact come from the clergy—with a courtly, if slightly shabby, gentility. Afternoon teas served by the first lady, sport coats with leather patches, the "first dog" curled lazily by the fireplace in the president's office, pipe-smoking strolls around campus, and evening philosophy discussions with attentive undergraduates are all part of the presidential mystique.

Today, the stereotype is different, but it is no less a stereotype. Today, the politician / celebrity / cheerleader / schmoozer / indefatigable-fundraiser view predominates, particularly for public university presidents, and as with most stereotypes, there is a germ of truth in the picture. Yet what is curiously missing from the stereotype is any sense that the job requires real knowledge. People who would never think of picking, say, a neurosurgeon on the basis of her bedside manner assume that a university president's job calls for little more than a collage of desirable social skills and innate personality traits. But if one's goal is to find a president who can transform an institution to make it suitable for a changing environment, then a deep understanding of academia's inner workings is called for. The job calls for a high level of sophistication, experience, and knowledge.

Although trustees may have searched for corporate CEOs or other senior executives in their business or recruited heads of community and volunteer organizations, they often find that their experiences do not carry over to the peculiar landscape of academia. To the uninitiated, trying to maneuver among campus advocacy groups, constituencies, and divergent expectations during a presidential search is to tiptoe through a minefield. An entire industry has popped up in the past few decades to lend a helping hand. Management consultants specializing in academic searches collect large fees for providing guidance on publicizing a vacancy, drafting a position description, seeking out interested candidates, checking background references, and negotiating a presidential contract. To trustees apprehensive about going it alone, search consultants can provide real service in setting up and carrying out a methodical process.[3]

But crafting a process is the easy part. How important is it that the new president be outgoing and comfortable with large groups, remember names and faces, and be a dynamic and inspiring speaker? How important is it that the president be a budget whiz, or a distinguished scholar? How young or old should the president be, and what kind of previous experience is relevant? Do scientists make better presidents than humanists, or vice versa? Do former governors, or generals, or corporate CEOs make good college presidents? How about unmarried or divorced candidates, or gay candidates, or candidates who ride motorcycles and drive pickup trucks? Here board members are pretty much on their own. The general answer, however, is that brilliantly successful university presidents have driven pickup trucks, been gay, and led armies in battle—and so have disastrous presidents.

Presidential Types to Avoid

Successful presidents are variations on the same theme. They are a mulligan stew of skills and personality traits whose ingredients satisfy the particular tastes of their school; their seasoning is neither too savory nor too bland. The ingredients that make for *unsuccessful* presidents, on the other hand, are out of balance. Their recipes have too much of some ingredients and not enough of others. Looking back on a disappointing presidential experience, it is usually possible to highlight the qualities that carried the seeds of failure. Here are a few examples.

- *The razzle-dazzle president.* This is the president with a flashy, outgoing manner who lacks substance. Such persons ride into office on a wave of favorable editorials and rave comments by alumni and business leaders. Their first year in office is marked by hope and excitement. They spin off strategic plans, promise institutional excellence and transformation, and impress the campus community with their enthusiasm.

  But inevitably, as they begin to make decisions, the bloom comes off. The strategic plan turns out to be mostly fluff. The promised transformation doesn't happen. And after a year or two, the school becomes embroiled in problems, poorly handled crises, and neglected needs. An atmosphere of cynicism displaces the earlier enthusiasm, faculty complaints multiply, and trustees start worrying that they made a mistake. About this time, seeing the handwriting on the wall, the president accepts an offer at another school in order to avoid the impending crunch. The hallmark of this style is a propensity to jump ship every few years.
- *The cheerleader president.* This president sees every half-full glass as completely full. To internal and external audiences alike, every program is top-notch, every faculty member is an outstanding scholar and

teacher, next year's teams are headed for certain victory, and the school is great and getting greater. Such presidents can have staying power, because everybody likes to be called a winner, but their school languishes because of its leader's reluctance to acknowledge and tackle problems and shortcomings.

- *The politician president.* Adept at reading tea leaves, politician presidents bend with the winds. Faced with difficult decisions, they appoint task forces to do their dirty work. They command little loyalty from their vice presidents, who tire of being asked to deliver the bad news. Politician presidents are always looking out for number one. They fortify their power base with favors and friendly notes to influential supporters, and while they may stay in their job for years, their lack of vision and reluctance to make unpopular decisions make their school stagnate.

- *The risk-averse president.* This president sees catastrophe lurking behind every decision. These cowardly lions always take the safest route. Fearing lawsuits, they never stray far from their general counsel. They take great care never to irritate the faculty, they capitulate to the demands of activist groups, and they do not overrule bad committee recommendations. Their jobs tend to be joyless and stress filled, because they measure success not in terms of accomplishments but in terms of disasters avoided. Their institutions do not advance, because the safest path for them is the status quo.

- *The bull-in-the-china-shop president.* These presidents are the opposite of risk-averse presidents. Far from fleeing confrontation, they charge toward problems like an out-of-control railcar. Ironically, such presidents often have good academic values and a clear vision for their school. But their noble intentions generally come to nothing because they lack the sensitivity and strategic abilities to carry out their agenda. Congenitally unable to pick their battles, bull-in-a-china-shop presidents are generally short-timers who may well leave their school in disarray.

- *The celebrity president.* Often well-connected scholars with national reputations, or persons with a high public profile, these prima donnas come with an ego as big as their senses of entitlement. Celebrity presidents surround themselves with personal staff, spend lavishly to redecorate the presidential home, like to fly on private aircraft, and enjoy hobnobbing with high-ranking politicians and business leaders. Skilled at negotiating on their own behalf, they are likely paid a very high salary, but their arrested senses of propriety mean that when their excesses are splashed across the newspapers, as they often are, they flame out like a shooting star. The celebrity president is an unwise choice for a private university but can be a disaster for a public one.

- *The insecure president.* Insecure presidents often present a tough demeanor, but the giveaway of their spongy interior is the way they handle criticism. For them, it is "my way or the highway." They surround themselves with docile vice presidents and deans, lash out at critics, and walk around with a chip on their shoulder. Insecure presidents are quick to take offense, and they see those who oppose their decisions as members of the enemy camp. Their office tends to be staffed by fearful and disloyal subordinates. Unable to build teamwork in their administration, isolated from candid advice, and unwilling to admit their own mistakes, they endure a presidential tenure that is predictably unsuccessful.

Obviously, these caricatures are painted with primary colors. Real college presidents, like everybody else, are a complex palette of strengths, weaknesses, idiosyncrasies, and mannerisms. However, the academic president's job is different from most jobs, because there is less latitude to accommodate human frailties. In most walks of life, we can muddle along pretty well even if we have a chip on our shoulder, an outsized ego, or a beanbag for a brain. But because of the nature of the job, the president's office tends to amplify personality shortcomings, turning them quickly into dysfunctional behaviors that can stall an institution's progress. In a presidential search, one challenge is to recognize the signs of these personality shortcomings and decide how much credence to give them.

Patterns of Unsuccessful Searches

Presidential searches in academia tend to follow patterns that make it difficult to evaluate candidates with appropriate care. Here is a list of the most common problems that lead to disappointing outcomes:

1. Candidates are evaluated by criteria that do not adequately bear on the actual skills, personality qualities, and levels of sophistication that the job calls for. As we will see, this problem often points to a structural problem in traditional search committees caused by the academic community's desire to be broadly involved in the selection process.
2. Trustees, hoping to address specific campus problems, focus on too narrow a range of candidates' strengths. In other words, if trustees want

the new president to emphasize endowment growth (or to improve relationships with the state legislature, rein in the football coach, or form
partnerships with the business community), they place undue weight on
the specific experiences relevant to that goal. A variation on this practice
is to search for somebody who is the mirror image of the outgoing president. The notion here is that if the outgoing president was particularly
good at doing A, B, C but not so good at doing D, E, F, then the new
president should reverse those strengths.

In principle, emphasizing particular skills is not a bad idea, unless the
desire gets out of hand. Success in the job calls for a president to have
a balance of strengths and no significant deficiencies. A president who
may be adept at wooing large donors ultimately does the school no
good if he or she is unable to attend to the school's academic agenda or
lacks the judgment to handle campus crises.

3. Trustees recruit a reform president whom they charge with making unworkable or inappropriate changes. An example of this mistake is the hiring of a tough ex-CEO as president, in the hope that a corporate bulldog
   can infuse the school with business strategies of cost control, accountability, productivity, and bottom-line efficiency. This practice, however
   desirable it might seem in the abstract, almost never works and can lead
   to disaster. General Dwight Eisenhower may have been a brilliant com-
   mander of World War II European forces, but when he tried his hand at
   leading Columbia University the enemy soon had him on the run.

4. An internal candidate has a close relationship with board members and
   is appointed president without being subjected to sufficient scrutiny.
   Internal presidents are often desirable for troubled small colleges, since
   they are known quantities who are already familiar with the school's
   problems. But for well-known colleges and universities, insiders usually
   do not measure up against the best candidates drawn from a national
   pool.[4] Furthermore, internal candidates often carry baggage that can
   undermine their effectiveness, and obviously they lack the fresh insights
   and perspectives that outsiders bring to the table. Trustees also run the
   risk of alienating the faculty if it appears they are circumventing normal
   campus search expectations.

5. Trustees rely too much on their own instincts about presidential qualifications and do not solicit advice and recommendations from those
   who have a deep understanding of the president's job and the internal
   problems of the institution. This is a common pattern, for two reasons.
   First, trustees seeking change and frustrated by an academic culture that

seems to go overboard to promote democracy and inclusiveness can conclude that campus advisers will only criticize or reject the credentials of those who might change that culture. And second, trustees can overestimate their understanding of the president's job and the knowledge it requires, as well as their own ability to evaluate the credentials of candidates. Running a university or college is a bit like coaching a football team, in that everybody thinks he can do it.

6. Trustees select a president in part to send a symbolic message about institutional priorities. Most commonly, this practice centers on issues of gender and race. Knowing that college presidents have mostly been Caucasian males, trustees hope to redress this imbalance and symbolize their commitment to inclusiveness by appointing a female or minority president. Despite the fact that this practice is rather common and nearly always well intentioned, I believe it is ill advised. Presidents are not the symbolic leaders of their school; they are the *real* leaders. When trustees select a president for reasons unrelated to his or her ability to do the job, then they are shortchanging their institution. If a woman, a Hispanic, a Nobel laureate, or a member of another underrepresented group turns out to be the most competent candidate, then by all means select that person. But if not, then select the person who *is* the most competent, because ten years down the road the only message anybody will remember is how well the president carried out the duties of the office.

7. Trustees who have never conducted a presidential search before and are fearful of violating campus protocol and attracting criticism simply parrot the procedures used in the previous search. Depending on the process used previously, this may or may not be a bad idea. However, the failure to stand back and look objectively at the shortcomings of the prior search will merely perpetuate flawed or ineffective practices.

The Traditional Presidential Search Committee

The idea that representatives of all constituencies should have a formal voice in selecting the university's leader grows out of the tradition of shared governance. The same expectation also drives academic searches for department chairs, deans, vice presidents, center and program directors, and other university officers. It is the primary reason that an appointment of a dean can take up to year, cost tens of thousands of dollars, and involve hundreds of hours of committee time.

The rationale for this cumbersome process is that students, faculty, staff, alumni, and other constituencies are seen as coexisting in a harmonious, egalitarian balance. Thus, if no alumni were appointed to the search committee, the other members could upset this balance by choosing a candidate with no interest in alumni affairs. And even if that did not happen, a cloud of suspicion could damage the alumni community's response to the new president. An instinctive goal of traditional search committees, therefore, is to search out candidates who express a commitment to all the represented constituencies. As a result, during interviews, the student member will inquire whether the candidate intends to teach a class or have an open-door policy for students. The African American member will ask how the candidate fostered diversity in her previous job. The faculty senate representative will search out the candidate's enthusiasm for shared governance. From around the table such questions will come, and while they may all appear to be different, in fact they are really the same question: *As president, will you support my constituency and advance its interests?* Candidates who believe, say, that the faculty union is a barrier to excellence, or that racial preferences in admissions are unfair, or that the basketball program harms the school's reputation will sidestep these important issues and give bland, cautious answers to avoid stepping on toes.

Constituency-based committee members, having little in common with each other and lacking broad insight into the president's job, often overemphasize the importance of a candidate's demeanor. Thus they gravitate toward candidates who project a distinguished aura, seem to have an enthusiastic, commanding presence, appear self-confident and assured, remember their names, and appear friendly and approachable. Of course, these are desirable traits that one might hope for in any incoming leader. But these qualities often have more to do with public image and the ability to interview well than the potential to advance an institution. Some of the best university presidents in the country have been shy, introspective intellectuals, cranky curmudgeons, or others whose physical appearance, social demeanor, and mannerisms did not conform to the popular stereotype. It is hard for constituency-based search committees to assess a candidate's decisiveness, planning skills, and ability to identify and motivate good people, to tackle problems, to delegate appropriately, to understand the nuances of university finances, and to exploit opportunities.

Furthermore, committee members who have only a superficial understanding of academic administration are often swayed by candidates who espouse an egalitarian but unrealistic philosophy of collegiality:

> I see my greatest strength as being a consensus builder. I believe universities move forward when everybody pulls in the same direction, with a commitment to a shared vision forged by the president. To me, this is the essence of academic leadership. It is what I have always tried to achieve throughout my career, and it is the strength I would bring to your campus.

The fact is that any presidential candidate who seriously espouses consensus building as a management strategy has little hope of implementing significant changes at his or her institution. Academic communities are fractious places filled with smart, strong-willed, and outspoken people who seldom see eye to eye on any substantive issue. The notion that such people can be transformed into lemminglike followers because of an articulated presidential "vision" is an unsophisticated expectation that flies in the face of long experience. Any university leader who really thinks consensus building is possible will avoid controversial decisions, be content with the status quo, and capitulate to outspoken interest groups.

That is not to say, of course, that communication skills and persuasiveness are unimportant for university presidents. But these skills should be used as tools for making change, not in pursuit of an idealized but naive notion of campus harmony. The traditional search committee gravitates toward consensus builders, because its members do not want to risk hiring a leader who might step on the toes of their constituents—even if doing so is what the institution needs to solve its problems and move forward. And even if the committee is determined to recruit a decisive problem solver, constituency-based committees often find it difficult to analyze a candidate's ability to transform a campus. Promises are not plans. It may please committee members to learn that, as president, a candidate will create a ten-point strategic vision for the future, place increased attention on undergraduate teaching, mend town-gown relations, be an aggressive fund-raiser, and reduce bloat in the administration. But in and of themselves, such pledges are about as meaningful as a mayoral candidate's promises to end corruption and rehabilitate the inner city. The devil is in the details, and a democratically balanced committee may not have the requisite expertise to know whether ideas about, say, using federal indirect cost recovery to stimulate faculty research are well thought out and doable.

Why Less Is More

Trustees charged with hiring a university president are caught in a bind. On the one hand, they may be determined to recruit a decisive leader who will face up to their institution's problems and steer it successfully through turbulent waters. And, instinctively, they may realize that a broad, inclusive search process that folds in many segments of the academic community may not yield that kind of candidate. But on the other hand, trustees want to be respectful of the academic culture of their institution, and since that culture can seem inscrutable and intimidating to outsiders, treading cautiously and not appearing to violate hallowed norms may seem the wisest strategy.

Furthermore, trustees who are unaccustomed to public criticism may be especially leery of upsetting faculty members, especially given the perception that professors are likely to pounce vocally on those with whom they disagree. Thus, after weighing the pros and cons, board members often take the safest route by deferring to campus constituencies, hoping that somehow they will be able to identify and recruit the best candidate despite the obstacles. But doing so is a mistake. Hiring a president is the most important action a college or university's governing board ever takes, and if there is ever a time for board members to protect their right to do it and display their independence and courage, this is the time. Choosing the right person for the job has to take precedence over the desire to placate campus interest groups.

In my opinion, the best presidential search committee is no formal committee at all; instead, trustees conduct the search in secrecy, advised by persons of their own choosing (about whom I will shortly have more to say). The worst presidential search committees are large, broadly representative groups with elected members. Between these extremes is a continuum of alternatives. If university rules or practices mandate a public search committee, and if trustees have the latitude to select the committee, then a small group of five to eight members is best, consisting of faculty members, trustees, and senior administrators chosen from among the most competent and thoughtful people the school has to offer. Students, alumni, staff members, and faculty senators, if chosen just to represent constituencies, should be added only if unavoidable.

Realistically, such people, despite their best intentions, bring little to the table and invariably lead to the constituency-based problems discussed previously.

Trustees should not fear that appointing a small committee will unleash a hornet's nest. Anybody can see the practical virtues of keeping a committee small, and with five to eight members, it is will be obvious that not every constituency can have its own representative. Paradoxically, large committees often generate more complaints than small committees do. If there is a professor from the physical sciences on the committee, then why not one from the life sciences? And if both are on the committee, then how about one from engineering, or medicine, or the branch campuses, and on and on? Large committees encourage the campus to parse itself into an ever finer grid of interest groups. Small committees discourage this tendency. So long as the committee makes a good-faith effort to solicit advice from across campus, and so long as the committee members are admired and respected, complaints are likely to be muted.

What Kind of Advice?

If, in the best of circumstances, trustees have the option of conducting a presidential search in complete confidence, that freedom does not mean that they should evaluate candidates by relying exclusively on their own judgment. In soliciting advice, the idea is to choose individuals who understand the depth and scope of responsibilities of the presidency, who are capable of evaluating the scholarly and administrative credentials of the candidates, and who have a deep understanding of the problems and needs of the institution. Whether these individuals meet as a group or act as independent consultants to the trustees is not important.

With respect to understanding presidential responsibilities, the best perspective can obviously be provided by a person with actual experience in the job. A highly regarded emeritus president, or a sitting president at another institution, can assess the personal qualities of candidates, their level of sophistication and experience, and their leadership skills. Sitting presidents or ex-presidents can recognize superficial thinking and are not likely to be impressed by candidates who lack substance but are able to interview well and make a favorable initial impression.

The scholarly credentials of presidential candidates can be assessed only by faculty members. Although university presidents are sometimes selected from outside the academy, highly ranked colleges and research universities nearly always choose leaders who have a prior academic career. For almost any type of academic institution, the majority of presidential candidates will have a history of teaching and research, and the prior work of these individuals, even if it took place decades earlier, provides important insight into their administrative style. Candidates coming from business schools, or colleges of education, or chemistry departments, for example, have been shaped by radically different academic cultures that will inevitably affect their approach toward administrative leadership. Although trustees may choose either to emphasize or to discount a candidate's prior academic record, it is always important that they have an objective evaluation of it.

Trustees may be tempted to solicit faculty advice from the leaders of their school's legislative body, which is typically a faculty or university senate. The rationale is that senate leaders, having been democratically elected by their colleagues, are seen as representing the collective voice of the faculty. Furthermore, such persons are often anxious to influence the presidential selection and will eagerly volunteer their services. Despite the temptation to keep the peace by acquiescing to such requests, trustees should consider looking elsewhere for faculty counsel. Representatives from faculty or university senates are often interested in advancing their legislative body's influence over the institution, and this desire sometimes manifests itself as opposition to strong administrative leadership. In extreme cases, especially at public universities, the campus senate can consider itself almost as a shadow administration that is locked into a chronic adversarial posture with the school's real administration. In this circumstance, trustees will get more objective and informed guidance by soliciting advice from the school's most accomplished professors: senior professors who hold endowed chairs or professorships, those who head important academic programs, or those who have won prestigious awards for their scholarship and teaching. The school's academic vice president can help identify these persons.

It is essential that trustees consult with some of the school's senior administrators—deans and vice presidents, generally—in order to place candidates' administrative credentials in the context of campus problems and needs. Trustees have a broad-brush understanding of their school, but the views of people in the trenches can also provide an important perspective. Presidents have to deal with turf battles between vice presidents, deans who have lost control of their college budget, departments with tenure-heavy faculty but declining numbers of majors, soaring laboratory costs for new professors, and myriad other issues that never make it to a trustees' meeting. A school's senior administrators can help educate candidates and assess their ability to deal with these kinds of problems. The school's most effective and highly regarded deans and vice presidents make the best advisers in this category, which, if at all possible, should also include the school's chief financial officer.

The general message of this chapter, therefore, is that presidential leadership is so crucial to the well-being of colleges and universities that trustees should do everything possible to maximize the chances of picking the right person for the job. Doing so, however, means resisting the academic forces that would advance candidates unsuited to a changing environment, and instead identifying those who have the decisiveness, insight, and strong hand that the job now requires. This is not an easy assignment. Not only may trustees have to work around ingrained campus practices and traditions, but they must subject candidates to a different and more intense kind of scrutiny than has been the norm. In essence, they have to think deeply about the future needs of their institution and then look beyond a candidate's public demeanor and interviewing skills in order to assess the qualities that are germane to those needs.

Reforming the Academic Culture

A Tale of Two Companies

Jungle Jim's International Market is arguably the most successful and imaginative independent supermarket in America. Owned by Jim and Joani Bonaminio, Jungle Jim's is a sprawling multiacre carnival of buildings in Fairfield, Ohio, north of Cincinnati. Part supermarket, part theme park, part specialty boutique, Jungle Jim's is a bizarre amalgam of thousand-dollar hot sauces, Thai noodles, plastic monkeys in palm trees, exotic live fish, singing Elvises, gourmet coffees, and souped-up hot rods. And, of course, African safaris. Jungle Jim's is better than Alice's Restaurant, because at JJ's you really *can* get anything you want.

Like all business owners, Jim Bonaminio tries to obtain maximum performance from his 350-person workforce. He wants his employees to show up on time, to not dawdle at their desks, to have a can-do attitude, to accept responsibility, to care about the quality of their work, and to be loyal to the company and its goals. And he also wants them to have fun. Nonsalaried employees at Jungle Jim's can earn "Goofy Tickets" by doing especially good work. Going the extra mile, coming to work early and staying late, having new ideas, and being especially helpful to customers will earn an employee a Goofy Ticket. At the end of the month, everybody's Goofy Tickets are put in a hopper. The winners get to spin a "wheel of fortune" and a chance to win prizes ranging from five hundred dollars to a case of Pepsi. Employees love their Goofy Tickets because the game is fun and rewarding. But most importantly, Goofy Tickets are good business because they build morale and raise the performance bar for the company's workforce.

Underlying "Goofy Tickets" are important business principles that are anything but goofy:

1. To motivate employees, whether janitors or Nobel laureates, carrots work better than sticks. When human beings are forced to change their behavior in order to avoid penalties, the resulting sullenness, resentment, and passive-aggressiveness generally outweigh any positive gains the organization might garner.
2. People will put their heart into activities they enjoy. If employees have fun at their job, the payoff is a strong sense of community, high morale, and loyalty to the organization.
3. Motivational strategies have to be matched to the organization's culture. The brilliance of Goofy Tickets is their fit with Jungle Jim's zany corporate personality. But try out Goofy Tickets on the Princeton English Department and one suspects the results would be far different.

My second tale is drawn from the Danaher Corporation, a perennial favorite of Wall Street, founded by brothers Mitchell and Steven Rales. With more than $10 billion in annual sales, Danaher owns nearly ninety manufacturing subsidiaries in the United States and Europe. What has made Danaher one of the most profitable and fastest-growing conglomerates in the world is its extraordinary ability to contain costs and maximize the efficiency and productivity of its acquisitions.

One of the Danaher companies is Videojet Technologies, a premier manufacturer of industrial coding, printing, and labeling machines. When visitors stroll along the immaculate corridors of Videojet's Chicago factory, what strikes their eye is that virtually every wall is covered with charts and graphs featuring some aspect of the company's performance. One graph may plot the record of improvement in the number of seconds customers are left on hold when they call the company's switchboard. Another may show the progress in decreasing the number of steps a worker takes when unloading cargo from a delivery truck and placing it on a warehouse shelf. All the company's operations, large and small, are relentlessly scrutinized and optimized. This culture of self-improvement is pervasive and encompassing, yet employees do not feel hemmed in or regimented by it. On the contrary, Videojet's workers take pride in making their company more productive. "In my other jobs, nobody ever asked my opinion," one loading dock hand told me. "Here, my boss takes my suggestions seriously."

The Danaher model for higher productivity, lower costs, and greater efficiency is grounded in several concepts:

1. The key driver of productivity and efficiency improvement is information. An organization cannot improve itself unless it collects the information that will provide benchmarks for its performance and track the changes it is undertaking.
2. The organization's culture has to be change-oriented at all levels, because the people who are actually doing the work are most qualified to solve problems and to know what questions to ask.
3. Employees have to be empowered to make changes. Empowerment breeds initiative, creativity, and commitment. Workers who are not empowered to make a difference in their working environment do not care about improving that environment.

Jungle Jim's International Market and the Danaher Corporation illustrate the two sides of the productivity coin. One side focuses on employee performance and uses words like *incentive, reward, motivation,* and *initiative*. The other side focuses on systems and processes, and here the words are *optimization, reorganization, data,* and *benchmark*. No successful enterprise can afford to neglect either side of the coin. A doctor's office may have the most industrious and caring receptionist in the land, but if patients have to wait thirty minutes in a crowded waiting room for their appointments, they will eventually switch doctors. To make their institutions more efficient, productive, and adaptable, therefore, higher education's leaders must work both to break down the ingrained conservatism of the academic culture and to restructure the processes and systems to increase organizational efficiency.

Changing the academic culture is the most difficult part of the equation, but not for the reasons commonly assumed by those outside academia. Critics of public universities often point to lax personnel policies as the primary cause of higher education's inefficiencies. The lack of professorial accountability, they claim, breeds laziness and abuse. Tenure locks in the "dead wood" on the faculty. Teaching loads are too light, professors study arcane, irrelevant topics, and nobody really cares about what students and taxpayers want. To such critics, higher education's problems could be fixed if universities would only learn better to supervise their workforce and enforce performance standards.

But the critics are misdirecting their attention. While there are unproductive employees and troublemakers on any university or college campus, just as there are in any organization, individual performance problems are not the primary cause of higher education's inefficiencies. On the contrary, as a group, university and college professors are self-starters who take their work extremely seriously. Those who are inclined to think otherwise should keep in mind that in their earlier lives college faculty members were the brainy kids in the class who turned in their homework on time, sat on the front row, asked lots of questions, and aced the exams. There is little reason to think that they changed their spots when, after preparing for their career for a decade or more in college and graduate school, they finally started drawing a paycheck.

But the systems and processes of academia are another story. Although individual professors on average work diligently, they are part of a culture that places a low value on organizational efficiency. Thus, understanding that culture and modifying it in a way that is acceptable to the higher education community is a prerequisite to addressing higher education's systemic problems.

There They Go Again

There is almost nothing that will more quickly provoke suspicion, rolled eyes, and ridicule from professors than an announcement from their campus administration of a new program to improve productivity. In academia, *productivity* and *efficiency* are fighting words, and the reasons go to the heart of the academic culture. The first reason is that *efficiency* and *productivity* are words from the business world. To professors, business represents the triumph of pragmatism over idealism. In business, employees are paid so that they will advance the interests of their employer; the primary goal of business is directed at the business itself—to increase profits and earnings, to grow sales, and to outdo the competition. By contrast, the goals of the university are not aimed at making the university better and more successful but rather at serving the needs of society. To professors, the point of their job is to advance knowledge and transmit that knowledge to others. While they may take pride in their school's reputation and accomplishments, they see themselves as actors on a larger stage.

To professors in some academic disciplines, especially in the humanities and social sciences, the business culture can seem distasteful. Many professors dislike the clichés and catch-phrases of business—"doing more with less," "thinking outside the box," "dressing for success." They dislike the business customs of tagging little homilies on the end of e-mails, striking deals on the golf course, dressing in business suits and carrying briefcases; all of these aspects of the business world symbolize a culture they had hoped to avoid when they chose an academic career. In their view, to import the business notions of productivity and efficiency into the academy would be to push them in the direction of a lifestyle with which they are uncomfortable and for which they are ill-suited.

A second reason productivity talk raises suspicions is that it potentially threatens faculty autonomy. As discussed previously, professors cherish their right to pursue knowledge for its own sake, to structure their classes as they deem best, and to come and go at will. To them, increasing efficiency could mean loss of control, mandatory schedules and regimentation, and marching to somebody else's drumbeat.

But the biggest concern professors have about increasing efficiency is a potential loss of academic quality. They know that in one sense it is easy for a university to become more productive. Increasing class sizes will reduce the unit cost of instruction, as will trimming journal subscriptions in the library or replacing tenured professors with inexpensive part-timers. Universities can become more efficient by eliminating specialty seminars with low enrollments, phasing out academic programs that do not pay their own way, increasing teaching loads, and cutting out faculty travel to professional meetings.

If improving productivity means reducing the academic enterprise to a set of indices, benchmarks, and cost ratios, and then measuring gains by numbers on a spreadsheet, then most faculty members will want nothing to do with it. Professors treasure the individuality and idiosyncrasy of academic life, and they will object to anything they see as a dehumanizing influence on that life. Just as the relentless pursuit of efficiency and cost reduction has led to the proliferation of cookie-cutter shopping malls and bland restaurant franchises, its impact on academia, professors fear, would be to homogenize and strip away the soul of their institution. Given this predisposition, selling the idea that actual good— and in some cases survival—could come by making their school more productive and efficient is an uphill battle.

Laying the Groundwork for Change

How then is it possible to modify and improve upon an academic culture populated by smart, creative individuals who are motivated by ideals more than by money, who have deep, intense interests, value substance over form, have little patience for conformity, think for themselves, do not defer to authority, and see their work not as a job but as a calling? Clearly the challenge is to find the incentives and rewards that will motivate this unique workforce to buy into desired changes and work willingly toward implementing them. But the first step is to explain clearly why change is necessary and, even more important, why change does not mean abandoning core academic values. To win the hearts of academics, one first has to educate them.

Here the essential point is to differentiate between explaining and persuading. University faculty members are predisposed to resist persuasion, especially from their school's administration. A more effective tactic is for an administration to lay out the facts as honestly as possible and let the school's faculty draw its own conclusions. For example, it is widely believed in professorial circles that universities give preference to administrative needs over academic needs, that the growth in the numbers of administrators—associate deans, assistant vice presidents, etc.—comes at the expense of putting more professors in classrooms and holding down class sizes. Why, professors often wonder, do presidents and provosts employ high-priced nonacademic professionals to staff administrative offices, while they are quite willing to allow inexperienced graduate students to teach classes? Concerns of this sort need to be addressed candidly and honestly. The growth in administrative ranks, the cost of that growth, and the reasons for the larger numbers must be explained clearly. If the reasons are sound—to comply with new federal and state mandates, to cope with growing mental health needs of entering students, to provide better budget oversight of collegiate athletics, to pump up the fund-raising staff for an upcoming campaign—then the faculty can understand that administrative growth is driven by a growth in institutional responsibilities and not merely by a desire of administrators to feather their nests. Faculty and staff salary trends should be analyzed, especially if there is slippage relative to salaries at other institutions. Swelling health care and energy costs, growing regulatory burdens, ever-expanding technology and network demands, a rising backlog of deferred maintenance—all of the cost pressures that consume the attention of the administration should be put on the table for scrutiny.

It is also important not to neglect the revenue side of the picture. Historical patterns of state subsidy should be explained, as well as the impact of tuition controls and the increased competition for students. Long-term revenue projections of the institution should be widely disseminated, showing what the future will hold in five or ten years. These messages should be as explicit as possible. It is easy to dismiss a general statement that budget problems are in the offing in a few years. But one cannot ignore a careful analysis that predicts a $30 million shortfall in the general fund in 2011 and lays out what the consequences will mean in terms of layoffs, hiring freezes, increases in class sizes, and cutbacks in services.

What all of this means is that the first step toward cultural change in academia is education. No change can take place unless the university community understands fully the extent of the forces on its institution and, barring structural changes, the inevitable long-term impact of those forces. This story must be broadly delivered. It must be shared with faculty and staff members, office supervisors, program directors, department chairs, and deans. A one-hour speech from the president or a presentation by a senior fiscal officer to the faculty senate budget committee will not do the trick. Fully developing and explaining a realistic picture of the institution's future is likely to take a year and the combined efforts of many people.

Using Personal Incentives

Although faculty members resist being categorized, like all human beings they will respond to incentives and rewards that match their interests and needs. For young professors building their career, the strongest incentive is peer recognition and approval, and to gain this recognition new faculty members will instinctively pattern their behavior after colleagues whom they most respect. If their mentors and senior colleagues take their own teaching obligations seriously, then they will do so also. If their senior colleagues publish widely, speak at international conferences, and obtain federal grants for their research, then these activities will become a standard against which junior faculty will calibrate their own professional advancement.

Shaping peer recognition can thus be an important tool for a university administration in redressing problems with the institutional culture. Often, this practice entails avoiding unintended negative incentives. If, for example, a chemistry department recruits a senior professor to fill an endowed chair and then excuses that professor from teaching introductory chemistry, then the department's junior faculty will internalize the message that avoiding teaching is a signature of professional success. On the other hand, if the department formally recognizes the teaching accomplishments of its top professors and assigns them periodically to teach introductory courses, then junior faculty will internalize the more positive message that commitment to teaching goes hand in hand with research achievement.

Another example pertains to committee leadership and other faculty service duties. All universities have professors who enjoy serving on committees and readily volunteer for committee assignments. Sometimes these professors are also first-rate teachers and scholars, but frequently they are not. Long-term associate professors who never satisfied the requirements for promotion to full professor sometimes fall into this category. Presidents, provosts, and deans should generally avoid choosing such persons to play highly visible roles on important faculty committees. To do so would be to promote role models for junior professors that are inconsistent with the larger institutional goals of teaching and research excellence. Using a school's top professors to send consistent desirable messages to the rest of the faculty should be an important part of any administrative strategy to improve the institutional culture.

It is unlikely that university professors are as motivated by monetary rewards and incentives as are nonacademic employees in business and industry. Even so, it is important that college and university administrators seeking to change an institutional culture learn to use personal financial incentives skillfully. University faculty members are salaried employees, and in public higher education annual salary raises tend to be modest, with little variation among colleagues in the same department. Although over time the salary spread between a department's most distinguished and least distinguished professor can be appreciable, a professor's base salary normally reflects prior accomplishments and reputation. From an administrator's viewpoint, salary raises are a way to recognize past achievement but not to provide strong incentives for future performance. In other words, if a college dean hopes to persuade a distinguished senior professor to chair a time-consuming search committee, the promise of an extra percent or so salary raise is unlikely to entice the professor to say yes.

In business, cash bonuses are important strategic tools for motivating salaried employees to take on extra responsibilities and special assignments. However, in universities, bonuses are normally not part of employees' compensation packages, except perhaps for coaches, athletic directors, endowment fund managers, and senior administrative officers. Universities would gain a useful tool for effecting institutional change by implementing a vigorous cash bonus policy for faculty and administrators. One example of how a bonus plan could work will be discussed subsequently in the context of streamlining governance procedures. A key point, however, is that in order to be effective, bonus incentives must come to a sizable fraction of an employee's annual salary. A bonus payment to a professor of a thousand dollars may be appreciated but will not be a strong motivating influence. A bonus of $20 thousand or $50 thousand is another matter.

Using Group Incentives

As the financial condition of public universities has deteriorated, professors have become increasingly concerned about the working environment in their departments. Faculty offices and seminar rooms have grown dingier, and equipment budgets have become depleted, making it difficult to upgrade computers, office duplicating machines, and other office equipment. Travel budgets have suffered, reducing faculty participation at professional conferences; colloquium and seminar schedules have been trimmed, as have subscriptions to professional journals. In general, professors at public campuses have experienced an erosion in their departmental working environment that mirrors that of their overall university budget.

Providing opportunities to reverse this erosion can be an effective way to motivate a department faculty to enhance its productivity and efficiency. For example, many academic departments routinely assign the same course teaching load to all faculty members, so that active scholars supervising PhD students teach the same amount as professors without active research programs. This practice is usually opposed by deans and provosts, but faculty resistance in departments can make it hard to implement a more equitable system. However, if a dean makes the acceptance of differential teaching assignments a prerequisite for approving a new faculty position, or increasing an operating budget, or increasing teaching assistantship stipends, then the department resistance is likely to soften. Tit-for-tat negotiations can be very effective at changing institutional behavior, but to work these negotiations must be specific. It is generally not successful to ask for a change in practices merely to satisfy a larger good. For example, if a large department has for years assigned eight faculty members to its curriculum committee, then it probably will resist a dean's proposal to reduce the number to four simply to serve some abstract notion of efficiency. However, if the dean promises to use the money saved to increase the department's travel budget, then the faculty are likely to be more accomodating. In academia, forces to maintain the status quo are powerful, so that incentives to change it must be immediate, recognizable, and specific.

Upgrading Institutional Research

The Videojet Technologies example at the beginning of this chapter illustrated the importance of gathering information in order to improve the systems and processes of an organization. If Videojet maps out one end of an information-gathering continuum, most universities and colleges map out the other end. Institutions of higher learning are so decentralized and encompass such a diversity of activities that comprehensive data collection is a formidable challenge.

Furthermore, the university culture discourages the kind of information gathering that might lead to significant change, especially in academic departments. Faculty concerns about administrative intrusions into their domain translate into apprehension about gathering the information that might make such intrusions possible. Faculty members in, say, a physics department are likely to become uneasy and suspicious if their dean starts inquiring about variations in faculty teaching loads, percentage of graduate students from non-English-speaking countries, books and articles published by faculty members in the past year, number of hours spent advising undergraduates, GRE scores of entering graduate students, number of faculty on research leave, and enrollment trends in honors courses. These are the kind of statistics that invite department-to-department comparisons and can spell trouble for departments that don't appear to be measuring up.

But that is exactly the point. Universities cannot manage their resources efficiently unless those in charge have the information to make informed decisions. If governing boards and senior administrators really want to reduce costs, speed up institutional reaction times, and make their campus more efficient and productive, then a good place to start is the Office of Institutional Research, as the data-gathering branch of the university's administration is frequently called. This is the office that prepares reports on building usage, enrollment trends, credit hours taught, federal grant support, and other statistical and summary information for use by the administration. At larger institutions, these functions are likely to be spread over several offices, with the finance office preparing "what if . . . ?" models of budget options, the university foundation preparing reports on endowment growth and gift-giving trends, and so forth. While these offices provide useful global information, such as the historical record of corporate gifts or state-by-state breakdowns of student applications, they generally do not collect data that could inform many important lower-level decisions.

For example, a dean of a large college who is considering making a major investment in the school's economics department, or perhaps weighing a request for new faculty positions or deciding whether to reappoint a department chair, needs to know how effectively the department uses its resources. Responsible administrative decisions will rest on the answers to several tangible and intangible questions about departmental performance. In the area of scholarship, has the number of faculty grant proposals to federal agencies been increasing, and what has been their success rate? What is the department publication record in refereed professional journals, and how does it compare to that of other departments? How many professors gave invited lectures in the past year at major professional conferences, consulted with government and business, spent sabbatical leaves at prestigious institutions, served on national panels, and spoke on their research at other universities? Have these numbers been going up or down?

In the area of instruction, has the number of undergraduate department majors been growing or shrinking? How about the numbers of MS and PhD students? Have recent graduates been successful at landing jobs? Have credit hours taught in the department been growing or shrinking? Have average class sizes, teaching loads, and classroom utilization rates been increasing or decreasing? In the fiscal area, has the department been living within its budget? What is its pattern of carry-forward year-end balances? How do equipment expenditures, travel expenditures, maintenance costs, and faculty salaries compare to those in other departments? Have alumni been generous in their gifts to the department?

The dean also needs to know answers to important nonquantitative questions. How well does the department mentor its junior faculty? Has the department been successful in filling faculty appointments with top-notch candidates? Is the department faculty collegial and united? Are the department's promotion and tenure recommendations candid and believable? Is the department chairperson a go-getter who is willing to set limits and make unpopular decisions in order to advance the department?

The answers to such questions can provide administrators with an understanding of the health and vitality of an academic unit. Most provosts and deans have a general idea about the performance of the major departments in their institution, but when one considers that a large public university can have a hundred academic departments spread over several campuses, a weak information-gathering system means that hearsay and subjective impressions too often form the basis for administrative decisions that can entail hundreds of thousands or even millions of dollars.

Thus an important step a university can take to become more efficient and productive is to improve its information and data-gathering systems. Most universities and colleges already collect a wide range of data about teaching, finances, research, student life, personnel, and auxiliary support services. Furthermore, most universities conduct a formal program review of individual academic units every few years. The challenge, therefore, is not so much to collect the raw data as to collate, organize, and present it in a way that supports administrative decisions. Upgrading the decision-making infrastructure should be a clear priority for institutions struggling to adjust to a changing environment.

How to Streamline University Decision-Making

In the election of November 2006, the voters of the State of Ohio approved Issue 5, a statute banning smoking in and near the state's public buildings. The passage of Issue 5 raised several compliance issues for Ohio's public universities. While the law clearly prohibited smoking in campus buildings and environs, it left open the question of smoking in parking lots, gardens, walkways, and so forth. Thus, the passage of Issue 5 provided an opportunity for the public universities in Ohio to review their antismoking policies. Should a university comply narrowly with the law and prohibit smoking only in and around its buildings, or should it comply more broadly with the spirit of the law and extend the smoking ban throughout the campus?

These kinds of administrative decisions come up almost daily in academia. Such decisions have nothing to do with academic freedom. Classroom content is not at stake, nor is the right to pursue knowledge for its own sake, nor is the right to speak out and voice opinions on any subject. But a campus antismoking policy is one of a class of issues that has the potential for creating campus controversy, albeit in this case a minor controversy. The larger question, therefore, is how universities should go about making decisions that are potentially controversial. In this instance, Miami University's response was to conduct a formal survey of campus opinion on the subject and create a university senate ad hoc committee on smoking. The committee met for a semester and then recommended a campuswide smoking ban as well as a variety of other measures to help campus smokers shake their habit. These recommendations were accepted by the president and eventually passed on to the board of trustees for final approval.[1]

In academia, administrators tend to avoid taking potentially controversial actions unilaterally, since doing so would likely draw the charge that they have ignored the collaborative expectations of the shared governance doctrine. Thus, in this example, rather than making the smoking policy decision themselves or delegating it to the human resources office, Miami University administrators passed the responsibility to a large committee. Passing decisions to committees as a way to temper public criticism is a common pattern in academic administration. The rationale is that broadly representative committee-based decisions are more likely to be accepted by the community than are unilateral administrative decisions. In this context, "acceptance" does not mean compliance so much as an absence of organized opposition and criticism.

But the cost to the institution of this decentralized practice is considerable. There is, of course, the actual dollar cost associated with committee-based decisions, and when the value of the committee members' time is added to the indirect costs of clerical and staff support, space for meetings, and so on, even a minor decision such as amending a smoking policy can cost a university tens of thousands of dollars. Furthermore, committees often make peripheral recommendations that entail future expenditures—in this case creating stop-smoking programs for campus employees—without considering either the implementation cost of their recommendations or whether the issue should really be a priority given the university's other pressing needs. Administrators can be boxed into accepting committee recommendations they would not otherwise support, simply because the political cost of rejecting them would be too great.

There are also numerous intangible costs associated with committee-based decisions, and these are no less significant than the direct dollar costs. Democratically balanced committees are prone to skirting or watering down difficult decisions that might upset a constituency, even if forthright action is justified by circumstances. Committee deliberations on even straightforward matters can stretch out for many weeks or months, as members research topics and draft and revise lengthy reports. And, of course, committee service diverts faculty members from the more central activities of teaching classes, advising students, and conducting research.

As is so often the case in academia, the challenge is to find the appropriate balance point. When university administrations overrely on group decision making, they waste resources, slow down responsiveness, and do not implement desirable but controversial changes. On the other hand, if administrators act too unilaterally, the result can be precipitous decisions that have unintended adverse consequences and lead to angry, fractious communities. The cultural vector of academia almost always points in the direction of wider collaboration and more committee involvement. At public universities especially, decades of cutbacks and declining resources have pressured campus leaders toward relying more heavily on committee-based decisions. Few members of a campus community will complain about positive administrative actions such as approving new faculty positions, increasing travel budgets, or opening new campus recreation facilities. But as financial necessity has forced more and more bad news on public campuses, their communities have become sensitized and defensive about negative decisions. As a result, even though the realities of university life call for stronger and more decisive leadership, the campus tolerance for unilateral administrative action keeps drifting lower.

Thus, transitioning toward a more appropriate balance point is a necessity for public universities seeking to respond strategically to their changed environment. Here are my recommendations to university administrators for making that transition. The principal concept is that universities and colleges can be weaned off excessive reliance on committee decision-making if the monetary and nonmonetary costs associated with committee decisions are understood.

1. *Calculating the direct and indirect costs of committee decisions.* So long as the time required for group decision making and collaboration is viewed as open ended, there is no incentive to consider whether the potential outcomes of the process justify its high price tag. To illustrate this point, consider the University of Michigan's Office of Lesbian, Gay, Bisexual, and Transgender Affairs. When the office decided in 2005 to change its name, it embarked on an elaborate consultative process that stretched on for three years and involved Web sites, surveys, bulletin boards, discussion groups, and forums. The actual total cost to the university of changing the name of this small nonacademic office probably exceeded a hundred thousand dollars. Had this cost been explicitly computed and reviewed in advance, it is likely that a more streamlined process would have emerged. Knowing the true price of governance makes it difficult to ignore whether those paying the bills—in this case, students and Michigan taxpayers—are receiving adequate value for their money.

   It is a straightforward accounting exercise to compute the actual dollar cost of committee-based recommendations and decisions, along with their ancillary forums, meetings, and discussion groups. Combining the number of meeting hours (either actual or anticipated) with the prorated salaries of the members, and adding a percentage for overhead expenses, will result in a dollar value that can used as an administrative tool to conserve committee time and ration it for important purposes. How this computation can be carried out in practice will be discussed shortly. The important point, however, is that tracking the price of all university committees should be a routine pro forma exercise for an institution's budget office.

2. *Learning to evaluate criticism.* One driver of excessive dependence on committees is university administrators' reluctance to subject themselves to criticism for making unilateral decisions that allegedly flout shared-governance principles. While this reluctance is understandable, the prospects of criticism should not inhibit leaders from making appropriate unilateral decisions. In academia, almost any administrative decision can be challenged as insufficiently collaborative by those who

oppose it; that fact alone is not a reason to avoid taking unilateral action provided, of course, that the action is grounded in reason and principle.

The strongest tool administrators have to forestall and rebut unwarranted criticism is to make every effort to explain publicly the reasons behind their decisions. It is human nature to attribute others' unwelcome actions to impulsiveness, base motives, incompetence, or insensitivity. But if an administrator's decision is seen as grounded in rational thinking, with a careful weighing of alternatives, then most critics will eventually accept it, even if they would have preferred a different outcome. Probably the single greatest reason for faculty opposition to their campus leaders is the failure of the administration to lay the groundwork and explain carefully the rationale for its actions. It may also be helpful for decision makers to bear in mind the positive side of criticism. When one's actions are in clear public view, the prospect of criticism widens one's perspective. Learning to see the consequences of a decision from many viewpoints helps put the brakes on impulsiveness.

3. *Recognizing and resisting upward delegation.* Upward delegation is a management problem in nearly all organizations, but universities and colleges are particularly vulnerable to this syndrome. Here is how it works. A dean, say, who is struggling to cope with an acute fiscal crisis informs the chairperson of English that he must trim $50 thousand out of his budget and asks him to submit a plan for the reduction. The plan arrives, but instead of reducing expenditures, the chairperson asks for a budget *increase* of $20 thousand. It is impossible, the chairperson says, to reduce his department's expenditures. To do so would involve canceling required writing seminars for freshmen who have already signed up for the courses. The syllabus has already been approved by committees, the adjunct instructors have already been hired, and the classrooms have been reserved. To protect these and other vital programs, the dean will have to come up with more money for the English Department and cut some other department's budget.

This is a textbook example of upward delegation in academia. In essence, the department chairperson has attempted to bump his problem up to the dean. Rather than thinking creatively about restructuring his department's budget—cutting back on some services, offering some courses less frequently, trimming travel and operating expenses, canceling service contracts on office equipment, reducing formal course requirements for students, curtailing a visitor program, selectively increasing class sizes, etc—he has proposed a business-as-usual plan that requires no fundamental changes in the department. Of course, if the dean insists on drastic measures, he will comply, but the dean will have to come up with the plan, and the dean will be responsible for the resulting backlash from students and faculty members.[2]

Universities are susceptible to this phenomenon because the culture discourages decisive action by administrators and also because faculty and students are quick to audit, critique, and second-guess administrative decisions they dislike. In our example, changing teaching loads, curricular requirements, office support, and the like normally calls for lengthy discussion among department members. Committees would have to meet; alternatives would have to be explored and pros and cons debated. There is no mechanism for a department chairperson to take action on the short timeline required by a fiscal emergency. For him, the most expedient and safe course of action is to pass his problem to the dean and present himself to his colleagues and the outside world as the staunch defender of his department against the unsympathetic officials higher up in the administration.

Upward delegation comes in many disguises and is surprisingly hard to recognize. Most university administrators feel a strong sense of dedication to their institution and can switch into a problem-solving mode almost out of instinct. The key to resisting upward delegation is to keep in mind the appropriateness of the problem. Asking oneself habitually whether a presented problem really is an issue that a president (or provost or vice president or dean) should be handling is the best way to recognize the syndrome. If the answer is no, then it is important not to engage, no matter how interesting or important the problem may appear to be in the abstract. It is also helpful to remind upward delegators that that making unpopular but necessary decisions is part of their job responsibility and one of the performance criteria against which they are evaluated.

4. Understanding when unilateral action is appropriate. Administrators should not shy away from making unilateral decisions that are straightforward, benign, and easily justified, or for which there is a precedent. This may seem an obvious point, but it is surprising how frequently academic committees are appointed to belabor the obvious or to confirm what is already widely anticipated. Thus, asking a committee to review an obviously dysfunctional program or office, to recommend a minor policy change (such as amending a provision of a student handbook), or to debate an issue on which extensive debate has already taken place is to waste

institutional resources. Administrators should think carefully about their true motivation for appointing committees. If the advice of a committee is not really needed, then it should not be created merely to send a symbolic message about collaboration. Carried to extremes, this common practice is not only wasteful and inefficient but also manipulative. One disrespects the true value of shared governance by going through the motions of consulting one's colleagues when their advice and counsel is not the real point of the exercise. Appointing a committee when the major reason for doing so is merely to diffuse the responsibility for making an obvious decision wastes time and is the signature of a weak leader.

Another appropriate moment for making unilateral decisions is when it is unlikely that a group consensus on a course of action can be obtained. I learned this lesson a few years ago when gender-equity issues created unsustainable budget problems for my university's intercollegiate athletics program. Because of the sensitivity of the issue to students, alumni, and sports fans, I asked the university senate for recommendations about the advisability of eliminating several varsity men's teams. The senators debated the pros and cons of the issue for months but could not come to closure. In the end, they directed the decision back to me without a recommendation, and I proposed to my board the phase-out of three men's varsity teams. Hindsight suggests that I should have realized that community debate on contentious topics can stretch on endlessly without resolution.

On important or controversial issues, such as eliminating varsity sports, it is clearly necessary to encourage public comment and, especially, to give those who would be most affected by an impending change an opportunity to voice their opposition and make proposals for alternate courses of action. However, the process and structure for this dialogue should be carefully spelled out in advance, with the understanding that on a certain date an administrative decision will be made. The failure to set firm ground rules in advance is what leads to uncontrolled, protracted opposition, including at the extreme demonstrations, student occupation of buildings, and so forth.

Other good occasions for unilateral administrative decision making arise when circumstances leave little other choice: when the timeline for action is unavoidably short, when the administrator already has the necessary expertise and adequate understanding of the issues, and when budget considerations leave one without other reasonable options. However, the fact that unilateral action is necessary does not remove the obligation for the decision maker to explain and justify the reasons for taking that action.

5. *Understanding when to appoint committees.* The most important reasons for appointing a committee are these: (a) the topic requires the collected knowledge and experience of a group; (b) the workload to research an issue is too great for one or two people; and (3) a topic needs to be evaluated from different perspectives before a decision can be made. There is thus a strong rationale for appointing search committees (provided the members are selected because of their knowledge of the position), curriculum committees, ad hoc committees on complex issues (such as student alcohol abuse), and committees pertaining to racial and ethnic diversity, intercollegiate athletics, investment policy, accreditation, and campus life. Committees are necessary to review research proposals and to approve additions and changes to the curriculum. And, of course, committees are essential for reviewing faculty credentials for promotion and tenure. The point is that, whatever the topic, the guiding principle should be a necessity for group judgment.

That said, administrators should also be on the lookout for alternate ways of obtaining necessary group advice. Instead of convening a committee to plan next year's weekly colloquium schedule, it is far faster and more economical for the department chairperson to solicit suggestions informally and then draw up a list of potential speakers. And it nearly goes without saying that when committees are unavoidable, they should be kept as small as possible, the timetable for recommendations specified in advance, and recommendations and final reports stipulated to be as brief as possible.

But despite all of the above, there will still be times when administrators feel compelled to create committees simply because the academic community expects formal involvement and will be incensed if this wish is not honored. Highly controversial topics, matters that have a significant impact on campus life, and the appointment of senior academic administrators almost always carry expectations of broad community involvement. It would be an error of judgment, however, to satisfy this community expectation by appointing committee members primarily to represent diverse campus constituencies, rather than for their expertise and knowledge. As discussed previously, democratically balanced committees whose members bring no special insight or knowledge to the task at hand can not only slow an institution's forward motion but do it lasting harm.

In these situations, a better strategy is to convene a small working committee of knowledgeable members and then to explain to the larger community that the committee has been asked to consult broadly across campus. Thus, instead of appointing an inexperienced undergraduate student to a committee charged with recruiting a school's chief financial officer, appoint somebody with actual knowledge and experience in financial matters who will then consult with student groups to solicit their views. If the cost savings and other practical benefits of this approach are explained to the community, then widespread grumbling about "not being consulted" will be defused. The stakes are too high for unqualified people, however well intentioned, to influence important university decisions about leadership and institutional direction.

Strategies for Reducing Service Bloat

In higher education, professors are evaluated by their department chairpersons each year for their professional contributions to teaching, research, and service, with the relative importance of these categories varying according to institutional mission. Most universities and colleges, public and private, expect a balance of strengths in each of these three areas. At universities and colleges that have a significant research mission, research excellence is valued more highly than teaching and service. Although university presidents, provosts, and deans often emphasize the importance of teaching in their public statements, the reality is that the dollars flow toward the school's top researchers. Outstanding scholars are rare birds that bring national prominence to an institution. Good teachers may reap the highest praise from students and alumni, but good teachers are more common than good researchers and they do not command a large "market value" outside of their campuses.

But if faculty research excellence is generally valued more than instructional excellence, at least in monetary terms, service achievements fall well below either activity. For faculty members, on-campus service generally means serving on departmental or university committees. Normally, professors receive their regular committee assignments at the beginning of each academic year, and these assignments may be supplemented throughout the year with ad hoc appointments to search committees, task forces, or commissions. Other on-campus service activities may include helping to organize workshops and conferences, hosting visitors, serving on university or faculty senates, and advising student groups and Greek organizations.

Most of these activities serve a useful and in some cases vital purpose in keeping the gears of the university turning smoothly. However, as we have seen, service can be carried to excess, resulting in committees that are larger than necessary, that meander without focus, that are preoccupied with minor matters, that delay or skirt important decisions, and that contribute unnecessarily to higher costs and inefficient use of institutional resources. Eliminating this unneeded and unproductive service "bloat" is thus a necessary step in shaping universities to accommodate a twenty-first-century reality of diminished public support and intense competition.

In truth, many professors view their committee responsibilities as a distraction from their primary teaching and research activities. Of course, there are other faculty members who enjoy serving on committees, who like the social interaction, and who have an organizational flair and the interpersonal skills needed to work productively with groups of people. University leaders are good at recognizing such persons and often encourage them to make a transition out of the classroom and into the ranks of the school's administration. But more typically, faculty members see their service obligations mostly as a required and sometimes thankless chore. Thus, if colleges and universities can increase their productivity, reduce their costs, and speed up their responsiveness by scaling back on excess service activities, they will find their faculty mostly agreeable to this idea. The challenge is to create the incentives that will induce professors to restructure their time more productively, without sacrificing either their autonomy or their influence over their school's direction. My proposal for creating these incentives entails the following five steps:

1. *On-campus service expectations.* The first step is to remove on-campus service as a formal criterion for promotion and tenure of probationary professors and as a component of merit salary raises for tenured senior faculty. In essence, this change would recognize formally what often is acknowledged in practice—that routine, day-to-day service is one of the continuing obligations of the academic profession but does not warrant special recognition or reward. Being helpful, whether by serving on committees, mentoring junior colleagues, or offering advice to a dean or provost, is part of the civic dues one pays to be a professor. Although

there is a general informal acceptance of this idea in academia, formalizing it in an institution's promotion, tenure, and faculty performance documents would achieve several useful goals.

First, it would make very clear to beginning tenure-track professors that they should spend their probationary years concentrating on their teaching and research. Inexperienced faculty members want their colleagues and department chairperson to see them as helpful, but this desire can easily be corrupted into a loss of focus that can harm a career. Entry-level women and minority faculty members—who often find themselves loaded down with committee assignments because of institutional diversity goals—would benefit especially from this policy change. Second, removing on-campus service as a factor in annual performance reviews would encourage all faculty members to weigh the importance of a service assignment before agreeing to it. Making it easier to say no would empower faculty members to ration their time judiciously. This step alone would tend to discourage oversized or superfluous decision-making groups. And finally, this change would mean some senior professors could no longer buttress their annual performance reviews by pointing to routine service on committees or legislative bodies. Some faculty members try to make the case that service is a viable substitute for teaching and research. Most academic administrators, however, believe that their school is better served if professors spend their time teaching, advising students, and building their research program.

Two caveats. First, this proposal would exclude only *on-campus* service from performance reviews. I believe faculty outreach to the community (if consistent with a school's mission) and service to academic societies and government are important professional activities that deserve to be recognized and rewarded. Second, the proposal is not meant to apply to chairing committees, taking on special service assignments, or otherwise going beyond the norm. How these more significant service responsibilities would be recognized is explained below.

2. *Bonus payments for committee chairs.* Most universities and colleges do not have a policy for paying the chairpersons of departmental and university committees, although sometimes they do receive a modest salary bump if the committee is especially important. In my proposal, all committee chairs would be compensated each year for their work with a bonus payment. For example, the chair of a departmental curriculum committee might be paid $2,000, while the chair of a presidential search committee

could receive $10,000. There are several reasons for this recommendation. The obvious one is that chairing a committee entails extra responsibilities that deserve compensation by the institution. If on-campus service above normal expectations is not recognized as a performance criterion for merit salary increases, then it is only fair that committee chairpersons be compensated through some other mechanism. Bonus awards are one-time payments and are thus well suited for committee leadership that is necessarily episodic.

3. *Committee record-keeping.* The more important reason for compensating committee chairpersons is that the institution then has the right to set requirements and standards for the work performed. In my proposed scheme, each committee chairperson would be asked to fill out a brief (online) form after each committee meeting, listing the following:

   a. the date and duration of the meeting and the names of members in attendance
   b. a meeting agenda and informal minutes of what was accomplished during the meeting
   c. a brief final summary report of the committee's accomplishments, after its work has been completed

   The reasons for requiring this information are to enable the institution to place a dollar value on each committee meeting and to allow department chairpersons or other administrators to assess the value of the committee's work relative to its costs. With the submitted information, the institution's budget or accounting office could easily compute the actual expense incurred by the committee's activities. Although setting up an automated system to prepare cost records would require an initial effort by the school's technology staff, subsequently all of these records could be obtained and processed with minimal continuing expenses.

4. *Computing the cost of governance.* After the committee's final meeting, the university's budget office would prepare a summary report to inform all parties of the total cost of the work performed by the committee. When this information was rolled up across all committees (and other decision-making bodies, such as university senates and department faculty meetings), the actual institutional cost of governance would be known. A dean of engineering, for example, would know exactly what fraction of the total engineering college budget was being spent on governance, with a department-by-department breakdown of the expenses. There

would be no additional workload on the faculty or staff required to obtain this information, with the exception of the minor effort required of committee chairpersons, for which they would be compensated. Thus, the implementation of this budgeting tool would essentially be invisible to the campus, in the sense that it would impose no unwelcome paperwork burden on any faculty or staff member.

5. *Spending money to save money.* Once governance costs are known by an institution, governance can be budgeted like any other expenditure. Thus if enrollment declines or state funding cutbacks force a public campus to retrench, the campus administration will be in a position to mandate reductions in governance expenditures, just as it does for operating budgets, personnel, building renovations, and so forth. Furthermore, once governance costs are computed routinely, if a history department chronically spends more on governance than do the English and political science departments, the dean and department chairperson will be in a position to work together to bring the costs into line.

That said, controlling governance expenses is a bit more complicated and subtle than controlling ordinary discretionary expenses, because nearly all governance costs are associated with salaried personnel who will be paid whether they are serving on committees or not. Suppose, for example, that a dean wants to cut the yearly governance costs of our hypothetical history department by $20 thousand. The most direct way would be to ask the department chairperson to reduce next year's governance expenses by that amount, with the understanding that a failure to meet the goal would result in a corresponding $20 thousand reduction in the department's annual budget. To protect the department budget, the chairperson would have to reduce committee sizes and redirect any committee work that could be accomplished by other means.

However, even if the chairperson met the dean's goal, the university would not save money in the short tem, because the department's budget would not be reduced; although the department's professors might spend fewer hours serving on committees, they would be drawing the same salaries as before. Yet in the long term the university would save considerable dollars, because the faculty time freed through the reduction of governance costs could be reallocated to other activities, presumably teaching, advising students, and research. After a few years, overall, the university would be able to fulfill its responsibilities with fewer professors and with no increase in total workload per professor.

In the long term, reductions in governance expenditures go right to the institution's bottom line.

A variation on this approach would provide positive incentives for academic departments to reduce voluntarily their governance expenditures. Suppose that the university's accounting system showed that our history department typically spent annually $100 thousand on governance and that the dean wished to reduce that amount permanently 20 percent, to $80 thousand. As an incentive, the dean would strike a bargain with the department. If the department meets the 20 percent reduction goal, the dean will transfer the savings, in this case $20 thousand, into the department budget, to be used for bonuses for faculty and staff, upgrading computers, hosting visitors, outfitting offices, or any other use the department wishes. These dollars would add to the department's existing budget, which would not be otherwise affected.

Once the department had successfully reduced its governance costs to $80 thousand, that would become the new base on which further reductions would be computed. Thus the $20 thousand payment to the department would be a one-time payment, but the governance expense reduction would be permanent. To prevent game-playing and to compensate for out-of-the-ordinary governance needs (such as search committees for new faculty), the chairperson would submit a plan for the proposed reduction which would have to be approved by the dean. Service reductions would be purely voluntary, but departments opting out of the plan would be giving up the opportunity to infuse precious new dollars into their budget.

It is easy to think of variations on this scheme, but the basic idea is to spend up-front dollars on incentives to create permanent cost reductions: in other words, spending money to save money. In the long term, the university would recoup its investment many times over because of the need to employ fewer people to do the same work as before. What makes all such productivity-enhancing plans possible is the ability (and willingness) of the institution to track its governance costs explicitly. Streamlining faculty governance is thus an illustration of the core business principle mentioned in connection with the Danaher Corporation at the beginning of this chapter: the only way for any organization to make substantive improvements in its efficiency and productivity is through collecting information that quantifies its performance.

A Journey of a Thousand Miles

A recurrent theme of this book is that the financial underpinnings of American public universities have been weakened by an academic culture that places a low premium on cost discipline and improving efficiency. Although this culture provides necessary safeguards for academic freedom and faculty autonomy, it also has acquired self-destructive attributes that hamper schools' efforts to rein in annual tuition increases and respond to changing realities. My premise is that it is possible to make universities more efficient and productive without either sacrificing important academic values or eroding the qualities of the academic lifestyle that have historically attracted smart, creative individuals to the profession.

Two of the legs supporting this productivity stool have already been identified. The first is the *leadership leg,* which proposes new mechanisms for identifying higher education leaders who are change-oriented and better able to understand and react to the larger environmental forces that are adversely shaping their institution's future.

Second is the *information leg,* given that the key to controlling costs and productivity is collecting and quantifying university performance data. The crucial part of this exercise is learning to value time by explicitly pricing faculty and staff labor as if it were any other limited resource. Once time is appropriately valued, many inefficient practices will become apparent, one example being the unnecessarily cumbersome governance activities already discussed. Others might include the overuse of expensive instructional methodologies, such as labor-intensive team teaching or small discussion group formats in large introductory courses. Although many professors see these teaching techniques as pedagogically superior to the traditional "sage on a stage" lecture format, they also have a high cost that may lead to undesirable trade-offs in budget-strapped departments—for example, forcing the replacement of regular full-time faculty with temporary part-time instructors. When the true cost of instruction is known, departments can make informed choices about whether such trade-offs are warranted.

Other practices, such as faculty differential teaching loads, already touched upon, are also easier to implement if faculty time is valued explicitly. The devaluation of time is the reason that universities often provide miserly administrative support for their faculty. Directors of an industrial laboratory know that it makes financial sense to give its engineering professionals full technical and secretarial support, but in academia highly paid engineering professors are likely to type their own manuscripts, make their own travel arrangements, and keep their own appointment calendar. Unless labor is valued explicitly as a cost item, such penny-wise-and-pound-foolish practices are unlikely to change.

The third leg of the productivity stool is the *accountability leg*. Accountability in the public sector is a continuing concern to elected officials, but in the context of academia their focus tends to be on professorial accountability, or the presumed lack thereof. From my perspective, however, the more significant productivity issue pertains to inadequately holding accountable department chairpersons, deans, vice presidents and provosts, and presidents. Upward delegation, buck-passing, and indecisiveness are the most obvious symptoms of college and university administrators who are not held accountable for their performance. For example, consider the situation where a provost turns down the tenure application of a probationary faculty member in his or her sixth year of service. This unfortunately common situation, aside from being a devastating personal experience for the faculty member, reflects badly on the department chairperson and dean who put the candidate forward in the first place. After all, the department chairperson most likely had a hand in hiring the candidate, monitoring the candidate's year-to-year activities and performance, making certain the candidate was appropriately mentored by senior members of the department, and giving accurate and candid assessments to the candidate of any shortcomings in teaching or research. The dean is at fault for not insisting on higher academic standards in the department and for recommending a candidate who did not meet the larger university standards for professional achievement. In other words, a failure to receive tenure is not only a sign that a candidate did not measure up to institutional expectations but also a likely symptom of weak administrative leadership. One can come up with analogous examples throughout academia: unsuccessful searches, unresolved personnel issues, inadequate communication, unbalanced budgets, poorly executed plans, unmet goals, sloppy record keeping, and avoidance of problems. If a school's leaders are not held accountable for these leadership shortcomings, there will be little reason to improve or correct them.

But expecting a high degree of accountability does not mean creating a harsh, judgmental environment where slip-ups and mistakes are not tolerated. On the contrary, accountability thrives in an environment marked by honesty, trust, and candor. University administrators, from presidents and chancellors on down, appreciate clearly stated expectations and straightforward assessments of their work. More often than not, administrative failures can be attributed to poor communication and misunderstanding or to inadequate help and advice. But whatever the reasons, formalizing performance reviews so that goals are clearly stated and progress objectively evaluated is a necessary ingredient in moving an institution forward.

It should be clear by now that there is no magic bullet that will redress the inefficiencies of higher education. Reforming the undesirable aspects of the academic culture is a journey of a thousand miles taken with small steps. But the effort is worth making because the stakes are so high, especially for public campuses. Taxpayers and their elected representatives have lost patience with their state universities because they are the ones who ultimately have to pay the price for the system's shortcomings. Every time students and taxpayers write a check for a tuition payment they cannot afford, sit in a dingy, overcrowded classroom, or stand in a long line to register for classes, they are reminded that something is wrong with the nation's public colleges. They may not understand the problems or the historical patterns that have led to these problems, but ultimately they are in the driver's seat, and those of us in academia ignore their voices to our peril. That said, addressing the cultural problems of academia is only half the challenge. The other half is to rethink the failed business model that no longer ensures an adequate flow of resources to the nation's public campuses. And that leads us to my next and final chapter.

A Proposal for Deregulation of Public Universities

The Scotch Boutique

On October 14, 1978, NBC's *Saturday Night Live* featured a now-classic skit about the Scotch Boutique, a store in a shopping mall that sells only Scotch brand adhesive tape. The store is newly opened, with Scotch tape dispensers neatly arranged along the shelves and a huge image of a Scotch tape dispenser above the door. The store's owner, Mr. Walker (played by Fred Willard), wearing a red plaid vest that matches the pattern on the tape dispensers, enthusiastically greets his customers, who one by one wander into the store looking for recording tape and are dumbfounded to learn that only cellophane tape, "the sticky kind," is sold. As the skit progresses, the store's cashier, Jenny (Gilda Radner), and stock boy, Kevin (John Belushi), express reservations about the store's future, but Mr. Walker is unfazed. "I can't go on surrounded by quitters and—and doubters," he says. After an emotional soliloquy by Mr. Walker, the skit ends with the group expressing solidarity and resolving to get back "to business as usual," which of course is no business at all.

Mr. Walker believes that service, teamwork, perseverance, a

good product, an attractive facility, and sound management will fulfill his lifelong dream of owning a successful business. He is so committed to his dream that he is blind to what is obvious to everybody else—that the Scotch Boutique is not based on a sound business plan.

The Failed Business Plan of Public Higher Education

Americans are so invested in the dream of an inexpensive taxpayer-supported college degree within reach of all citizens that, like Mr. Walker, they too are blind to the fact that their dream is no longer based on a sound business plan. But unlike the business flaws of the Scotch Boutique, which are outrageously transparent, the flaws of public higher education's financial underpinnings are not self-evident. Public higher education's basic financial premise—government appropriations that enable universities to discount their charges to students (augmented in recent years by tuition controls to make sure they do)—has until the past few decades worked well. In fact, in a larger context, governmental support of colleges and universities goes back to the earliest days of the medieval academies. It is a time-tested formula still embraced by most countries of the world, and of all those countries none has implemented the formula more successfully than the United States.[1]

But even if the public, their elected representatives, and academicians can be forgiven for holding fast to their dream, it is now necessary to face up to the unpleasant truth. *The business model of public higher education, no matter how successful it was in prior decades, is not working now, and no amount of yearning or waxing eloquent over past successes will make it work in the future.* As we have seen, the symptoms of the failed plan are unaffordable college tuition, deteriorating physical plants, lagging professor salaries, growth in the numbers of temporary adjunct faculty, the defection of top scholars to private universities, complaints by elected officials about bureaucratic and change-resistant university administrations, and campus atmospheres increasingly marked by divisiveness, polarization, and employee unrest.

All of these symptoms are the result of shrinking resources driven by fundamental economic and demographic changes in American society. In earlier chapters I have explored at length the complex dynamic between government and academia that this long-term decline in funding has set in motion. To recapitulate, here are our principal concerns about the shortcomings of the traditional business model.

1. Government subsidies to universities are not contingent upon institutional performance. Thus, this key revenue source carries no financial incentive for institutions to prune weak or unneeded programs, enhance efficiency and productivity, stay focused on mission, and be innovative and responsive to student needs.

2. A government subsidy shields universities from the beneficial influence of competition. The result is bureaucratic growth and a focus on lobbying and maintaining the subsidy, rather than competing with other universities to improve performance and enhance value.

3. Government appropriations for campuses use taxpayer funds inefficiently because they benefit wealthy, middle-income, and poor students equally. Blanket appropriations for campuses indirectly subsidize students who can afford to pay their own way, thus diverting state resources from those who cannot. Furthermore, appropriation decisions are generally based on business cycles, legislative negotiations, and lobbying rather than a considered response to actual campus needs.

4. Government subsidies raise a university's cost of doing business. The extra revenue from a subsidy increase is immediately swallowed into an institution's permanent cost base, allowing it to increase future expenditures without having to prune weak programs or make internal reallocations.

5. Government subsidies are episodic, varying from year to year in accord with the legislative timetable. This unpredictability hampers thoughtful, long-range financial planning, and in times of cutbacks it often leads to sudden undifferentiated retrenchment that reduces quality.

6. Over the years, subsidy declines have not only driven up public university tuition charges but exacerbated an academic culture of defensiveness and resistance to change. Shrinking resources have led frustrated public university professors, adjunct instructors, and teaching assistants to form unions and dig in their heels to protect themselves against deteriorating working conditions over which they otherwise would have little influence.

7. The tuition controls imposed by most states are a form of price-fixing that, in combination with government subsidies, means that public universities have virtually lost control over their major revenue sources. To the extent that total revenues have been less than needed to build or maintain quality, the result has been a long-term decline in public universities that shows no sign of reversing.

8. Government efforts to rein in campus spending and increase accountability have been counterproductive, resulting in a regulatory burden

on universities that has raised costs, expanded bureaucracies, stifled creativity, and handicapped initiatives by individual schools to excel and distinguish themselves academically.

9. Dependence on public revenues has discouraged campus leaders from being entrepreneurial and innovative. Instead, a campus culture has evolved that rewards laissez-faire administrators who focus on peace-keeping, lobbying, and image management.

The century-old financial model by which American public universities have been funded can no longer provide an affordable high-quality college education for many lower- and middle-income Americans. The grim assertion of this book is that this syndrome is irreversible so long as the current funding model remains unchanged. On the other hand, its positive message is that another model exists that can better respond to the forces undermining the nation's public campuses.

Departments of Wishful Thinking

Every few years, most state governments or higher education authorities create a strategic plan intended to strengthen their state's public universities and align their missions with state needs. These plans tend to follow a similar template; they usually begin with a statement of vision and academic values, followed by an assessment of problems and deficiencies, then a list of goals and strategic priorities, and finally end with recommended assessment and benchmarking criteria. Such plans often begin with a rhetorical flourish reminiscent of presidential speechwriting:

> Alaska is a great land, vast in area and rich in history and cultural diversity. Alaska has provided a harsh test for its men and women; the Alaska Natives who have sustained vibrant lives and rich cultures in one of the most formidable climates on Earth; the miners, risking all for the promise of riches, the soldiers and airmen taking back invaded American soil; the searchers for black gold, finding it at last near the shores of the Beaufort Sea; and the many others seeking adventure in this most challenging place we call "The Great Land." Alaska provides a harsh test for a University system as well.[2]

The smorgasbord of goals and strategies in these plans suggests that nearly all states want the same thing: The State of South Carolina, for example is interested in "creating a well-educated citizenry, raising the standard of living of South Carolinians, improving the quality of life, meeting changing work force needs, creating economic development opportunities, [and] positioning the state to be competitive in a global economy . . ."[3] The State of Virginia wants to "improve alignment between higher education and the Commonwealth's workforce need," and also to "strengthen academic program quality and accountability through assessment."[4] The State of New Mexico would "increase student access and success," "innovate to meet current and future educational needs efficiently and effectively," and "provide programs and services integral to state and regional economic needs."[5]

State strategic plans often skimp on the exact mechanisms whereby these goals would be implemented. Frequently, it seems the proposed mechanism is simply another, more finely tuned goal. For example, New Mexico would position its public universities "to be ranked in the upper echelon" by creating "funding mechanisms that encourage research institutions to be top tier" and by developing "incentives to keep our best New Mexico students in our state institutions."

It is not hard to see why such plans seldom accomplish their objectives. One reason is that when one scratches the surface, beneath almost every recommendation is a call for an infusion of additional state money, either directly or indirectly. To create innovative new programs, revamp administrative practices, renovate facilities, build collaborations, recruit "world-class" faculty, and the like generally means hiring more people, awarding more construction contracts, investing in more capital equipment, and making other changes that cost money. When such proposals are injected into the legislative process, they run smack into the competing demands of K–12 education, health care, law enforcement, highway construction, federal entitlements, and all the other pressures on state budgets. In this competition for scarce resources, higher education seldom fares well.

A second reason these plans generally fail is that their "strategies" are not so much realistic blueprints for change as wishes for problems to go away.

Problem: Universities need to strengthen their faculties.
Strategy: Universities will start hiring world-class scholars.

Problem: The world needs to bring peace to the Middle East.
Strategy: People will put aside their religious differences.

Problem: My friend is depressed.

Strategy: Your friend will stop moping and pull herself together.

But there is a deeper reason why, despite the best efforts of state strategic planners, public universities have been unable to arrest their long downward slide; my own state of Ohio illustrates this reason. On November 7, 2006, Ohio voters elected Democrat Ted Strickland to be governor of Ohio. Governor Strickland believes deeply in the importance of higher education to the economic well-being of his state, and soon after taking office he declared that he would make higher education a high priority in his administration. This news was enthusiastically welcomed by the state's higher education community, which had felt neglected or even disparaged by former administrations.

The first step the governor took to implement his priority was to create a formal "University System of Ohio," an umbrella structure that draws together the state's fourteen public universities, twenty-four branch campuses, and twenty-three community colleges. The governor appointed a respected, long-time state politician to be chancellor of this new system and, to highlight the importance of the new structure, made the chancellor a member of his cabinet. The goal of this new system was to build "the highest quality, student-centered system of higher education in the country."

Word of the governor's new statewide system created immediate ripples of concern among the state's public universities, which had always treasured their autonomy and independent status. University presidents, especially, are well aware that institutional quality goes hand in hand with autonomy and that statewide systems, such as in the State of New York, tend to breed clumsy bureaucracies that create a leveling effect, encouraging mediocrity and inhibiting campus innovation and achievement. The governor and chancellor tried to dispel these concerns by asserting that control and regulation of the campuses was not their intention—that the goal of the new system was to facilitate collaboration, avoid needless and wasteful duplication, and discourage unhealthy competition among the state's public campuses.[6] Unfortunately, these reassuring words did not fully assuage campus anxieties, since these are the familiar goals of all state "systems," including those that are the most stifling and bureaucratic. Many public university presidents in Ohio continued to worry that the camel had just stuck his nose in the tent and it was only a matter of time before the rest of the beast would follow.

However, Governor Strickland backed up his pledge to make higher education a priority by raising the state appropriation to higher education by 8.8 percent in the first year of the Ohio biennial budget—a surprisingly large and welcomed increase, especially considering the state's beleaguered economy.[7] However, in exchange for this infusion of new state dollars, the governor instituted a two-year freeze on public university tuition increases. By doing so, the governor hoped both to help the universities by raising their subsidies and to provide some relief to taxpayers who struggled to afford their college expenses. (Although this trade-off strategy played well to the public, it put the state's campuses under a significant financial squeeze, the reason being that campus tuition revenues are significantly greater than their state subsidies.)

Soon after taking office, the governor and chancellor announced a comprehensive ten-year strategic plan for Ohio public higher education.[8] The 109-page document in many respects reads like those from other states. It promises to improve student access, quality, affordability, efficiency, and leadership in the new state system, and it would create "compacts" between the state's colleges and businesses. The plan reiterated the desire of the governor to "emphasize cooperation over competition" and went out of its way to pledge that it would "eliminate, not create, levels of bureaucracy and regulation, while focusing all our institutions on accomplishing a single set of statewide goals." The plan promised to respect the diversity among the state's public institutions. "Allowing this diversity to flower," the plan read, "will achieve one of the state's most cherished goals—lowering the cost of a college education." By the plan's end in 2017, per-capita state appropriations to higher education will have increased to the national average (in 2006, Ohio ranked fifth from the bottom in per-capita support of its public campuses[9]), while tuitions will have decreased to among the bottom ten in the nation (Ohio currently ranks ninth highest in tuition charges). Of course, these positive benefits will come to pass only if the plan's goals are met, and as we will see, that is a very big "if."[10]

The Ohio strategic plan for higher education is an interesting and telling document. It is clearly well intentioned and reflects a strong commitment by the governor and his advisers to improve the educational opportunities for Ohio citizens by strengthening the state's public higher-education system. Yet the plan fails to maintain a philosophical consistency in its approach, in essence trying to come down on both sides of the coin. The plan promises to respect the freedom and independence of the state's schools, while simultaneously pledging to reap efficiency, lower prices, focus missions, and reduce competition through central coordination. In public higher education circles, "to coordinate" is viewed as government-speak for "to control."

But the larger problem is that the plan's core strategy is to try to turn back the clock—to see the solution to public higher education's problems as increased government subsidy (and involvement) as a way to moderate tuition charges. In other words, the plan would increase state schools' dependence on their government appropriations, would thereby reduce "unhealthy" competition by weakening the forces of supply and demand, and would "coordinate" the missions and priorities of campuses rather than let the marketplace and student needs shape those priorities. Unfortunately, Ohio's new strategic plan for public higher education, although grounded in good intentions, would take the state in exactly the reverse direction from that proposed by this book. As I have emphasized repeatedly in earlier chapters, the continuously eroding condition of the nation's public universities shows clearly that this traditional strategy is no longer viable.

On January 23, 2008, the hammer fell on Ohio. On that day, scarcely a year into his term, Governor Strickland announced that a shortfall in tax revenues though mid-2009 would be in the range of $733 million to $1.9 billion and that state-supported entities should brace themselves for potentially massive budget cuts.[11] As of mid-2008, the impact of this revenue shortfall on Ohio's public campuses was still unclear. However, even if the state's campuses weather the immediate fiscal crisis, the handwriting on the wall could not be more clear: in the long run, neither Ohio nor any other state, despite the best efforts of governors and other elected officials, can reverse the economic and demographic forces that have invalidated public higher education's historic business model.

The Goals of Public Higher Education

By way of introducing my proposals for deregulation and economic reform, it is useful to consider precisely what we hope to accomplish. At the most general level, what is it that Americans really want from their public universities? Table 3 shows my version of the answer.

Historically, American public universities and colleges have generally done a good job meeting these goals, and even in recent decades they have continued to meet the first four. The slippage brought about by the

Table 3. Desired goals for American public universities and colleges

- to provide a high-quality education that is responsive to the curricular needs of students and matches their abilities and career interests
- to encourage personal growth, critical thinking, and responsible citizenship
- to provide research and curricular programs that advance knowledge and serve the economic and workforce needs of communities and states
- to preserve academic freedom, open inquiry, and the free exchange of ideas
- to enroll Americans from all economic, racial, and social backgrounds, without saddling them with debt
- to make realistic demands of taxpayers and to be sensitive to the other growing pressures on state treasuries
- to make efficient use of resources, to stay focused on mission, to plan carefully for the future, and to strive always to become more productive
- to be adaptable and responsive to a new environment of global competition and demographic change
- to attract and retain creative, intelligent, and independent-minded professors

breakdown of public higher education's economic model is mostly with the last five goals, and in one sense this is fortunate because it means that irreversible damage has not yet occurred. The challenge is to rework the model in a way that will not only prevent further damage but also remediate the erosion that has already taken place. And that raises the crucial issue of constraints.

Nearly all major societal problems—pollution, global warming, inadequate health care, poverty, crime, racial inequality, illiteracy—could be alleviated or solved given enough resources, and the problems of public universities are no exception. Because of this obvious fact, buried within most proposed cures to public higher education's ills is an implicit assumption that more public money is potentially available and the major challenge is somehow to shake it loose from federal and state coffers. This assumption is what drives public universities to hire lobbyists, motivates college presidents and chancellors to write editorials calling for appropriation increases, underlies state strategic plans such as the one I have been discussing, and leads student interest groups to call for expanded loan and grant programs. Behind these hope-springs-eternal strategies is the belief that the key to more money is to get the message out more persuasively. If people could only be made to understand how higher education fuels economic growth, creates jobs, raises personal incomes, and creates opportunities for the disadvantaged, then surely they would be willing to pay higher taxes, subordinate other needs, and make whatever sacrifices are called for in order to invest in this crucial resource.

But this belief unfortunately flies in the face of experience. As we have seen, the needs of public universities nearly always come up short in comparison to caring for the elderly, repairing roads, fighting crime, preserving vital public services, and maintaining public schools. After states take care of their immediate needs, there isn't enough money left over for them to invest adequately in the long-term well-being of their public universities. Even if the family savings account holds the key to our children's future, the leaky roof always commands a higher priority in our household budget. Thus, any viable reform strategy has to be constrained by these economic facts of life, even if these are not the facts we would prefer.

Working Goals and Assumptions

With this thought in mind, let us then delineate the working objectives of our proposed financial model. In comparison to public higher education's current business plan, here is what we want our model to accomplish:

- the model should be revenue neutral, so that it does not adversely impact other essential public expenditures
- the model should use taxpayer dollars efficiently, so that public money is not expended to advance unnecessary or low-priority objectives.
- the model should honor the principle that government's first responsibility is to the public and not to the preservation of unneeded or dysfunctional government institutions
- the model should make use of the beneficial power of competition and market forces to increase the productivity, efficiency, and quality of service of public universities
- the model should limit the regulatory influence of government to no more than needed to maintain social equity and accountability
- the model should increase the responsiveness and nimbleness of public campuses to changing social and economic circumstances
- the model should provide incentives to enhance campus entrepreneurship, innovation, productivity, and efficiency
- the model should increase choices for public college students by expanding their educational options

- the model should make higher education more affordable, especially for middle-class taxpayers who do not qualify for financial aid programs aimed at low-income citizens

Outline of the Proposed Model

The driving concept underlying my proposal is to replace the current subsidy-based mechanism for financing public universities with a performance-based mechanism that would hold universities responsible for their own financial destiny.[12] In this proposal, state governments would continue to support public higher education as before, but in the form of scholarship awards to students rather than as direct appropriations to campuses.[13]

In order to maintain their revenues, universities would compete with each other for these new scholarship dollars by tailoring their course offerings, degree programs, student services, and extracurricular activities to the needs of the scholarship recipients. Keeping costs low, embracing efficient business practices, and maximizing productivity would be rewarded, since any resulting savings could be redirected to making the institutions more competitive and thereby more attractive to students. Universities that offered the greatest value to students—attractive programs at an affordable price—would prosper, while those that failed to do so would see their enrollment shrink. With a government lifeline lacking, the end result for institutions that could not compete successfully would be bankruptcy, rather than perpetual subsidy-sustained mediocrity.

In order to adapt to this new competitive environment, public universities would acquire increased flexibility—primarily the freedom to set their own tuition and fee schedules, determine salaries and compensation, establish enrollment and admissions guidelines, implement curricular and programmatic changes, and assume greater fiscal autonomy over capital expenditures. In recognition of this increased freedom, public universities would be subject to greater oversight, in the form of campus-specific boards of trustees (as already exist in some states). These governing boards would have the ultimate responsibility for approving budgets, personnel appointments, and operational policies and also for assuring a desired level of public accountability.

An inevitable outcome of increased self-reliance would be greater academic segmentation, as public universities learned the importance of focusing on their competitive strengths. For example, regional urban universities might conclude that responding to the educational needs of low- and middle-income adults in their community is more beneficial than attempting to compete for students with a nearby flagship research university. Decisions about investing in, for example, a nanotechnology institute, distance learning center, or new student union would be driven by the realistic potential of these investments to increase competitiveness (by attracting students or federal research grants) rather than by vague perceptions of prestige or a president's or legislator's personal desires.

In this new scenario, public higher-education dollars would be expended both efficiently and fairly. By setting scholarship criteria, governors and state legislatures could meet specific state needs by directing dollars to particular groups of students. If, for example, states wanted to provide tuition relief to debt-laden middle-class taxpayers, then scholarship criteria could include a financial means test that favored this group. Similarly, scholarships could be directed toward students studying engineering, agriculture, nursing, math and science education, or any other area of state importance. State-supported institutes, centers, research projects, or vital but low-enrollment academic programs (for example, in agriculture or nursing) would not be changed by this proposal. Let us now consider some of these features in detail.

Deregulation and Oversight

In this model, each state university's system of public four-year universities would devolve into a consortium of semiautonomous, publicly owned but independently governed tax-exempt corporations. In states such as Ohio and Michigan, where public universities already have considerable autonomy because of their separate governing boards, this change would be relatively straightforward. In states that have multicampus systems overseen by a single governing board, such as California, the proposal would entail creating a separate governing board for each major campus. In other words, the Berkeley, Los Angeles, San Diego, and other campuses in the University of California system would be overseen by individual boards of trustees.

As is true of most governing boards, these campus-specific trustees would have appointing authority for the campus chancellor and fiscal oversight responsibilities for their institution. The trustees would have the final authority to set tuition and fees for their campus, approve personnel policies and compensation, award construction contracts, accept gifts, approve curricular and programmatic changes, and set admissions and graduation requirements. These are the kinds of important oversight functions that systemwide governing boards have difficulty providing because of the broad scope of their responsibilities and interests. For example, the twenty-six regents of the University of California are mostly political appointees who serve twelve-year terms, with other ex officio members representing various state agencies and constituency groups. Such broad-based groups are necessarily focused on statewide policy matters and are not in a position to oversee the detailed needs and operations of individual campuses.

Furthermore, it is the nature of appointed statewide boards to reflect the social and political interests within their state. Experience suggests that such groups can become embroiled in partisan wrangling, disputes over social issues, and activist agendas that can adversely affect individual institutions and their students. While it is appropriate for a statewide board to wrestle with policy matters pertaining to, for example, immigration, affirmative action, taxation, and workforce and business needs—all of which have ramifications for public higher education—it is not desirable for individual institutions to be buffeted about by the crosscurrents of the fractious public debate that often precedes the development of these policies.

In my proposal, statewide governing boards, such as California's Board of Regents, would continue to deal with important public policy issues involving higher education. They would continue to monitor the health of the state university campuses and the degree to which campuses are serving the needs of the public. They would also retain authority over allocation of the state's higher education budget. However, as discussed below, tuition- and fee-setting authority would become a prerogative of the campus-specific governing boards. This shift of tuition-setting authority is essential if campuses are to survive in a deregulated environment that places an emphasis on campus strengths and performance rather than on public appropriations.

A Tuition and Fee Strategy

As mentioned in chapter 1, most states regulate the tuition and fees charged by their public universities, either by direct fiat or by capping allowed tuition increases. Although the purpose of tuition controls is to shield students and taxpayers from prohibitive educational costs, the growing unaffordability of public higher education, especially for struggling middle-class citizens, has clearly shown the ineffectiveness of this strategy. Like virtually all forms of price controls, the practice inevitably undermines the stabilizing influence of the marketplace. When goods are price-fixed, as they were in the former Soviet Union, the results are supply shortages, shoddy products, long lines of frustrated consumers, and social unrest. Similarly, tuition controls in public higher education, as discussed in prior chapters, erode educational quality, discourage initiative, and grow bureaucracy and inefficiency. Furthermore, state-controlled tuition provides no financial incentive for institutions to be attentive to their students' needs, productive, and focused on their strengths.

As they weigh the consequences of tuition controls, therefore, legislators are confronted with a Hobson's choice: either to continue tuition controls and live with the adverse impact on their state's public campuses, or to end controls and see the public burdened by fast-rising tuition charges. In the end, legislators normally try to split the difference. They permit significant tuition increases in order to stave off acute fiscal disasters at their campuses, but not so significant as to prevent long-term erosion of quality. By the same token, significant but not unbearable tuition increases shield students to some extent from short-term pain but compound over the years to make college ever less affordable.

In the proposed model, public universities would be given the flexibility to establish their own tuition charges but only as one component of a larger plan. Absent the other components, this freedom would only exacerbate the unaffordability problem. The key to breaking the cycle of rising tuition and deteriorating campuses is thus not only to deregulate public universities but also to create a competitive environment that gives students additional educational options. When students have choices about where to attend college, the powerful forces of competition come into play. Under my scenario, public universities could not charge whatever they want but only what the marketplace will tolerate. And as I have shown in chapters 2 and 3 and in appendix B, the price-restraining power of a competitive marketplace is virtually unstoppable; organizations either keep their prices as low as possible or eventually go bankrupt. Furthermore, competition forces organizations not only to minimize prices but also to increase efficiency and productivity and to deliver a quality product (or service) that meets the needs of customers. As my analysis has demonstrated, market forces will not allow any latitude for universities to increase tuition charges beyond the minimum necessary to accomplish these objectives.

Thus, empowering public universities to set their own tuition and fee schedules is a necessary but not sufficient condition for implementing this new business plan. The remainder of the plan is to lower the barriers that insulate public universities from the beneficial forces of competition. Lowering these barriers requires phasing out the direct state subsidy of public universities, thus removing the government lifeline that keeps failing campuses on perpetual life support; and it requires increasing the purchasing power of students through awarding them state-administered scholarships. Let's consider each of these additional measures.

Replacing Government Subsidies with Scholarships

In the model I am proposing, the annual (or biennial) government appropriation to four-year public universities would be gradually withdrawn. Although the phase-out period would be subject to negotiation, six years is a reasonable starting point, since that is the time-to-graduation for which graduation statistics are normally compiled. Pegging the phase-out rate to the six-year graduation rate would provide time for institutions to accommodate the new system without undue disruption. Furthermore, states could readily phase in the new system so that it would affect only newly enrolled students; if this was done, universities would continue to draw subsidy for currently enrolled students until they graduated or disenrolled.[14]

To make up the loss of revenue caused by the subsidy decline, universities would obviously have to raise their tuition charges. If one assumes that a state university's total tuition revenue is typically twice its state subsidy, then a six-year subsidy phase-out (a reduction of 17 percent per year) would translate into a tuition "surcharge" of about 8 percent per year for six years for all students.[15] This surcharge would be above and beyond the university's customary tuition increase. Thus, after six years, the gross tuition of each public university would be increased by roughly 50 percent in order to make up for the loss of government subsidy.

It is important to understand that this tuition increase would not translate into a increase in the average out-of-pocket sums that students pay to attend college. Nor would the subsidy phase-out translate into a decrease in the average revenue received by state universities. This model is designed to be revenue neutral, which means that the money the state saves by reducing its direct appropriation to campuses would be reallocated to students in the form of state-administered scholarships. Thus, students would use their scholarships to offset their increased tuition bills on a dollar-for-dollar basis; on average, students would see no increase in their out-of-pocket college costs as a result of the new plan, and universities would see no average decrease in their total collected revenues. In this sense, the new plan simply provides a different pathway for states to direct taxpayer dollars to their public universities.

But under this new system, if students end up paying the same amount to attend college and public universities receive the same total revenues, what is to be gained by the exercise? There are several important benefits. The first is that public dollars are expended efficiently in this model, because they can be directed to specific state goals, such as providing financial relief to middle- and low-income students or promoting state workforce needs, such as in engineering or science education. That is, although the average total scholarship dollars paid to students (and thereby passed on to universities) are unchanged in the new model, there can be significant student-to-student variations in the scholarship awards.

Of course, if some students receive larger-than-average scholarships, then others must receive smaller-than-average scholarships. This variability is one of the important features of the plan. Under the current system, all students benefit equally from subsidies to universities, and there is no mechanism for differentiating among students on the basis of their financial needs, interests, talents, abilities, or any other attributes. Although states could always award across-the-board scholarships to all students, thus perpetuating the uniform treatment of the current subsidy-based system, the new model would give state officials the option of targeting dollars more strategically. In an era when state higher-education dollars are in chronic short supply, this is an important mechanism for stretching those dollars productively to meet state needs.

The second major consequence of replacing appropriations with scholarships is that it links state revenues to university performance. Under the current business model, the only way universities can increase their state appropriation is through lobbying, in essence pleading for more money. Under the new system, universities have the opportunity to increase their revenues by making themselves more attractive to scholarship-bearing students. Although under this proposal the amount of state money going to public universities is unchanged, individual campuses could not automatically count on getting their proportional share. But schools that skillfully identified a market niche for themselves and then offered top value to the students in that niche could significantly expand their revenue base.

The third benefit of the new model is that it introduces healthy competition into the public university environment. In part, this competition comes about because universities would have a strong financial incentive to make themselves attractive to scholarship holders in order to recoup the revenue from their lost subsidy. But equally important is the fact that the scholarships give students more educational options. Later we will explore this mechanism in some detail.

The Importance of Failure

One has only to look at the dismal state of failed inner-city schools to see the end result of institutions kept alive only by a government appropriation. When bankruptcy is not a lurking possibility, an institution's leaders are denied an important incentive for making strong, strategic decisions. As we have seen, there are powerful forces in public higher education that discourage strong leadership. These forces do not reflect an administrative unwillingness to make decisions so much as the realization that ultimately the stakes are not high enough to justify confronting the inevitable campus resistance. When there is little public university leaders can do to influence their revenues, and when survival of their institution is not on the table, the leadership mindset takes on a different tenor from that found in private universities, where the reverse is true. The focus is on dividing up the pie instead of making the strategic decisions that would grow the pie.

Furthermore, the rationale for making expenditure decisions is very different when financial imperatives are removed from the equation. It is not uncommon for public university presidents to embark on costly construction projects for their campus—spending hundreds of millions of dollars to build a showcase concert hall, a student union, a conference center, or sports facilities, sometimes designed by signature architects. In some cases these facilities are based on crucial campus needs, but often they reflect mostly subjective desires. In the abstract, it may be desirable to renovate the football stadium or build a new student union, and if the school believes it can pay off the bonds, then why not do it to please the sports fans, alumni association, and student government leaders, or to build a legacy for a president? This is the kind of rationale that often drives large capital expenditures at public universities.

But decisions based on this kind of thinking are not strategic, and in this respect they are very different from those grounded in financial imperatives. A bank will never build a new branch office to please the mayor and residents of the community or because the bank's local employees wished it to do so. Instead, it will analyze the traffic flow, area demographics, and competition from other banks. In the end, the decision will be based on whether the new office will grow market share and make money—in other words, to advance the bank's overarching strategic goal.

In academia, an analogous criterion might be whether a proposed new student union or intramural sports complex will expand enrollments by helping to attract students. However, if the university is already at capacity enrollment with a surplus of applicants and if students are already pleased with the overall level of amenities provided them, then the impact of the expenditure on the university's larger goals is small. Currently, there is little financial incentive for a campus administration to explore whether the $50 million for a new building could be better invested on something that would strengthen the institution's revenue base. Expenditure decisions that are not strategic do not have the potential to grow revenues. Do the student dining halls really *need* to serve sushi to first-year students? It is easy to answer yes when the answer does not bear on revenues, and since revenues for public campuses are mostly determined by state legislatures, that is nearly always the case.

Hence the importance of failure. In my model, a public university would become a tub sitting on its own bottom, its success or failure the sole responsibility of its leadership and governing board. With skillful management it could grow revenues and flourish, but if its leaders made too many wrong-headed decisions, the institution would see its revenues drop and its students siphoned off by competitors who offered better value and a superior educational product. In a competitive market, the specter of bankruptcy in the background is the ultimate driver of strong, focused leadership.

Of course, one would hope that in this new deregulated environment no universities would ever fail. But assuming that some might, would their states really let them go bankrupt? Public universities exist in a political environment where decisions seldom reflect abstract economic principles. Realistically, the Texas legislature would never let its flagship state university in Austin fail, at least to the point of seeing it declare bankruptcy and liquidate its assets. On the other hand, if tiny West Texas A&M University (enrollment 7,400) in Canyon, Texas, was unable to meet its payroll, it might be another story. Small regional state universities could be hard-pressed to muster the political muscle needed to push bailout legislation through their state government.

But even for state flagship campuses, the theoretical potential for bankruptcy, however remote, would provide a powerful incentive for campus administrators to exert strong strategic leadership. Currently, public university leaders are not held accountable for falling revenues, the reason being that they have no control over those revenues. Furthermore, because it is the nature of the legislative process that revenues cannot generally even be predicted, unexpected deficits tend to be forgiven.

When I was president of Miami University, the Ohio legislature would periodically cut our appropriation and clamp our tuition charges to a level below what we needed to conduct business. My job as the university's senior officer was then to retrench the institution by reining in expenditures enough to balance our budget. Under deregulation, however, any decline in revenues would have been my responsibility, and my governing board would have held me accountable for the decline. Why had I not attended to growing our applications and reputation to increase our pricing power, to making the long-term investments that would have stabilized and grown revenues? In short, my trustees would have expected me to display the kind of strategic vision that government backing and control render unnecessary. Deregulation, with the theoretical possibility of financial failure, raises the bar for management by making an institution's leaders fully accountable for the institution's destiny.

A Hypothetical Example

As discussed, a key element in the proposed new model entails the replacement of the state appropriation to public universities with a state-administered scholarship program for state residents. This dollar-for-dollar swap would increase the competitive environment of campuses, since universities could no longer count on automatically getting their share of the state higher-education budget. Instead, universities would have to compete with each other to attract these scholarship dollars; the

competition would reward strategically focused leadership and improvements in institutional efficiency and productivity.

This proposed scholarship program is not directly analogous to a
school voucher program, whereby students receive a cash credit that
they can apply toward any school of their choice. Students receiving
these scholarships could use them only at colleges that accepted them
for admission. Furthermore, the scholarships would not be entitlements
but rather awards based on specific state-established criteria, both as to
eligibility requirements and award amounts. These criteria would enable states to improve college affordability by selectively underwriting
the college expenses of students most in need of financial assistance.[16]
To the extent that the scholarships' selection criteria include financial
need, they would extend the range of affordable colleges for recipients.
The more choices students have, the more effective are the competitive
pressures that hold down tuition increases and enhance productivity. Let
us use some numbers from the State of Ohio to illustrate how a state-
administered scholarship program might work in practice.

In recent years, the Ohio General Assembly has allocated about
$1 billion per year in the form of direct appropriations to the state's thir-
teen public four-year universities, an amount that averages out to about
$3,500 per enrolled Ohio student. (Ohio students pay tuition to make
up the difference in the cost of their education, to the tune of about
$8,000 on average in 2007.[17]) In our scenario, state universities would no
longer receive a government subsidy, meaning that this indirect discount
to students would disappear. Because universities have to maintain their
revenues in order to stay in business, Ohio students would therefore see
an average increase of $3,500 in their tuition bill, bringing their gross
yearly tuition bill to $11,500, again using 2007 as a reference point. This
increase would be offset by the new state-administered scholarships, the
funds for the scholarship program coming from the $1 billion reclaimed
by the state from the phased-out institutional subsidies. This fund transfer from one category in the state budget to another would have no deleterious impact on the Ohio treasury.

However, focusing only on averages obscures an important benefit of
the program. A key feature of my hypothetical example is that no students would actually receive the average scholarship of $3,500. We will
assume instead that the state hands out the new scholarships solely on
the basis of financial need, with the neediest 50 percent of students receiving scholarships of $7,000 and the remaining 50 percent receiving no

scholarships at all. Thus, in this simplified example, the half of the Ohio public college population most in need of financial assistance would see their net out-of-pocket costs of attending college drop from $8,000 (the tuition paid before implementation of the new program) to $4,500 (the new $11,500 tuition less their $7,000 scholarship). A reduction in college costs of this amount would be a huge step in making college more affordable for these students.

On the other hand, the students in the upper-income half of the population, who did not receive scholarships, would be required to pay full tuition; for them, college costs would rise from $8,000 to $11,500. Although nobody wants to pay more money, an increase in tuition charges for these upper-income students would not materially affect their ability to obtain a college education. Thus, through these scholarships, the state would have used public funds to assist students who are most vulnerable to the rising cost of a college degree, while requiring the upper-income students who do not have pressing financial needs to pay the full costs of their education. In essence, the program would have significantly increased the affordability of a college education for precisely those students for whom college affordability is a major problem.

In the example, I have divided the college population into two income groups, one of which receives scholarships and one of which does not. Although this division illustrates the concept, it would be too draconian for a real program. A more realistic program would stratify scholarship applicants into different income categories, with students in each category receiving scholarship assistance that was appropriate to their actual financial needs. Miami University, for example, has implemented a somewhat similar scholarship program (described in appendix A) that divides applicants into five need categories, each of which is pegged to a different award amount. In the Miami model, all students receive some scholarship aid, but the neediest students receive more.[18]

The key point is that this kind of scholarship program would give lawmakers the flexibility to direct taxpayer higher-education dollars to advance state priorities, whatever those priorities might be. In Ohio and Michigan, for example, lawmakers could target scholarship dollars to the middle-class residents who have suffered greatly from the layoffs, foreclosures, and personal bankruptcies caused by the decline of their state's traditional manufacturing economy. Other states might have different priorities, and their scholarship programs would therefore have different criteria. What is clear, however, is that the current system of directing public dollars directly to state institutions implements no priorities at all and, as I have discussed at length, has the corollary impact of discouraging competition and thereby aggravating institutional inefficiency.

Scholarship Applicability

In this new scenario, it is obviously important to specify precisely which institutions could receive the new state-administered scholarships. The straightforward answer is to allow students to use their scholarships only at public four-year universities in the issuing state, in effect keeping the money circulating within the state's public university system. At first blush, this restriction seems equitable, inasmuch as the state's four-year colleges paid for the scholarships through their loss of state appropriation.

There are other considerations, however, that argue for a broader range of institutional acceptance. Specifically, my recommendation is that these state-awarded scholarships should be valid at any four-year, accredited, nonprofit institution in the issuing state, including private universities and colleges. The rationale for this recommendation is that it would increase the educational choices available to state residents by opening up to them the offerings of private institutions that they otherwise could not afford. Furthermore, this recommendation would raise the competitive bar for a state's public campuses by removing the intrinsic price advantage that insulates them from private competitors.

From a public policy perspective, state governments should not care whether their residents are educated at public universities or private universities. The goal of policy makers should be to educate as many citizens as possible, and if a private university or college can provide a better combination of value and curriculum for some residents than can a public university, then so be it. The government focus should be on advancing the interests of the taxpayers rather than protecting the interests of government-owned institutions. That said, it is still important to consider the potential impact of such a fundamental change in the ground rules on a state's public campuses. The concern, of course, is that public universities might see their students siphoned off by nimble private competitors, resulting in a destabilizing loss of operating revenue. Given that states have only a limited amount of public money to spend on higher education, would giving some of that money to private sector students undermine the fiscal base of a state's public institutions?

This concern, although understandable, is not supported by the numbers. In the United States, private colleges and universities enroll only about 20 percent of the nation's four-year college students. In addition, nearly all private colleges and universities have a residential campus, with enrollment ceilings determined by the capacity of their physical plant. If, in our scenario, private institutions could accept applicants bearing state-issued scholarships, then those schools would see an increase in the number of lower- and middle-income applicants who could now afford their higher tuition charges. On the other hand, because of capacity limitations, these schools would necessarily displace other students, who would enroll at public universities. In other words, although the socioeconomic diversity of their student bodies might increase, private campuses would see little if any net increase in their enrollment, and there would therefore be no deleterious impact on either the enrollment numbers or the revenues received by public universities.

On the contrary, the scholarship program would almost certainly increase total enrollment at public universities, because more state residents would be in a position to afford a four-year degree. An increase in educational attainment of residents is, of course, an important goal for all states. But there can also be too much of a good thing, because enrollment increases put pressures on fast-growing states that already have capacity problems at their universities. Under this new system, therefore, state planners would have to examine closely their university expansion plans to make sure they have adequate resources in place to absorb additional students. Furthermore, two-year campuses might see a decline in enrollment, since some of the four-year enrollment growth would no doubt come from price-sensitive community college students who upgraded their educational goals. The point is that any significant change in the business plan of public higher education, no matter how beneficial, will have consequences that require careful planning and accommodation.

There is still one more consideration. If all college-bound students in a state, including those planning on attending a private institution, are eligible to apply for state scholarships, then the pool of potential scholarship applicants would increase by roughly 20 percent. The question, then, is whether this increase in applicants would dilute the scholarship pool excessively by spreading the available dollars among a larger number of recipients. Fortunately, the answer is mostly no. The majority of private colleges and universities have selective admissions and cater mostly to the educational needs of students who can afford a net tuition that is at least twice that charged by public universities. Relatively few of these students would qualify for scholarships in a state-administered scholarship program whose award criteria are primarily based on unmet financial need.

Potential Downsides

As noted previously, the transition from direct appropriations to student scholarships (as the key source of government support) represents a de facto philosophical shift from viewing public higher education as mostly a public good to viewing it as mostly a private good. In practice, given that state support has steadily declined in proportion to tuition revenues over the past three decades, this shift is much smaller than it might have been in years past. Nevertheless, with my proposal's increased emphasis on market forces and competition, it is not unreasonable to inquire about any potential impact on institutional missions.

To put it starkly: if universities are given a stronger financial incentive to attract tuition and scholarship revenues, are they likely then to abandon their historic mission of serving the larger needs of society and reshape themselves to satisfy the desires of entering freshmen? Or, phrasing the issue differently, how will universities under the new model treat thinly enrolled disciplines such as philosophy and classics, or majors whose graduates face meager or highly competitive job prospects, such as music? Might not these socially important departments be jeopardized if market forces are allowed to prevail over academic considerations?

Although these are reasonable concerns, I believe they are easily answered. The first point is to observe that *private* universities are able to balance successfully academic priorities with the financial necessity of attracting fee-paying students. This balance is achieved because safeguarding academic values, setting academic priorities, and establishing curricular and degree requirements are the responsibilities of the university faculty, whereas keeping the institution solvent is the responsibility of the university administration. At times, of course, these roles come into conflict, sometimes resulting in tense negotiations. However, the checks and balances built into governance at reputable universities and colleges normally result in an accommodation that is acceptable to both the faculty and the administration. That this accommodation is reached at private universities, which receive no direct instructional subsidy and thus are especially dependent on tuition revenue, suggests that it will also be possible at public campuses under my proposed reforms.

The second point is that in many if not most states the instructional subsidy to public universities is proportional to their enrollment. This fact means there are already strong financial incentives for public campuses to attract students in order to prop up revenues. Thus, while the particular mix of incentives might change under my reforms, depending on the implementation, both funding systems have incentives to be responsive to student needs. It is highly unlikely under my model that institutions would put their academic curriculum and degree offerings in the hands of nineteen-year-olds just because those students have new, state-administered scholarships. Obviously, students are consumers of higher education, and their needs should be carefully weighed by all institutions of higher learning. But it is not plausible to suppose that public universities, with their strong traditions of faculty governance, would suddenly accept the notion that students are "customers" who know what they want, are always right, and must be deferred to because of the dollars they hold. There is nothing in my proposal that would subvert the faculty's responsibility to set curricular priorities and standards.[19]

The more serious problem, I believe, is the current tendency of state governments to regulate campus speech, dictate curricular content, and, in the extreme, mandate personnel decisions surrounding controversial professors. One of the reasons for wanting to shift public dollars away from direct appropriation and into scholarships is to weaken the undesirable financial leverage that state governments can now exert over their campuses.

Social and Philosophical Issues

By now, readers will surely have noticed that in my proposed scholarship program, which is based on a revenue-neutral assumption that does not require increased state funding, the improvement in college affordability for middle-income and low-income students comes at the cost of higher tuition charges incurred by wealthier students. This "ability to pay" is in fact an important ingredient in my proposed strategy, but like all government actions that would treat taxpayers differentially, it raises fundamental philosophical issues about the proper role of government.

One function of government is to tax the population in order to pay for government services. In this regard the ability to pay is always an im-

portant consideration: those with the biggest homes pay the most prop-
erty taxes, and those with the highest incomes pay the most income taxes
(at least in principle). There are continuing arguments over the amount
and the degree, of course, but the principle of progressive, nonuniform
taxation is a clearly established part of any democratic society.

In other respects, democratic governments aspire to treat their citizens with complete, uniform equality. No citizens, rich or poor, are exempted from the rule of law. All citizens have the same voting rights, and
no vote counts more or less than any other vote. We are all expected to
obey the rules of our society, such as speed limits, and we all expect the
same even-handed treatment from the courts and from government offices and officials. In these respects a citizen's ability to pay should have
no bearing, and when it does, it is a cause for great alarm.

The picture becomes more complicated, however, with respect to
how government returns to the population the money it has collected.
Obviously, services provided by some agencies, such as local police and
fire departments, the Food and Drug Administration, and the National
Science Foundation, benefit all citizens equally. Other government programs, such as the Food Stamp Program and Medicaid, benefit selected
groups of citizens. The rationale for this deliberate discrimination on
the basis of need is that, indirectly, all of us benefit when all of our fellow
citizens are healthy and well nourished. To cite an example used by my
philosophy professor many years ago, everybody suffers if we fail to care
for the indigent smallpox victim living in our midst.

The issue is further complicated with respect to the government's
role in education. In the United States, all citizens are required by law to
attend school. And although taxpayers pay different amounts to support
those schools—again, with a continuing public debate over the criteria
and the amounts—a public education through twelfth grade is considered to be a "free" entitlement of all persons living in this country. There
are many people who would like to extend this educational right to include a college degree. The rationale is that in our new, knowledge-based
economy, America's historic commitment to providing opportunity for
all citizens now has a higher threshold of educational competency than
it once did. By analogy with K–12 education, some argue that states
should now also provide a free college education to all who want it.

Superficially, it is hard to argue with this logic, just as it is hard to
argue with the idealistic notion that a truly democratic society should
provide a base level of health care or housing, or adequate retirement

income, to all citizens. Perhaps one day, when the country has grown wealthy enough or enlightened enough, all of these things will come to pass. But that day is not yet here, and the particular problem with higher education is that the country is moving backward. Fifty years ago, when a college degree was still considered something of a luxury, a public college education could be afforded by almost anybody who wanted it. Today, when a college degree has become vital to one's economic well-being, fewer and fewer people can afford it.

Thus my new business plan for public universities is at heart a concession to practical realities. Although in an ideal world none should be barred from receiving an education because of financial circumstances, in the real world the next best thing is to minimize the burden. And minimizing the burden means using taxpayer dollars to help those who really need the help, even if some who do not need help may lose benefits they previously enjoyed. Ultimately the issue comes down to the democratic principle that treating people fairly is not always the same thing as treating them equally. Today, public universities are supported by appropriations that treat all students equally. The proposed scholarship program would replace that mechanism with one that treats them fairly.

Postscript

I began this book reminiscing about my first days as a university president and my gradual awakening to the subtle chronic disease that is slowly debilitating America's public universities. Throughout these chapters I have asserted that the disease cannot be cured by addressing the symptoms only and that trying to do so is as futile as giving cough drops to a tuberculosis victim.

During the intervening months, I have seen near-daily examples of public higher education's malaise. On one day, an online news story reminded me of the large salary disparity between public and private university professors.[1] On another, a study by the Collaborative on Academic Careers in Higher Education showed an analogous disparity in faculty career satisfaction. A University of North Carolina survey concluded that public college professors are increasingly feeling "burned out" and unhappy with their work environment.[2]

As I was finishing the first draft of this book, the governor of California ordered all state agencies to plan for 10 percent budget cutbacks, with obvious implications for the state's public campuses.[3] During that same week, in the nation's capital, a "Hall of

Shame" was proposed by congressional leaders to draw attention to academic inefficiencies. "For too long, students, parents and taxpayers have been held hostage to the ever-rising cost of a college education," said Rep. Howard P. McKeon.[4] And as I wrapped up my manuscript revisions, California's budget was again in the news, with critics complaining that the new budget, with no increase in funding for higher education, did not deal with the state's long-term fiscal problems and relied too heavily on borrowing and one-time revenue sources.[5] Now, as I draft this postscript, the nation has entered a credit crisis and economic downturn of historic proportions. Exactly how these will play out is anybody's guess, but one does not need a crystal ball to see that the prognosis for public higher education is not good. Rising unemployment, failing businesses, and the collapse of major financial institutions all translate into reduced tax revenues for states and an even tighter fiscal squeeze on the nation's public universities. The need for a systemic overhaul of public higher education could not be more urgent.

America is built on the principle of equal opportunity for all its citizens, and it is a small step to assert that the key to that opportunity is the dissemination of knowledge. An educated citizenry is the strongest asset for sustaining our way of life, because as our thoughts go, so go our actions and values. This is a revelation that stretches back more than twenty-five centuries, to the teachings of Buddha:

> The thought manifests as the word,
> The word manifests as the deed,
> The deed develops into habit,
> And the habit hardens into character.
> So watch the thought
> And its ways with care,
> And let it spring from love
> Born out of respect for all things.

This is all by way of saying that the health of America's public universities is an important element in the preservation of American democracy. This book has been preoccupied with the inner workings of academia—with committee sizes, salary policies, presidential searches, trustee selection, supply and demand, and dozens of other details of academic life that are of little interest to most people. But it is important that those in positions of leadership now think seriously about these details, because the stakes are ultimately very high. If our public universities are allowed to decay, denying average Americans the knowledge they need to prosper and live together in harmony, then our children will one day inherit a world that is not worthy of the noble dream of our republic's founders.

Appendix A
The Miami University Tuition Plan

In the year prior to the introduction of Miami University's tuition initiative in 2004, the university had charged its Ohio undergraduate students yearly fees of $8,353. That year it charged nonresident undergraduates $18,100, a difference of $9,747. Technically, this difference is called the "nonresident surcharge." The concept of differential pricing for resident and nonresident students is universal among public universities. The practice is based on the assumption that taxpayers in each state do not want their tax dollars underwriting the educational expenses of nonresident students who attend a public university in that state. The nonresident surcharge is intended to preclude that possibility by requiring nonresident students to pay the full unsubsidized tab for their education.

It is surprising, therefore, that the nonresident surcharge generally does not equate to the per capita subsidy a university receives from its state government. At Miami University, for example, the nonresident surcharge in 2003 was roughly twice the per capita subsidy. In fact, the university stood to profit to the tune of nearly $5,000 for each nonresident student it enrolled, even after allowing for the fact that the state provided no subsidy for those students. These extra dollars helped underwrite the educational expenses of Ohio students. Putting it differently, Miami lost money on each of its Ohio undergraduates but made up the difference on the revenues it earned from nonresidents.

But if the level of state appropriations does not determine a public university's nonresident surcharge, then what does? The answer is supply and demand. Although state authorities usually control the tuition a public campus can charge state residents, they will almost always permit a campus to charge nonresidents whatever its administrators choose. And that choice is invariably governed by the competitive laws of the educational marketplace. If a university sets its nonresident tuition too high, it will not attract out-of-state students. If it sets it too low, it forgoes the opportunity to enhance revenues. In other words, the nonresident tuition is a reasonable measure of the actual market value of a university's educational offerings. This is a key concept underlying Miami's tuition plan.

Beginning with the freshman class of 2004, Miami University abandoned its traditional two-tiered tuition structure and replaced it with a single tier based on the nonresident tuition. For Ohio residents, this meant a tuition increase of about 120 percent above what they would have been charged before the plan's adoption. Although the university completely offset this increase by means of Ohio-only scholarships, the sticker shock of such a large tuition increase and its potential impact on the university's Ohio applicants obviously was foremost on the minds of university officials. I will have more to say about the sticker-shock issue shortly, but for now let us consider how the new scholarships worked.

These new scholarships were intended to make a Miami University education more affordable for Ohio residents, and it is important to clarify just what this goal means. In this context, "affordable" does not necessarily mean a lower out-of-pocket cost of attending the university, since under the plan many Miami students actually paid more to attend than they would have paid otherwise. Rather, "affordability" folds in a student's ability to pay, so that an increase in affordability means a lowering of a student's financial barrier to enrollment. To use the language of economics, the goal of the plan was thus to lower the *average price sensitivity* of the university's applicants.

"Ohio Resident Scholarship" Awards

Under Miami's tuition plan, every admitted Ohio applicant is offered two scholarships, both renewable for up to six years. The first is an Ohio Resident Scholarship (ORS) that is pegged to the per capita undergraduate subsidy received by the university from the Ohio legislature. This is an automatic scholarship, in the sense that it is the same dollar value for all students, rich and poor alike. In 2004, the initial ORS was set at $5,000, which was actually about $1,000 higher than the per capita subsidy that year. Per capita subsidy is a derived number that depends somewhat on model assumptions. We set our ORS baseline value to be on the high range of any conceivable subsidy calculation, to insulate ourselves from possible criticism that we had not fully credited the state with its support of Ohio students.

The ORS awards are intended primarily to highlight the indirect financial support residents receive from Ohio taxpayers for their college expenses. All state residents know that the legislature provides support to public universities, but neither students nor taxpayers have an easy way of knowing how significant (or insignificant) that support actually is. The ORS award, which is computed by dividing the yearly educational appropriation to the university by its full-time-equivalent resident undergraduate enrollment, quantifies this support in a way that is easily understood by students and their families. The ORS is recomputed each year, based on the fluctuations in state appropriations. Thus, when the legislature increases its appropriation to public higher education by, say, 3 percent, each student's ORS also increases by 3 percent. Decreases are treated the same way. In this way, the ORS shows the direct impact on student pocketbooks caused by changes in government support. Providing this linkage is one way for the university to mobilize support for public higher education.

However, there is another benefit as well. Before the ORS program, reductions in state support to the university were, to the extent allowed by the legislature, offset by corresponding increases in tuition charges. Not surprisingly, tuition increases are always unpopular with students and taxpayers. Although university officials tried to link each increase in tuition to declining state support, this explanation often seemed too theoretical to be fully credible. To students, it was the university that was raising their tuition charges and not the state. This tendency to blame the university for tuition increases was often exacerbated by elected officials, who frequently skirted the issue of the appropriation cutbacks they had approved and instead attributed tuition growth to wasteful campus spending and inefficiency.

With the ORS concept, however, declining state support does not result in a tuition increase; rather it results in a decrease in scholarship aid. The net impact on students is the same—higher out-of-pocket costs— but the ORS awards place the responsibility for a decline in state support on the shoulders of lawmakers. The dollar-for-dollar linkage between state support and an ORS award makes the connection between state funding and college costs unambiguous: cuts in state support to higher education result in lower scholarships, not higher tuition charges. The ORS award program therefore increases public support for higher education while it also buffers the university against criticism for state-driven tuition increases over which it has no control.

"Ohio Leader Scholarship" Awards

The other financial aid award in the program is the Ohio Leader Scholarship (OLS), whose amount varies primarily according to student need. Thus, each Ohio student receives both an ORS and an OLS, the combined total being credited against the university's published tuition. In the OLS program, accepted Ohio students are placed into one of five graduated need categories, based on standard federal guidelines. Needs assessment is made using the Free Application for Financial Student Aid (FAFSA), which evaluates numerous economic factors besides current income. Applicants who decline to submit a FAFSA are assumed to be in the lowest need category and thereby are offered the smallest scholarships. Those in the highest need category obviously are offered the largest scholarships.

In the initial year of the plan, the OLS awards to entering freshmen ranged from $5,000 (34 percent of the class) to $6,200 (21 percent of the class), a modest spread of $1,200. We deliberately kept the spread small in order to gain experience with the plan, with the intention of gradually widening it in future years. By 2007, the OLS awards ranged from $7,050 (36 percent of freshmen) to $10,476 (36 percent of freshmen), and the spread had nearly tripled, at $3,426. Since these scholarships could be credited only against tuition, the net price Ohio students paid to attend the university thus varied by the amount of the spread. In effect, the variable OLS scholarships enabled the university to implement differential pricing in order to make the university more affordable to students with unmet financial need.

However, because all Ohio students received some dollars from both scholarship programs, even the school's wealthiest students still received a significant financial benefit from the new plan. Furthermore, because of their guaranteed Ohio Resident Scholarship, wealthy students received the full benefit of the institution's taxpayer-based subsidy. The additional dollars paid out of pocket by upper-income students did not significantly affect their enrollment decisions, but the corresponding savings enjoyed by lower- and middle-income students had a significant effect on their ability to attend the university. In other words, the decrease in affordability for upper-income students was modest, whereas the increase in affordability for lower- and middle-income students was substantial.

A few conservative critics have interpreted the variable pricing aspects of the Miami tuition plan as implementing a "Robin Hood" strategy of taking money from the rich to give to the poor. Some have also drawn a parallel between the plan and taxes that fall disproportionately on upper-income citizens. Is the plan at core really just a wealth redistribution scheme? In fact, it is not, and the reason comes down to the plan's voluntary nature. In effect, the university makes a financial aid offer to undergraduate applicants, but the decision whether or not to accept that offer rests in their hands. Because Miami is a selective university, the school's applicants invariably apply to other institutions. If they get a better offer from another school or perceive another school as offering more value, then they are always free to decline their Miami offer. By contrast, taxes are imposed on citizens, who have no choice but to pay them. The role of choice is what differentiates the tuition plan from the wealth redistribution policies that economic conservatives often find objectionable.

Applicability to Other Universities

Among the nearly 650 public four-year universities in the United States, there are relatively few that would be able to implement successfully a Miami-like tuition plan, in toto. To those considering a similar plan, Miami's experience suggests there are three basic requirements:

1. The university should have selective undergraduate admissions, with a high percentage of the student body consisting of full-time students. Selective admissions means that the university has excess application pressure to serve as a buffer against the financial risk of a possible enrollment decline. Selective universities also have admissions offices that devote considerable effort to student recruitment. Furthermore, students at selective universities have more college choices than do students at

nonselective schools, who are often place-bound commuters and working adults. Such students may have few other college options and would
therefore not be able to assess value by weighing admissions offers from
other schools.

2. The university should enroll a significant number of out-of-state
    undergraduates. (At Miami University, about one-third of enrolled
    undergraduates live outside Ohio.) Nonresident students are important
    because many pay the high unsubsidized tuition and thereby establish
    the university's actual market value. For the tuition plan to be viable,
    the university has to defend its published tuition as appropriate and fully
    justified by the value of its educational offerings. It cannot do this if its
    tuition is seen as arbitrary or unreasonable.

3. The university's competitive marketplace should include private univer-
    sities and colleges whose "high tuition / high aid" practices are familiar
    to the university's applicants. In other words, applicants must have
    other schools against which they can benchmark and evaluate a school's
    acceptance letter and financial aid package. Large flagship research uni-
    versities, e.g., the University of Illinois, might have trouble implement-
    ing the plan successfully, because their peer institutions (in this case,
    other Big Ten universities) have traditional two-tiered tuition structures.
    Miami University has a reputation as being "privatelike," so the new
    tuition plan seemed natural to most of the school's applicants, the large
    majority of whom also applied to private colleges and universities. This
    perception also helped the university lay the groundwork with the Ohio
    legislature, as discussed below.

Political Considerations

In an era marked by voter complaints about the high price of college,
there are obvious political barriers to implementing a plan that calls for
a one-year increase in tuition of more than 100 percent. Elected officials
have to be concerned with public perceptions, even if those perceptions
are at odds with the facts, and they are likely to oppose otherwise desirable policy changes that are too subtle for voters to understand. In
this respect, Miami's tuition plan posed a particular challenge, because it
asked people to follow a logic that, in essence, stated that the university
would double its tuition in order to make education more affordable.
Although the math supported that claim, the message at first blush is
obviously difficult to swallow.

It took a year to lay the political groundwork for the plan. We prepared comprehensive briefing documents to explain the concept and met individually with the governor, key legislators, and their office staff. I participated personally in many of these meetings, but other senior officers—including my provost and chief financial officer—also played important roles. Our two legislative affairs professionals devoted most of their year to the effort. We also relied heavily on lobbying assistance from our trustees. As discussed in previous chapters, public university trustees in Ohio are gubernatorial appointees, and in 2004 all nine of our trustees were Republicans. (At that time, Ohio had been led by Republican governors for fourteen years.) Several of our trustees were also major supporters of Republican officeholders, an obvious benefit, since in 2004 both the Ohio Senate and the Ohio House were dominated by Republicans.

In obtaining state approval for our plan, we found it essential to have key lawmakers championing our cause. Our local state senators and representatives were crucial in this regard, as were the speaker of the Ohio House and the president of the Ohio Senate. We also mobilized support from our alumni, especially those who were elected officials and legislative staff members. In the end, the proposal attracted considerable bipartisan support. Conservatives liked the plan because of its privatelike emphasis on market forces and competition, while liberals approved of its favorable impact on low- and middle-income students. With one exception, all of the major Ohio newspapers were supportive of the concept. (Our lobbying efforts included visits to their editorial boards.)

That is not to say that the proposal did not have its share of critics. The most vocal legislative resistance came from a state senator who staked out immediate fierce opposition to the proposal and subsequently declined to reevaluate his stance. Most of the legislative concerns centered on the suspicion that the university would use the tuition increase to pump up its revenues surreptitiously, rather than to benefit students. In the end, however, the plan prevailed and was embodied as part of the Ohio Revised Code.

In hindsight, I believe legislative approval can in large part be attributed to Miami University's unique niche among Ohio's public universities. In Ohio, Miami has always been seen as fundamentally different from the other state schools. With its privatelike campus atmosphere, residential student body, selective admissions, and focus on the liberal arts, the university's niche gave it a license to experiment that other public universities did not have.

Marketing, Admissions Psychology, and Public Relations

Prior to the tuition plan's introduction, the university administration had attempted to predict its likely impact on student applications and enrollments. Although we were confident of the plan's success once it had been well established, we felt the transition years held the risk of significant application declines. Our best estimates were that the plan would have a negligible impact on nonresident applications (since the plan's provisions did not apply to nonresident students) but that applications from Ohio residents could decline by as much as 15 percent because of the sticker-shock problem alluded to previously. Our fear was that lower- and middle-income applicants would be spooked by the large published increase in our tuition and would rule out the university from consideration without ever computing the offsetting provisions of the scholarship awards.

As it turned out, our predictions were completely wrong. In the first year of the program, nonresident applications to the university surged 25 percent and our Ohio applications increased 8 percent. Furthermore, the quality of the applications rose, as measured by academic achievement metrics of ACT and SAT scores and high school grade-point averages. There were significant increases in applications from students from low- and middle-income families, and at the end of the application season, we saw large increases in freshmen from these price-sensitive categories. Enrollment of minority students jumped 25 percent, and that of students from first-generation college families surged a remarkable 40 percent. The reasons for these counterintuitive results say a great deal about both the psychology of college admissions and the peculiar calculus of college financing.

In projecting application decreases, we made several errors in reasoning. The first was to underestimate the financial sophistication of our applicant pool. Our experience now suggests that college-bound students and their families are acutely aware of comparative college costs. Since Miami applicants in particular tended to coapply to private colleges and universities, they were quite familiar with private-sector pricing practices. Private universities typically have high published "sticker prices," which are then substantially discounted by generous financial aid offers. From the perspective of applicants, Miami's new tuition plan simply mimicked this practice. (Here I should note that even today relatively few of the university's low- and middle-income applicants come from disadvantaged, impoverished backgrounds. A low-income Miami University applicant is more likely to be the son or daughter of an elementary school teacher than a child raised by a single parent in a poor inner-city neighborhood. In this respect, the financial sophistication of Miami's applicant pool is probably not typical of that at many public universities.)

Furthermore, in laying the groundwork for the new plan, our admissions, recruiting, and financial aid staff took great care to explain the program to high school guidance counselors throughout the state. Our representatives met individually with guidance counselors from many of the state's high schools and also hosted a statewide conference for counselors. These meetings, augmented by pamphlets, brochures, letters, and e-mail messages about the plan, meant that its workings were effectively disseminated throughout the state. All of these efforts served to defuse the sticker-shock problem.

Our biggest surprise, however, was our underestimate of the importance of psychology in influencing selective college admissions. After the plan was implemented, the university's published tuition jumped from $8,353 to $18,100 for Ohio residents. Despite this increase, the university could reasonably claim that the latter figure reflected the true value of a Miami University education, because thousands of nonresident students were willing to pay that amount. Thus, to new Ohio applicants and their families, Miami suddenly seemed like a fabulous bargain. If accepted, they would receive an $18,100 education, but because of the plan's scholarships they would pay less than half that amount out of pocket. In prior years, Miami had seemed merely the most expensive public university in the state. Now, applicants benchmarked the university against private universities, and it seemed like a comparative bargain. In the minds of applicants, Miami's "brand" evidently had acquired the cachet of a selective private university, and this cachet extended to both Ohio and out-of-state applicants.

The plan's scholarship awards reinforced this perception. From a marketing standpoint, consumers always prefer to buy an expensive item at a substantial discount, rather than an inexpensive item at little or no discount. Unknowingly, our new tuition structure played to this strong consumer preference. Moreover, the large scholarships in the plan were a source of pride to our applicants. Scholarship recipients are often named in local newspapers and have their names read at high school graduation ceremonies. We heard many reports of parents who were very pleased at this recognition for their college-bound student.

In short, the plan significantly improved the university's market position, resulting in an increase in both resident and nonresident applications. During my years as Miami's president I felt it essential not to dilute inadvertently this market strength. Thus, we never publicized the average discounted net tuition to Ohio residents, and in public statements we referred only to our single published tuition. We encouraged applicants to weigh their financial aid offers from Miami with those from other schools, and we showed them carefully their out-of-pocket costs. However, the arithmetic was always based on our published tuition. Had we publicized the discounted average tuition to the media or to Ohio residents, we would have lessened the perceived value of our educational offerings and undermined the favorable impact of the plan on applications. As noted already, our credibility was contingent on our being able to establish our tuition as reflecting true market value. Otherwise, our "sticker price" would have been seen by Ohio applicants as merely a marketing gimmick.

Appendix B

The Impact of Competition on Public University Tuition, Costs, and Revenue

In chapter 2, it was asserted that government appropriations and tuition controls provide disincentives for public universities to rein in expenses and enhance productivity. It was further asserted that removing these disincentives not only would enhance efficiency but also would provide a host of other positive benefits, including especially a moderation of annual tuition increases. Here we will explore this topic more deeply and consider explicitly how the forces of supply and demand, if allowed to act, can compel a university to constrain its prices. Legislators often are apprehensive about releasing state universities from tuition controls, fearing that if given the chance, public colleges would continue to raise tuition charges indefinitely. As we will see, the constraints exerted by competition and market forces show that this concern is largely misdirected.

Let me begin with a disclaimer. The goal of this appendix is to provide the more technically inclined reader with a brief tutorial on the inner workings of supply and demand in the academic marketplace. The figures that follow are idealized representations based on simple models of university costs, revenues, and so on, and as such are necessarily oversimplified. (The mathematical de-

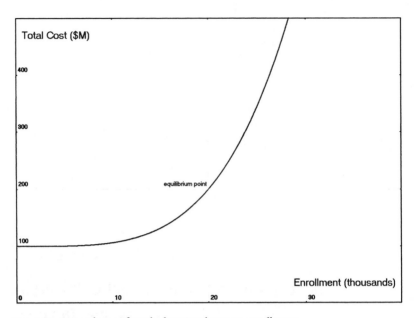

Figure B1. Dependence of total educational cost on enrollment

tails of the models are given in the endnotes.) To put it differently: my analysis deliberately strips away all of the real-word messiness in order to focus on basic concepts, in much the same way that physics teachers illustrate Newton's laws for first-year students by sliding imaginary blocks down frictionless planes.

Figure B1 shows qualitatively how total educational cost might vary with enrollment for the same hypothetical university described in figures 2 and 3 (chapter 2).[1] The vertical axis plots the total cost of educational operations, while the horizontal axis shows the number of enrolled students. The cost curve is flat at low enrollments, reflecting the large fixed costs that all public universities incur. These fixed costs include the maintenance of building and grounds, salaries of tenured faculty members, cost of utilities, and debt service on bonds. All of these costs and a host of others must be paid, independent of the number of enrolled students.

As the figure shows, costs increase as enrollments climb, slowly at first and then rapidly as more students are added. A school cannot continue to add students indefinitely without at some point hiring more instructors, building more classrooms and dormitories, and generally expanding its physical plant. As a school nears its enrollment capacity, its costs begin to skyrocket because of the need to make a large capital investment in expanding capacity.

Although universities must know their total costs in order to balance their books, other cost variables are more relevant to making tuition decisions. These are the *average cost per student* and the *marginal cost per student*. The relationship between these different costs is as follows:

Total cost, $C(N)$: The total cost of educating N students. It includes all direct and indirect expenditures associated with the university's educational operations but normally excludes research operations, room and board expenditures, and other expenditures that are not directly related to the university's instructional mission. At many universities, educational costs are rolled into an "Education and General" (E&G) budget.

Average cost, $C_A(N)$: The average cost per student is defined as $C(N)/N$. Because of a university's large fixed costs, $C_A(N)$ tends to decrease as N increases, resulting in significant economies of scale, until N approaches the school's enrollment capacity, at which point $C_A(N)$ begins to increase.

Marginal cost, $C_M(N)$: The cost the university incurs by adding one additional student to the student body, that is, by growing enrollments from N to $N+1$. (Mathematically, $C_M(N)$ is the slope of the $C(N)$ curve at position N and is given by the derivative $dC(N)/dN$.)

Figure B2 shows how these three costs vary with enrollment for our hypothetical university. The total cost is shown on the left scale, the average and marginal costs on the right scale. The figure shows that the average cost per student $C_A(N)$ falls initially, as the institution's fixed costs are spread over a growing number of students, but eventually rises as this savings is dwarfed by the expense of opening more class sections, hiring more instructional staff, and providing more support services for the additional students. The marginal cost, $C_M(N)$, is nearly zero at a very low enrollment, because the school can add additional students to near-empty classrooms without having to hire more personnel. In this part of the curve, the school's enrollment is far below its capacity, a disastrous situation, because average per-student costs are unsustainably high. The only hope for survival for any university or college that finds itself in this position is to try to dig itself out by increasing enrollments. Because the marginal costs are so low, the additional tuition revenue goes immediately to the school's bottom line.

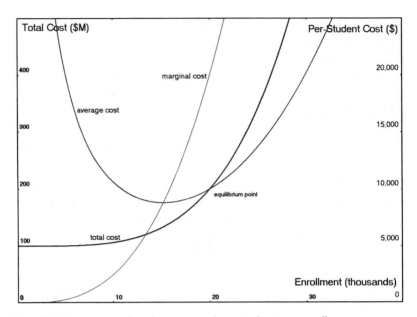

Figure B2. Dependence of total, average, and marginal costs on enrollment

As enrollment numbers climb, the marginal cost curve, $C_M(N)$, also climbs, eventually crossing the average cost curve, $C_A(N)$, at the bottom of its dip.[2] The crossing point of these two curves is strategically important; it serves as a warning flag that any enrollment growth beyond that point will raise the institution's average cost per student. Recall from chapter 3 that in order to avoid an operating loss, the university must balance its average per-student cost with its average per-student revenue. Thus growing enrollment past this crossing point, which is 15,000 students in our example, is likely to incur losses for the institution.

But that is exactly what is happening in our example. Recall from figure 3 that our hypothetical university took in a maximum revenue of $200 million when its enrollment was 20,000 students, corresponding to an average per-student revenue of $10,000. This is the equilibrium price point shown in figure B2. (The apparent intersection of the total cost and average cost curves on the figure at this point is accidental.) But at this enrollment level, the marginal cost of educating each new student is about twice as great as the additional revenue that student brings in. Thus, to balance its budget, the university needs to admit fewer students, even though it gives up revenue by doing so. This analysis may seem very theoretical, but buried within the theory is a very practical lesson:

once market forces begin to influence demand, administrators of public colleges need to understand how changes in enrollment affect both their costs and their revenues. Growing revenues may be exactly the wrong way to balance a budget.

The Revenue-Cost Balancing Act

Up to now, I have discussed campus costs in terms of their dependence on enrollments. However, there is another useful way of viewing cost, and that is to see how it varies with tuition. The logical connection between cost and tuition is straightforward: costs are driven by enrollment, and enrollment is tuition sensitive; therefore, costs are also tuition sensitive. To illustrate the connection between cost and tuition, we simply combine the cost vs. enrollment curve of figure B1 with the enrollment vs. tuition curve of figure B2 to obtain curve (A) in figure B3, which plots total cost, $C(T)$, as a function of tuition, T.[3] The resulting curve is unfamiliar but not difficult to understand. It shows that when a very low tuition is charged, the university's cost is high, because the low tuition attracts a large number of students, up to a maximum of 40,000 in the example. As the tuition rises, the total cost decreases, reflecting the fact that enrollments are dropping. Once tuition has increased to its cutoff limit of $20,000, beyond which no students enroll, the cost has decreased down to the fixed costs that are independent of enrollment.

Since both are a function of tuition, we can now compare the cost curve (A) and the total tuition revenue curve from figure 3, which is redrawn on figure B3. Plotting cost and revenue together in this way illustrates clearly how market forces set limits on a university's tuition-setting ability. The important feature to note on the graph is that the cost curve (A) intersects the revenue curve at two points. These intersection points define the edges of a band of allowed tuition charges, whose low and high values are designated on the figure by T_L and T_H. Inside this band, the cost of running the university is lower than the tuition revenue it collects; in principle, the university is initially free to set its tuition anywhere inside this band. The regions outside the band are "forbidden zones," where the university cannot operate. Should it attempt to set its tuition in a forbidden zone, it would not generate enough revenue to cover its costs.

Now suppose the university sets its tuition somewhere within the allowed band, say at the vertical line marked T_I on the graph. Here the university reaps a "windfall profit"—excess funds it does not need to

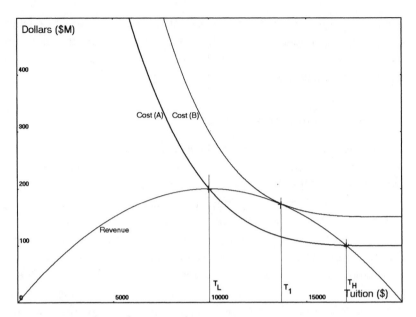

Figure B3. Dependence of revenue and cost on tuition

maintain operations. But, being a nonprofit enterprise that does not pay dividends, the university will reinvest these surplus dollars back into itself by expanding programs, improving facilities, or hiring new faculty and staff. In effect, these reinvested dollars add to the university's base cost structure and thus raise the total cost curve just far enough to reduce the spread between cost and revenue to zero. This new cost curve is shown in the figure as curve (B).[4] Although the university can initially price itself anywhere within the band between T_L and T_H, doing so results in a subsequent cost increase that reduces the bandwidth to the single point of intersection.

In reality, universities almost never see such revenue windfalls. Instead, university officials try to adjust tuition each year to balance the university budget, that is, to bring revenue into alignment with their existing cost structure. In our figure, this alignment occurs where the cost and revenue curves initially intersect, at either tuition T_L or T_H. But at these band edges there is a financial incentive for the university to raise its tuition (if at T_L) or lower its tuition (if at T_H) so that it can move into the interior of the band and generate excess revenue. Moving into the band then leads to the chain of events described in the previous paragraph, raising costs and again resulting in a single intersection point at tuition T_1.

Let us suppose, however, that university officials are able to resist the temptation to adjust tuition in order to reap excess revenue. As it turns out, there is another force at play that will compel them to do so. The cost of running a university does not remain static. Costs increase on a year-to-year basis, which is the normal budgeting cycle for awarding wage and salary increases to employees. Historically, this cost increase has exceeded the yearly inflation rate. Thus each year the university's cost curve will shift up a bit, and each upward shift will narrow the tuition bandwidth and also result in a tuition increase (if initially at T_L) or decrease (if at T_H).[5] Eventually, as costs ratchet up, the bandwidth narrows down, again to a single point of intersection.

And so, by hook or by crook, the university finds that the forces of supply and demand have removed all ability for it to set its tuition arbitrarily. There is one value of tuition, and only one, that it can choose and still balance its books. Once equilibrium is reached at T_I, any movement off this point in either direction will cause the university to incur operating losses.[6] The actual value of T_I depends on the price sensitivity of student demand and the university's cost structure, both of which are unique to the particular school. However, no matter what its actual demand and cost profiles are, the university can charge only one tuition value if it is to balance its budget.

But once this limiting point is reached, what happens the following year, after the university makes its next round of salary and wage increases? Assuming that student demand remains unchanged (so that the revenue curve doesn't shift), a gap will appear between the cost and revenue curves, which means that the university can no longer balance its books by adjusting tuition. Raising tuition will drive down enrollments, thus reducing revenue, while lowering tuition increases costs more rapidly than it increases revenue. In effect, the university is stuck with only one option, and that is to try to eliminate the gap by reducing its overall cost structure.[7] Thus we see that competitive pressures not only restrain tuition levels but also provide irresistible pressures for universities to rein in spending—in effect to become more efficient.

It is natural to wonder whether this idealized analysis, based on simplified mathematical models, bears any relationship to actual universities once all the real-world messiness previously referred to is folded back in. The answer is a qualified yes. Although the details will depend on circumstances, the forces of supply and demand cannot be resisted by any organization subjected to an active competitive market. In the automobile industry, for example, American manufacturers find themselves in just the situation described here. If they try to raise prices on their cars and trucks, then sales will drop and revenues will fall. If they try to lower prices, then the resulting growth in sales does not compensate for the increase in costs. The only possible solutions to their dilemma, short of declaring bankruptcy, are to improve their product line in order to boost demand, and to rework their cost structure, which they do by renegotiating union contracts, closing unproductive facilities, and laying off employees.

Universities face analogous choices. To remain economically viable in a competitive market, universities have to keep improving their educational "product," that combination of instruction and services that attracts students who are willing to pay tuition; they also have to rein in or eliminate expenditures that do not advance this objective. Both of these are desirable attributes, but they can come to pass only if the universities are actually required to compete. As we will see subsequently, the existence of government subsidies to public universities, combined with state-imposed tuition controls, undermines these beneficial competitive forces, allowing public universities to become both inefficient and unresponsive to the needs of students.

Private universities and colleges, of course, do not receive a direct appropriation from the government, and in addition they have the freedom to set their own tuition charges. They are thus fully subject to competitive market forces. That said, highly selective private universities (and a few selective public universities) enjoy such a surplus of applicants that they are able to fix their enrollments at a predetermined level. So long as their student demand remains high, they have the latitude to raise tuition without fear of driving down enrollment and losing revenue.[8] They are also freed to some extent by the need to restrain their operating costs. This, of course, is a luxury enjoyed by a relative handful of elite private universities and colleges. The large majority of private institutions must be acutely aware of the fiscal implications of competition and the need to control their expenditures.

How Tuition Controls Undermine Competition and Disrupt Market Balance

As previously discussed, public colleges generally have their tuition regulated by an external controlling authority, which suppresses market influences.

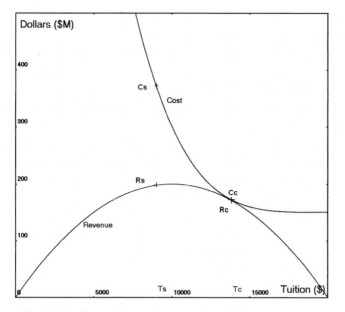

Figure B4. The impact of tuition controls on university budgets

The impact of below-market tuition controls is easily seen from the revenue-cost diagram labeled figure B4. In the figure, the initial market-determined tuition, T_C is the point where the cost and revenue curves coincide, and we denote the (lower) state-mandated tuition T_S.[9] The points on the cost curve associated with T_C and T_S are C_C and C_S, respectively, and the corresponding points on the revenue curve are R_C and R_S. At T_C, cost and revenue are in balance, so that $C_C = R_C$, as expected.

The figure shows clearly how the lowered tuition throws the market out of balance. Because of the increase in demand, the university will enroll more students than it originally expected. The cost of educating this larger student body rises to C_S, and the additional tuition revenue the university collects rises to R_S.[10] The impact of the tuition cap is thus to throw the university's budget out of balance by creating a gap between revenue and cost. The shortfall is given by the vertical line segment of length $(C_S - R_S)$. In order to balance its books, the university must reduce its expenditures by this amount. Because the biggest expenditure category is for personnel, employee compensation is typically most affected, although modest reductions can sometimes be absorbed by cutting operating and equipment budgets. In any case, through a combination of expenditure reductions, the university reduces its costs to R_S, thus bringing its budget back into equilibrium.

Because tuition caps are generally decided by state governments during budget deliberations, universities have difficulty folding them into their planning process. The resulting budget cuts are thus necessarily opportunistic; it is more possible to quickly freeze salaries and leave vacancies unfilled than to quickly eliminate weak or unnecessary programs. Because the largest component of any university's budget is personnel compensation, this is the area affected most drastically by cost reductions. Over the long term, the primary result of tuition controls is a lowering of the quality of the institution's faculty and staff.

Note that my example is meant to apply to nonselective public universities, whose enrollments fluctuate with demand. Selective universities (which are a rather small subset of all public colleges) intentionally price their tuition at submarket levels in order to stabilize their enrollment at the school's capacity. For them, the growth of demand following a tuition cap temporarily increases the size of their applicant pool but does not lead to cost increases associated with larger enrollments. Thus the gap they experience between cost and revenue is entirely due to decreased revenue. Over time, of course, tuition controls reduce student demand, because of their deleterious impact on the school's quality. In practice, tuition controls have a disproportionately greater impact on selective universities than on nonselective universities because they weaken the stature of the school relative to its competition.

Appendix C
Suggested Readings

Here, selected from a seemingly endless number of volumes about higher education, is a sampling of twenty-one, mostly recent, books that amplify on the themes in this book. Readers will note that many entries in this list are authored by former college presidents and administrative officers. This selection partly reflects my own biases as a member of that crowd. But it also reflects the reality that former university leaders, finally freed from their shackles, often feel a compulsion to write books about their experiences. Sometimes they write to share insights about academia, impossible to garner, they believe, in any other capacity; sometimes it is to reawaken their dormant inner scholar; and sometimes it is simply to vent after years of mouthing president-speak: "Thank you for stopping by to share your concerns, Senator Smith. Know that you are always welcome." (Translation: Now get out of my office and don't come back.") Other suggested readings are compilations of essays, mostly by senior scholars and university administrators, and also a few contributions by nonacademic critics. These are by no means the last words on the subject, but all have interesting messages that are worth paying attention to.

Altbach, Philip G., Robert O. Berdahl, and Patricia J. Gumport. *American Higher Education in the Twenty-first Century: Social, Political, and Economic Challenges.* 2nd ed. Baltimore: Johns Hopkins University Press, 2005.

Hersh, Richard H., and John Merrow. *Declining by Degrees: Higher Education at Risk.* New York: Palgrave Macmillan, 2005.

Priest, Douglas M., and Edward P. St. John, eds. *Privatization and Public Universities.* Bloomington: Indiana University Press, 2006.

St. John, Edward P., and Michael D. Parsons, eds. *Public Funding of Higher Education: Changing Contexts and New Rationales.* Baltimore: Johns Hopkins University Press, 2004.

The above four books are collections of essays, largely by respected scholars, college presidents and administrators, think tank researchers, columnists, and public policy experts. St. John et al. review the history of public university funding and financial aid, the changing political and social landscape, and new directions for policy studies. Altbach et al. look at the challenges facing America's colleges, with an excellent historical overview providing the setting for an analysis of the internal and external forces on academia. Not whether but how well public universities will privatize is the common theme behind the essays in Priest et al. As adequate public funding for higher education wanes, the authors believe the challenges of identifying alternate income sources, managing that income, and coping with market forces are the keys to survival for the nation's public colleges. The essays in Hersh et al. (meant to accompany a PBS documentary) look at declining academic standards, inadequate media scrutiny, the frantic admissions sweepstakes, complacent campuses, mounting public criticisms, and growing concerns about access and affordability. With a foreword by Tom Wolfe, the book brings together an unusually broad range of perspectives in service to a common theme: the clock is ticking and it is time for the nation to wake up before a precious national resource is lost.

Bok, Derek. *Universities in the Marketplace: The Commercialization of Higher Education.* Princeton, NJ: Princeton University Press, 2003.

The author worries that "something of irreplaceable value may get lost" in the contemporary university's relentless search for profit-making opportunities. As former president of Harvard, a school rife with fiercely independent entrepreneurs and fiefdoms, Bok certainly knows whereof he speaks. Here he weighs in against business deals that compromise academic values and standards and offers suggestions for reform.

Bowen, William G. *The Board Book: An Insider's Guide for Directors and Trustees.* New York: W. W. Norton, 2008.

This book is a bit out of the mold for this list, because much of it focuses on the governing boards of for-profit and other nonacademic entities. Nevertheless, the general principles and recommendations have broad applicability to institutions of higher learning. As a former Princeton University president and board member of several for-profit and nonprofit organizations, the author brings a wealth of personal experience to this topic, providing insight and guidance on the practices, problems, and pitfalls of serving as a university or college trustee.

Bowen, William G., and Harold T. Shapiro, eds. *Universities and Their Leadership.* Princeton, NJ: Princeton University Press, 1998.
These essays are from a 250th birthday celebration of Princeton University ("a pearl among America's research universities, shining true when so many others are accused of being made of paste"); the contributors mostly include presidents and academicians from the sherry-sipping end of the higher education continuum. If one can overlook their sometimes ponderous tone, the writings are thought-provoking, with an informative historical bent.

D'Souza, Dinesh. *Illiberal Education: The Politics of Race and Sex on Campus.* New York: Free Press, 1998.
Horowitz, David. *Indoctrination U.: The Left's War against Academic Freedom.* New York: Encounter Books, 2007.
Kimball, Roger. *Tenured Radicals: How Politics Has Corrupted Our Higher Education.* 3rd ed. Chicago: Ivan R. Dee, 2008.
Love them or hate them, the titles of these books speak for themselves. This trio of works by outspoken conservative authors and public intellectuals is the tip of a large iceberg of conservative complaints about American higher education. D'Souza's book, initially published in 1991, led off the attack on campus political correctness, while Horowitz, scorned on many campuses for his reform proposals, has mobilized critics against academe's presumed politicization. Kimball, armed with the credentials of a public intellectual who has ties to the upper echelon of American conservative thinking, joined the fray and raised the stakes. Although some books in this category can be strident polemics, there is no doubt that as a group they have shaped lawmaker complaints and attitudes about the nation's universities and colleges.

Duderstadt, James J. *A University for the 21st Century.* Ann Arbor: University of Michigan Press, 2000).
Duderstadt, James J., and Farris W. Womack. *The Future of the Public University in America: Beyond the Crossroads.* Baltimore: Johns Hopkins University Press, 2003.
In these two books, the authors, a former president and a chief financial officer of the University of Michigan, bring experience and insight into analyzing the problems facing public universities and their potential solutions. I usually find myself in near-total agreement with their candid and thought-provoking views. These are well documented and readable—if at times a bit gloomy—treatises on the prospects of meaningful reform in the political cauldron of American public higher education.

Duderstadt, James J. *The View from the Helm: Leading the American University during an Era of Change.* Ann Arbor: University of Michigan Press, 2007.
For those who have wondered how university presidents ("people who live in big mansions but beg for a living") spend their days, nights, weekends, and holidays, this book lays it all out in detail. The University of Michigan is one of those nearly ungovernable public behemoths, and the author is one of an unusual breed, having proved himself able to keep it on course.

Ehrenberg, Ronald G. *Tuition Rising: Why College Costs So Much.* Cambridge, MA: Harvard University Press, 2002.
The author is a leading economist of higher education and brings the perspective of both a prolific scholar and a former chief financial officer of Cornell University. Despite the title, this is not specifically a book about why college tuition keeps rising. It is, rather, about the internal and external forces that drive up university expenditures, a soup-to-nuts overview ranging from air conditioning systems to endowment policies to faculty governance. Filled with graphs and charts, it is nevertheless quite accessible to the lay reader.

Fish, Stanley. *Save the World on Your Own Time.* Oxford: Oxford University Press, 2008.
In this little book, Stanley Fish, academe's answer to Andy Rooney, takes up that most fundamental of questions "What is it that universities should do?" He finds that what they should do is often very different from what they do do, and for that reason this book is useful reading for college trustees and administrators. The boundaries of academic freedom and the proper role of teachers in the college classroom are two of the main topics. What distinguishes Fish from other pundits is not that he holds strong opinions; everybody has strong opinions. It is that Fish's views are philosophically grounded in well-framed principles and concepts.

Kirp, David L. *Shakespeare, Einstein, and the Bottom Line: The Marketing of Higher Education.* Cambridge, MA: Harvard University Press, 2003.
Written by a Berkeley professor of public policy, these case studies achieve the difficult feat of being both scholarly and engaging. With lively and elegant prose, the author, assisted by a coterie of student coauthors, explores the commercialization, salesmanship, and competition in entities ranging from McDonald's Hamburger University, where graduates receive a "diploma" in hamburgerology, to the New York University philosophy department, where presumably they do not.

Newman, Frank, Lara Couturier, and Jamie Scurry. *The Future of Higher Education: Rhetoric, Reality, and the Risks of the Market.* New York: Jossey-Bass/Wiley, 2004.
Based on a four-year study, this book is a candid appraisal of the transformation of American higher education brought on by globalization, for-profit competitors, changing societal needs, and declining state budgets. The authors do not let universities off the hook, attributing some of higher education's challenges to the comfort of universities with the status quo, their reluctance to have their performance assessed, their inability to plan strategically, the priority given to research over teaching, and the proliferation of unneeded, low-quality doctoral programs.

Paulsen, Michael B., and John C. Smart, eds. *The Finance of Higher Education: Theory, Research, Policy, and Practice.* New York: Agathon, 2001.
A compilation of essays by eighteen authors, mostly well-known economists, many with college administrative responsibilities, this 588-page tome looks at federal and state policies, student access and college choice, tuition-pricing strategies, human capital, investment, productivity, costs, and supply and demand. Although much of

the theory is heavy going and not aimed at lay readers, this collection provides an interesting overview of a rapidly developing and sophisticated branch of economic analysis.

Rosovsky, Henry. *The University: An Owner's Manual.* New York: W. W. Norton, 1990.
This well-known commentary for lay readers on the culture and practices of academia is as applicable today as when it was first published in 1990. The author is an economics professor and former Harvard dean, and he writes with the clarifying and balanced insight of a seasoned academician-turned-administrator who loves the academy but isn't fooled by its shenanigans.

Vedder, Richard. *Going Broke by Degree: Why College Costs So Much.* Washington, DC: American Enterprise Institute Press, 2004.
The author is an opinionated and colorful conservative critic of the contemporary university. Unlike many critics, however, Vedder backs up his opinions with the careful hand of a serious, data-driven economist. Bulging with tables and graphs, this book cheerfully takes on some of higher education's sacred cows. An admirer of Milton Friedman and a strong believer in the beneficial power of markets, Vedder comes to many conclusions similar to those in this book.

Zemsky, Robert, Gregory R. Wegner, and William F. Massy. *Remaking the American University: Market-Smart and Mission-Centered.* New Brunswick, NJ: Rutgers University Press, 2006.
The lead author in this thoughtful and readable work is a senior, well-known higher education scholar. For modern universities to succeed, the authors argue, they must now embrace market principles, but only in a way that preserves their historic mission of serving the larger public good. The market brings in the necessary dollars, but how those dollars are spent requires a distinctive humanistic set of social values.

Notes

PREFACE

1. Shannon Colavecchio-Van Sickler, "Too Cheap to Be Great," *St. Petersburg Times,* October 8, 2006.

2. Nathan Crabbe, "Trustees Tweak UF Budget Cuts," *Gainesville Sun,* May 15, 2008.

3. Maria L. La Ganga, "A Money Gap and a Brain Drain: UC Berkeley, Long on Reputation but Short on Funding, Is Losing Talent," *Los Angeles Times,* October 28, 2006.

4. Scott Carlson, "As Campuses Crumble, Budgets Are Crunched," *Chronicle of Higher Education,* May 23, 2008.

5. Average pay of full-time professors at public doctoral institutions in 2006–7 was $105,174. At private doctoral institutions it was $126,444. *Chronicle of Higher Education,* 2008–9 Almanac Issue, 3.

6. Ibid.

INTRODUCTION

1. Until the beginning of the twentieth century, nearly all the beneficiaries of the Morrill Act were male Caucasians. Significant numbers of women began to enroll in public universities around the turn of the century, and minority Americans about a half-century after that.

2. College Board, "Federal Student Aid to Undergraduates Shows Slow Growth, While Published Tuition Prices Continue to Increase," press release, October 22, 2007.

3. Ralph R. Gutowski , "Restructuring Tuition and Scholarships," annual meeting of the Central Association of College and University Business Officers, Milwaukee, October 18, 2005.

4. According to U.S. Census data, among all states the per capita income in Ohio slipped from twenty-second to twenty-sixth place. The Ohio median household income (a three-year average from 2004 to 2006) ranked twenty-ninth.

5. Increasingly, public university students complete a baccalaureate degree by first attending community colleges, where they often take a patchwork of evening and weekend courses, and then transferring to a four-year college to complete their final degree requirements. This trend is one of the reasons a "four-year" public college degree frequently takes about six years to attain.

6. Although government subsidy to campuses has decreased as a percentage of total university income, the states had actually increased their funding of public campuses (in inflation-corrected dollars) for two decades up to about 2002. This upward trend then faltered as a series of budget crises overwhelmed state treasuries. Frank Newman, Lara Couturier, and Jamie Scurry, *The Future of Higher Education: Rhetoric, Reality, and the Risks of the Market* (New York: Jossey-Bass, 2004), 41.

7. Ronald G. Ehrenberg, *Tuition Rising: Why College Costs so Much* (Cambridge, MA: Harvard University Press, 2000. Although focusing on selective private universities, Ehrenberg provides a comprehensive synopsis of the internal pressures also driving up costs at public universities. At selective private universities and colleges, the author concludes, competition and the desire to excel is the major *external* driver of costs. Public universities also seek to excel, but such aspirations are dampened by government restrictions on revenues. In the absence of revenue flexibility, public university expenditures merely track whatever tuition and subsidy income the universities are allowed to receive from their state government.

CHAPTER 1

1. This assertion obviously does not apply to for-profit institutions, like the University of Phoenix.

2. "America's Best Colleges," *U.S. News & World Report,* September 1–8, 2008.

3. In 1997, Ohio's Central State University suffered a financial collapse. In response, the Ohio General Assembly passed "fiscal watch" legislation requiring each Ohio public university to report annually on three measures of its financial health: a "viability ratio" (calculated by dividing the institution's total debt into expendable net assets); a "primary reserve ratio" (calculated by dividing the institution's total expenditures into total net assets); and a "net income ratio" (calculated by dividing total revenues into the increase in net assets for the year).

4. See, for example, William Zumeta, "State Higher Education Financing: Demand Imperatives Meet Structural, Cyclical, and Political Constraints," in *Public Funding of Higher Education: Changing Contexts and New Rationales,* ed. Edward P. St. John and Michael D. Parsons (Baltimore: Johns Hopkins University Press, 2005), 79–107 and figs 5–4, 5–6.

5. Donald E. Heller, "State Support of Higher Education: Past, Present, and Future," in *Privatization and Public Universities,* ed. Douglas M. Priest and Edward P. St. John (Baltimore: Johns Hopkins University Press, 2004), 11–37.

6. Ronald G. Ehrenberg, *Tuition Rising: Why College Costs So Much* (Cambridge, MA: Harvard University Press, 2002), 273–74 and fig. 19.2.

7. Edward P. St. John and Eric H. Asker, *Refinancing the College Dream: Access, Equal*

Opportunity, and Justice for Taxpayers (Baltimore: Johns Hopkins University Press, 2003), 2, 232, table A.3.

8. Eric Kelderman, "Tuition Makes Up a Growing Share of College Budgets While Spending on Instruction Has Slowed," *Chronicle of Higher Education,* May 1, 2008.

9. At large research universities grant and contract revenue may be larger than tuition revenue, but that money cannot be used for undergraduate instructional purposes.

10. For an informative synopsis of how rising public-university tuitions influence institutional practices, see Don Hossler, "Students and Families as Revenue: The Impact on Institutional Behaviors," in *Privatization and Public Universities,* ed. Douglas M. Priest and Edward P. St. John (Bloomington: Indiana University Press, 2006), 109–28.

11. Ohio University economist Richard Vedder has observed that these kinds of "improvements" are seldom aimed at increasing productivity, that is, reducing the unit cost of instruction, and in fact often result in lowered productivity. Richard Vedder, *Going Broke by Degree: Why College Costs Too Much* (Washington: American Enterprise Institute Press, 2004), 26.

12. In the past decade, Ohio State University has become markedly more selective in its admissions practices and has been very successful at recruiting well-qualified undergraduates.

13. "State Tuition, Fees, and Financial Assistance Policies for Public Colleges and Universities, 2005–06," State Higher Education Executive Officers (SHEEO).

14. In the SHEEO survey, cited above, only the State of Michigan indicated that market forces were a primary tool in determining tuition rates.

15. Scott Carlson, "As Campuses Crumble, Budgets are Crunched," *The Chronicle of Higher Education,* May 23, 2008.

CHAPTER 2

1. Source: University of Minnesota Office of Institutional Research.

2. The era when student demand was only weakly dependent on tuition has long since passed. As noted by Edward St. John and Ontario S. Wooden, the decline in state support of higher education and in federal grant aid has "fueled a new period of unequal opportunity. There is substantial evidence that low-income, college-qualified students have been left behind in large numbers." St. John and Wooden, "Privatization and Federal Funding for Higher Education," in *Privatization and Public Universities,* ed. Douglas M. Priest and Edward P. St. John (Bloomington: Indiana University Press, 2006), 59. The authors also present a scathing critique of biased and flawed methodology used by the National Center for Education Statistics (the federal agency that reports on college access), which has come to an opposite conclusion (55–58).

3. By the 1960s, soaring national demand for higher education also buffered the potential restraining influence of growing tuition levels on college expenditures. As reported in *Time Magazine,* January 10, 1964, the blue-chip nineteen-member Educational Policies Commission, an independent committee of the National Education Association, observed that "the goal of universal education beyond the high school is no more utopian than the goal of full citizenship for all Americans, for the first is becoming prerequisite to the second." *Time* also noted that by 1964, the high school graduation rate in the nation had reached 65 percent (up from 6.4 percent at the turn of the century) and that 58 percent of these graduates were entering college.

4. The appropriation to higher education is a discretionary item in a state budget and is therefore funded with whatever remains in the treasury after nondiscretionary

expenses are covered. Federal entitlements, such as Medicaid, K–12 education, and pensions chew up large parts of a state budget. Other items may be technically discretionary, such as prisons, road maintenance, and the operating budgets of state agencies, but unlike higher education these have no other source of revenue and therefore receive higher priority than the state's public universities. As a practical matter, higher education is usually near the bottom of a state's major appropriation priorities.

5. Source: Ohio Board of Regents. Some of this growth entailed a movement into the state system by formerly private or municipal schools.

6. Richard Vedder, *Going Broke by Degree: Why College Costs Too Much* (Washington: American Enterprise Institute Press, 2004), 92–93 and table 5-1.

7. Donald E. Heller has observed that the number of American high school graduates is expected to peak in 2009. Heller, "State Support of Higher Education: Past, Present, and Future," in *Privatization and Public Universities,* ed. Douglas M. Priest and Edward P. St. John (Bloomington: Indiana University Press, 2006), 28.

This same leveling effect has been noticed by Vedder, who finds that, absent an influx of immigrants, the number of traditional college-age students will be roughly static until 2015. He further notes that the increase in participation rates in this age group (i.e., the fraction of the population that attends college) has slowed markedly in the 1990s and shows signs of saturating. Vedder, *Going Broke by Degree,* 94.

8. Although coming to his recommendation by a different route, Vedder has also proposed "defunding" public universities by gradually withdrawing their state appropriations. He analyzes the oft-expressed assertion that larger government subsidies stimulate state economic development but finds that the reverse is true. He also challenges the widely held view that state subsidies to universities enhance access for low- and middle-income students. Similar arguments lead him to propose eliminating most federal grants as well. Ibid., 194.

9. James J. Duderstadt, *A University for the 21st Century* (Ann Arbor: University of Michigan Press, 2003), 248.

10. In this context, a causal connection means that event A, an independent variable, "causes" event B, a dependent variable. By contrast, an associative connection refers to either of two situations: a random or accidental correlation between A and B (as in stock market peaks being associated with phases of the moon) or a situation where C causes A and C also causes B. In the latter case, A and B have a nonrandom correlation, even though there is no direct causal relationship between them. Economic indicators sometimes are based on such associations, e.g., when sales of luxury goods are used as a gauge of economic growth.

11. Vedder (*Going Broke by Degree,* 20) has pointed out that increases in third-party payments via expanded grant and loan programs may actually cause a net increase in college costs for students because they drive up tuition charges without increasing productivity.

12. In the figure, demand is modeled by a simple, straight-line dependence on tuition, i.e., $N(T) = N_0 (1 - T/T_0)$, where $N(T)$ is the number of enrolled students at tuition T, N_0 is the maximum number of students (at $T=0$), and T_0 is the maximum tuition beyond which demand is zero.

13. Readers will note similarities between figure 3 and the well-known Laffer curve of economics, which relates tax revenues collected by government to individual tax rates. Although the underlying concepts are similar, there are also important differences, as will become evident.

14. In this example, $T_0 = \$20,000$, and $N_0 = 40,000$ students. Then the revenue $R(T)$ is given by $R(T) = TN(T)$, where $N(T)$ is the number of enrolled students at tuition T. The expression for a straight-line demand curve is $N(T) = No(1\text{-}T/T_0)$. The maximum revenue R_M is obtained by setting $dR(T)/dT = 0$, which yields $R_M = N_0T_0/4$, at which point the number of enrolled students is $N_0/2$.

15. Don Hossler reports that the discount rate of some selective public flagship universities varies from about eight to seventeen percent. It is likely the discount rate for most non-selective public universities is significantly lower. Hossler, "Students and Families as Revenue: The Impact on Institutional Behaviors," in *Privatization and Public Universities*, ed. Douglas M. Priest and Edward P. St. John (Bloomington: Indiana University Press, 2006), 122–23.

16. Ibid., 117.

CHAPTER 3

1. There are actually many other parts of the Ohio higher education budget, some of which are "line item" appropriations that fund specific projects and facilities, such as the Ohio Agricultural Research and Development Center and the Ohio Supercomputer Center.

2. There is another technical assumption buried in the example, which is that the university operates near its full-enrollment capacity, so that its average per-student costs are equal to its marginal per-student costs. This assumption permits us estimate the financial impact of the tuition cap without having to know the details of the school's cost curve. (Marginal and average costs are discussed in detail in appendix B.)

3. In this example, we assume that the university receives no additional state subsidy because of the extra 600 enrolled students. In some states, however, subsidy is indexed to enrollment. In that case, the subsidy would increase in proportion to the larger number of students, thus reducing the net fiscal impact of the enrollment increase by (600 students) $\times$ (\$300/student) = \$180 thousand.

4. National Center for Education Statistics, Digest of Education Statistics, Tables and Figures, 2007, table 180.

5. National Center for Education Statistics, Digest of Education Statistics Tables and Figures, 2007, table 255.

6. In 1970, average per-campus enrollment was (4.23 million students)/(426 campuses) = (9,930 students/campus). By 2005, that number had grown to (6.84 million students)/(639 campuses) = (10,704 students/campus.) Thus, average per-campus enrollments over the entire thirty-five-year period increased by 774 students, or 22 students/year. This figure is a lower limit, because the NCES data include branch campuses in the 2005 data but exclude them from the 1970 data. The actual per-campus enrollment increase is closer to 100 students/year, when estimated branch campus effects are included in the computation.

7. National Center for Public Policy and Higher Education, January 2003 report.

CHAPTER 4

1. College Board, "Graph 16: Percent of 2008 College-Bound Seniors with High School GPAs of A+, A, and A– by Family Income and Parental Education," in Tables and Related Items, 2008.

2. Daniel Goldon, "At Many Colleges, the Rich Kids Get Affirmative Action," *Wall*

Street Journal, February 20, 2003; Robert Joiner, "Affirmative Action Double Standard," *The Affirmative Action and Diversity Project,* April 7, 2003, http://aad.english.ucsb.edu/docs/joiner5.html.

3. David L. Kirp and Jeffrey Holman, "This Little Student Went to Market," in David L. Kirp, *Shakespeare, Einstein, and the Bottom Line* (Cambridge, MA: Harvard University Press, 2003), 11–32.

4. American Intercontinental University website, www.aiuniv.edu.

5. See Kirp, *Shakespeare, Einstein, and the Bottom Line,* 240–54. Kirp provides an illuminating overview of the for-profit higher-education sector, using DeVry University as an example.

6. Cleveland State University admissions website, www.csuohio.edu/admissions/freshmen/requirements.html.

7. Peterson's, a Nelnet Company, 2008, www.petersons.com.

8. Michael Schwartz, testimony before the (Ohio) House Select Committee on Higher Education, September 9, 2002; the Ohio Board of Regents.

9. Ibid.

10. College of William and Mary, Office of Institutional Research, 2006–2007 Common Data Set.

11. University of Texas at Austin, Office of Information Management and Analysis, 2007–2008 Common Data Set.

12. James Vaznis, "UMass facing a daunting repair bill," *Boston Globe,* May 9, 2007.

13. Ibid.

14. Robert Zemsky, Gregory R. Wegner, and William F. Massy have noted that "medallion" private institutions—those with large endowments and an excess of applicants—can afford to subordinate market forces in order to emphasize the liberal arts, with their mission of serving the "public good." For private colleges at the lower end of the financial spectrum, however, survival often means focusing on marketplace demands by offering business, adult-learning, and job-skills curricula and eschewing the traditional liberal arts. Zemsky, Wegner, and Massy, *Remaking the American University: Market-Smart and Mission-Centered* (New Brunswick, NJ: Rutgers University Press, 2006), 54.

15. Sierra Nevada College, press release, March 27, 2007.

16. Princeton University, Budget Facts and Figures (2007), www.princeton.edu.

CHAPTER 5

1. Robert Birnbaum and Peter D. Eckel, "The Dilemma of Presidential Leadership," in *American Higher Education in the Twenty-first Century: Social, Political, and Economic Challenges,* ed. Philip G. Altbach, Robert O. Berdahl, and Patricia J. Gumport (Baltimore: The Johns Hopkins University Press, 2005), 555.

2. Robert Zemsky, Gregory R. Wegner, and William F. Massy, *Remaking the American University: Market-Smart and Mission-Centered* (New Brunswick, NJ: Rutgers University Press, 2006), 213.

3. The foundations of tenure are embodied in the "1940 Statement of Principles on Academic Freedom and Tenure" by the American Association of University Professors (www.aaup.org/AAUP/pubsres/policydocs/contents/1940statement.htm). The underlying principle in this statement is that tenure and academic freedom are essential to the "free search for truth," which in turn is essential to pursuing the "common good" of serving society. Although few challenge the principle, many question whether its

implementation is still consistent with practical realities. The major arguments are that (1) tight budgets have led to a caste system of tenured "haves" and often-exploited "have-nots," with universities increasingly preferring the latter in order to avoid making long-term financial commitments they cannot afford; (2) tenure's protection against arbitrary or politically motivated dismissal is no longer needed, given the strong protections of today's legal system; and (3) tenure protects the incompetent and unneeded, thus denying institutions the flexibility and financial resources they need to respond to changing circumstances. On the other hand, advocates of tenure point to an increasing tendency of elected officials to try to rid universities of politically unpopular or controversial professors, and the importance to society of giving professors the freedom to voice new and provocative opinions and theories.

4. Kanya Balakrishna, "Tenure Changes Accepted," *Yale Daily News,* April 5, 2007.

5. Yale University, "The Report of the Faculty of Arts and Sciences Tenure and Appointments Policy Committee," February 5, 2007.

CHAPTER 6

1. Grade inflation is a well-established national phenomenon, verified by many studies. Afflicting nearly all colleges and universities, grade inflation has been particularly acute in the Ivy League; for example, in 1996 46 percent of Harvard undergraduates received grades of A or A–, up from 22 percent thirty years earlier. Fewer than 12 percent received grades below B–. In 2002, the American Academy of Arts and Sciences issued an "occasional paper" on the subject (from which the above statistics are taken), prepared by two distinguished academicians who analyzed the problem and urged that it be addressed via discussion and education about faculty professional responsibilities on a school-by-school basis. See Henry Rosovsky and Mathew Hartley, "Evaluation and the Academy: Are We Doing the Right Thing?" *American Academy of Arts and Sciences,* 2002.

2. As an exception to this assertion, in 2004 Princeton University mounted a mostly successful assault on the grade inflation problem, when the faculty voted to adopt a common grading standard for all departments that limited A grades to 35 percent of an undergraduate class. (Upper-division independent studies classes were exempted.) A faculty follow-up committee reported a year later that A-range grades had, in fact, decreased significantly across the university, nearly to the target goal. Predictably, the student newspaper had opposed the change, arguing that Princeton attracted strong students who deserved high grades and that the new policy would be harmful to them after graduation.

3. Henry Rosovsky, *The University: An Owner's Manual* (New York: W. W. Norton, 1990), 262.

CHAPTER 7

1. Some of the material in this chapter is taken from my 2004 State of the University address to the Miami University community.

2. Stanley Fish, a law professor at Florida International University and former dean of liberal arts at the University of Illinois at Chicago, challenges the notion that academic freedom gives professors a broad license to do and say what they please. To Fish, academic freedom is much more prosaic, a "task-specific and task-limited" authorization that merely enables professors to do their specific jobs of teaching and research without interference. Fish, "Academic Freedom Is Not a Divine Right," *Chronicle of Higher Education,* September 5, 2008, B10.

3. John V. Lombardi, "University Improvement: The Permanent Challenge," Center for Measuring University Performance, Tempe, AZ, February 2000.

4. Robert Birnbaum and Peter D. Eckel, "The Dilemma of Presidential Leadership," in *American Higher Education in the Twenty-First Century: Social, Political, and Economic Challenges, Second Edition,*" ed. Philip G. Altbach, Robert O. Berdahl, and Patricia J. Gumport (Baltimore: Johns Hopkins University Press, 2005), 346.

5. Board of Trustees, "Relation of President and Faculty," resolution found in the Minutes of the Board of Trustees of Trinity College, Durham, NC, June 8, 1893. The resolution was subsequently published in *Trinity College Official Bulletin,* no. 14 (August 1893).

6. Although this example is based on a real academic department, I have changed a few nonessential details to preserve confidentiality.

7. Piper Fogg, "President of Texas University Suspends Faculty Senate," *Chronicle of Higher Education,* October 21, 2005.

8. Scott Jaschik and Elizabeth Redden, "No Confidence Vote at Antioch," *Inside Higher Education,* September 6, 2007.

9. Following a year of often acrimonious debate, Antioch College finally began shutting its doors on June 30, 2008, when efforts by faculty, students, and alumni failed to produce a financial solution to the college's fiscal woes. The trustees expressed hope of eventually reopening the college as a self-sustainable entity, independent of Antioch University, though this possibility seems increasingly remote. See James Hannah, "As Antioch College Closes, Former Profs Continue Teaching," *Cleveland Plain Dealer,* July 11, 2008.

10. Bill Schackner, "St. Vincent's President a Lightning Rod for Criticism," *Pittsburgh Post-Gazette,* April 2, 2008.

11. James Vaznis and Matthew O'Rourke, "Faculty Defiant on Proposal for UMass," *Boston Globe,* May 25, 2007.

12. Selena Roberts, "The Wal-Mart of College Sports," *New York Times,* June 3, 2007.

13. Robert Zemsky, Gregory R. Wegner, and William F. Massy have noted that the growth of college intercollegiate athletics in the twentieth century is a prime example of letting a once-academic mission (providing opportunities for undergraduates to participate in character-building team sports for pleasure and exercise) to be driven and ultimately dominated by marketplace commercialization. They further observe that once the powers of the market have taken hold, it is virtually impossible to "put the genie back in the lamp." Robert Zemsky, Gregory R. Wegner, and William F. Massey, *Remaking the American University: Market-Smart and Mission-Centered* (New Brunswick, NJ: Rutgers University Press, 2006), 58.

14. John Russo, "Speaking Out," *Advocate OnLine,* December 2002, www2.nea.org/he/adv002/adv01202/speaking.html.

15. The notion that earlier times were happier for public university professors may seem wrong to many women and minority faculty members, whose "earlier times" were marked by a discriminatory and unsympathetic working environment. As far as social equity is concerned, contemporary public (and private) universities are much improved over those of prior years.

CHAPTER 8

1. Final Report of the Ad Hoc Committee on Faculty Career Flexibility, submitted to the Georgetown University Faculty Senate, March 15, 2007.

2. Main Campus Election Commission of the University Faculty Senate, "University

Faculty Senate Main Campus Election Results," letter to Wayne Davis, president of the University Faculty Senate, May 2, 2006.

3. These numbers are taken from a 2004 study I commissioned, as background for an annual State of the University address to the Miami University community.

4. In 2002, Brown University President Ruth Simmons initiated a restructuring of the university's governance system with the goal of reducing by 50 percent the number of faculty committee assignments. A faculty task force issued its recommendations on September 10, 2002, and after extensive discussion and revisions the changes were implemented in July 2003. In 2008, the university's Faculty Executive Committee (FEC) released a comprehensive review of the governance reforms. Although the FEC saw many positive accomplishments with the new system, it scarcely mentioned the increased efficiency and savings of faculty time as benefits. Nor did it address the cost-savings resulting from the new system. Rather, the recommendations of the FEC were mostly aimed at *increasing* faculty participation and independence, with language sometimes bordering on hostile, e.g., "Nowhere is the Administration's lack of consultation with the Faculty and its disregard for the Faculty Rules and Regulations more conspicuous than in the management of the University's educational programs."

The Brown University experience is a case study of the difficulty of reducing governance expenses in an environment in which the default goal of faculty leaders is for more involvement and independence, with costs, if considered at all, a subsidiary concern. "Review of Faculty Governance: Report of the Faculty Executive Committee," Brown University, February 2008; "Minutes of the Faculty Forum on Faculty Governance," September 10, 2002; Mark Nickel, "Task Force Redesigns Faculty Governance," *George Street Journal*, September 13, 2002.

CHAPTER 10

1. Concern about the quality of governing boards is nearly ubiquitous among public university presidents. Former University of Michigan president James Duderstadt has observed that trustee selection has grown more contentious in recent years and that board members increasingly advocate political and ideological agendas. He also notes that there is generally no mechanism for removing board members, even for instances of misconduct or gross incompetence. James J. Duderstadt and Farris W. Womack, *The Future of the Public University in America* (Baltimore: Johns Hopkins University Press, 2003), 165, 175, 199.

2. In 2006, Ohio law was changed to increase to fifteen the number of Ohio State trustees. In addition, Miami University in 2004 began adding up to three nonvoting "national" trustees (i.e., chosen from outside Ohio) to its governing board.

3. Mary Beth Marklein, "College Trustees Feel Unprepared," *USA Today*, May 11, 2007.

4. Duderstadt and Womack, *Future of the Public University*, 176, have made the "radical suggestion," with which I concur, that presidents of public universities be given a voice in board selection, as is the current practice in private universities. The authors have also proposed, as I have here, that boards include at least one active or former senior academic administrator.

CHAPTER 11

1. *Chronicle of Higher Education*, 2005 survey of 688 presidents of four-year colleges and universities.

2. John Hechinger and Rebecca Buckman, "The Golden Touch of Stanford's President," *Wall Street Journal,* February 24, 2007.

3. "President's Profile," Rensselaer Polytechnic Institute Web site (http://www.rpi.edu/president/profile.html).

4. Boards must also be aware that unmarried presidents or presidents with spouses pursuing an independent career will need special support and assistance in order to manage the social expectations of the presidency.

CHAPTER 12

1. Julianne Basinger, "U. of Toledo President Resigns after Push from Trustees," *Chronicle of Higher Education,* June 23, 2000; and "A 17-Month Presidency Leaves U. of Toledo in a State of Unusual Disarray," *Chronicle of Higher Education,* August 4, 2000.

2. Harold Shapiro, former president of the University of Michigan and Princeton University, has a whimsical description of the university president as manager, the first sentence of which is "I manage to survive; I manage to plan, organize, staff, coordinate, budget, report, and make decisions regarding the future of this organization as part figurehead, part pastor of interpersonal relations, part spokesperson, part disturbance handler, part negotiator, part resource allocator and general disburser of institutional propaganda and positive reinforcement to students, faculty, alumni and trustees; I manage to be an unprincipled (at times) promoter and principled (at other times) huckster of the institution and its objectives; I manage to bring forward the historical traditions of the institution and give some of them new life and meaning in a different world; I manage to articulate a set of goals for the institution that, despite all odds, actually covers all the activities of what increasingly has become a general-service public utility; I manage an organization of bewildering scope with at least a little dignity, respectability, some authority, and (occasionally) wisdom." Harold T. Shapiro, "University Presidents—Then and Now," in *Universities and their Leadership,* ed. William G. Bowen and Harold T. Shapiro (Princeton, NJ: Princeton University Press, 1998), 87–88.

3. Academic search consultants are a controversial topic among university presidents and trustees. The best clearly earn their fees by helping to recruit top candidates, checking backgrounds, and helping search committees focus and set priorities. The worst appear mainly to trade in gossip about who is currently "on the market" and are less inclined to identify nontraditional candidates who may be well suited to the institution's needs.

4. Exceptions to this rule are the elite private universities, which have often have chosen their presidents from their own faculty ranks. Considering that these institutions usually attract faculty members from the top of the faculty job pool, it is not surprising that their internal choices for presidents measure up well by national standards.

CHAPTER 13

1. The Miami University smoking policy became effective August 1, 2008, and may be found at http://www.miami.muohio.edu/documents_and_policies/smokefree.cfm.

2. This example also illustrates the difficult dual role faced by academic department heads, who often feel caught between a rock and hard place. On one side, their faculty expects them to be standard bearers who will defend their department against administrative incursions, and on the other side their dean wants them to set limits, solve departmental problems, and help sell larger university priorities.

CHAPTER 14

1. That the practice is time-tested, however, does not mean it is universally praised. Since the 1960s, some economists have questioned whether the public subsidy of higher education is *objectively* merited by the social benefits. In a recent review, economist Maureen Woodhall notes that Milton Friedman in 1968 challenged this premise, and in 1973 the Carnegie Commission presciently observed that rising incomes would increasingly result in a displacement of higher education costs away from the taxpayer onto students. Maureen Woodhall, "The Contribution of Economic Thinking to Debate and Policy Development," in *Economics of Education: Major Contributions and Future Directions, June 20–23, 2006* (Dijon, France: World Bank 2007); and Carnegie Commission on Higher Education (1973), *Higher Education: Who Pays? Who Should Pay?* (New York: McGraw-Hill, 1973). Richard Vedder (*Going Broke by Degree: Why College Costs Too Much* [Washington: American Enterprise Institute Press, 2004], 196–201) has recently made similar arguments and observations.

2. University of Alaska System, "Building Higher Education for Alaska's Golden Anniversary," Strategic Plan 2009, September 18, 2003.

3. South Carolina Commission on Higher Education, "2002 Strategic Plan for Higher Education in South Carolina," 2002.

4. State Council of Higher Education for Virginia, "Advancing Virginia: Access, Alignment, Investment; The 2007–13 Strategic Plan for Higher Education in Virginia," 2007.

5. New Mexico Higher Education Department, "New Mexico Higher Education Strategic Priorities and Goals 2006–2010," 2006.

6. These objectives are unfortunately contravened by the findings of a recent study that statewide systems, although effective at managing growth and simplifying resource allocation, have been largely unable to prevent mission creep or program overlap; nor do they reduce costs, improve efficiency, or enhance quality. For these reasons, there is a "growing interest in shifting from dependence on regulation and oversight to using the market as a means of ensuring public purposes." Frank Newman, Lara Couturier, and Jamie Scurry, *The Future of Higher Education: Rhetoric, Reality, and the Risks of the Market* (San Francisco: Jossey-Bass/Wiley, 2004), 31–32.

7. Ohio Office of Budget and Management, "State of Ohio Budget Highlights: Fiscal Years 2008 and 2009," October 2007.

8. Eric D. Fingerhut, chancellor, "Strategic Plan for Higher Education 2008–2017," Ohio Board of Regents.

9. Paul E. Lingenfelter, "State Support of Higher Education," Association of Governing Boards, April 14, 2008, figure 10.

10. In most financial respects, Ohio's plan benchmarks itself against the national average for public higher education. While this might be a stretch goal for Ohio, if successful it would only bring Ohio's public campuses up to the lagging condition of public universities in other states.

11. Mark Niquette, "State Budget Might Suffer Massive Cuts," *Columbus Dispatch,* January 23, 2008.

12. Newman, Couturier, and Scurry have observed that, perversely, the chronic budget crises in a majority of states, although placing public campuses under severe strain, have made state governments receptive to considering alternative funding scenarios. Newman, Couturier, and Scurry, *Future of Higher Education,* 39.

The decline of government subsidies in higher education has led to an active debate about the pros and cons of "privatizing" public university systems. Douglas M. Priest, Edward P. St. John, and Rachel Dykstra Boon, (in *Public Funding of Higher Education: Changing Contexts and New Rationales,* ed. Edward P. St. John and Michael D. Parsons [Baltimore: Johns Hopkins University Press, 2004], p. 2) have defined privatization as "the process of transforming low-tuition institutions that are largely dependent on state funding . . . into institutions dependent on tuition revenues and other types of earned income as central sources of operating revenue." South Carolina Governor Mark Sanford in 2003 proposed letting some public campuses in his state privatize as a way of escaping government controls. Other states (Virginia, Colorado, Maryland, for example) have flirted with the idea in a limited way. The Darden Graduate School of Business Administration at the University of Virginia is an example of a subunit within a major public university that has willingly forfeited its public subsidy in exchange for increased freedom from state control.

The proposals in this book are a variation on the privatization concept. They would free public universities from state control of their tuition policies and wean them from state subsidy. However, the universities would still be wholly owned by their states and would continue to receive state support, redirected as scholarships to their students. (See also the following note.) Numerous writers have observed that the transition from state appropriations to scholarships represents a de facto philosophical shift, from viewing public higher education as mostly a "public good" that benefits all of society to a "private good" that benefits the scholarship recipients. Robert Zemsky, Gregory R. Wegner, and Willam F. Massy (*Remaking the American University: Market-Smart and Mission-Centered* [New Brunswick, NJ: Rutgers University Press, 2006], 7) see society as losing in this transition if universities capitulate excessively to marketplace forces, e.g., by allowing their missions to be driven too much by the wants of students.

13. Economist Richard Vedder credits Milton Friedman as first conceiving this basic approach forty years ago. In a 2004 book (*Going Broke by Degree,* 196–202), Vedder has elaborated on Friedman's idea by proposing an "alternate scenario" that resembles what is proposed here. Although Vedder's first choice is to get the government out of the higher education business completely, his backup option would have state governments replace direct subsidies to universities with "progressive vouchers" for students. Like the state-administered scholarships proposed in this book, the size of these vouchers would be based on a needs assessment of the recipients.

A historical note: In 2005, I outlined my suggestions for public higher-education reform in an opinion piece in the *Washington Post* ("How to Put College Back within Reach: Better Uses for State Education Dollars," December 30, 2005, A27). My suggestions seemed a rather straightforward generalization of the Miami University tuition plan (described in appendix A), which by then had proved its worth by achieving its primary goals. Professor Vedder, recognizing the parallelism between my proposals and his own ideas, arranged for me to present my proposals to Education Secretary Margaret Spelling's Commission on the Future of Higher Education, of which he was a member. Vedder's view of public higher education's needs grows out of his understanding of more than a half-century of analysis and debate among economists and public policy scholars about the pros and cons of vouchers (first embodied in the 1945 GI Bill), government appropriations, public versus private ownership of institutions, and market competition. In my case, as a physicist who was largely unaware of this running scholarly dialogue, my proposals grow out of my administrative experience trying to balance budgets, hold down tuition charges, cajole elected officials, rein in costs, and implement changes at my own institution. Thus Vedder and I have come to very similar recommendations via very different trajectories. In that sense, the proposals in this book, if realized, would represent a kind of unintentional experimental test of ideas growing out of decades of deep economic and public policy thinking.

14. New entering students would obviously include freshmen but might also include transfer students as well as upper-class students who are returning to college after an absence.

15. If universities chose to grandfather currently enrolled students and apply the tuition surcharge only to newly enrolled students, then the tuition surcharge for those new students would be about 48 percent. As explained in the text, this increase would be offset by scholarship awards that would on average exactly cancel the amount of the tuition increase.

16. As discussed previously, private universities and colleges routinely use a "high tuition / high aid" strategy to account for the ability to pay of their enrolled students. As public university tuitions have increased, use of this strategy has drawn increasing attention from many public higher-education reformers. For example, James J. Duderstadt and Farris W. Womack (*The Future of the Public University in America* [Baltimore: Johns Hopkins University Press, 2003], 124–25), have observed that low public college tuition is, in effect, a de facto subsidy for the affluent and that the high tuition / high aid model is fairer and more socially progressive. On the other hand, not all are enthusiastic about the concept. For example, William Zumeta ("State Higher Education Financing: Demand Imperatives Meet Structural, Cyclical, and Political Constraints," in *Public Funding of Higher Education: Changing Contexts and New Rationales*, ed. Edward P. St. John and Michael D. Parsons [Baltimore: Johns Hopkins University Press, 2005], 96–97) has noted several obstacles to carrying over the high tuition / high aid concept to the public sector: political opposition because of the ingrained low-tuition preferences of legislatures; the potential adverse "sticker stock" impact on low-income students; the challenges of identifying acceptable need-based aid criteria; and the weak political clout of low-income aid recipients in making the case for larger financial aid appropriations from their state government.

17. Ohio Board of Regents, "Fall 2007 Survey of Student Charges." For the 2007–8 academic year, the average annualized full-time undergraduate tuition for main campus students at Ohio's thirteen public universities was $7,984.

18. The federal government has developed a comprehensive means test for evaluating students' need of federal aid. Known as the Free Application for Federal Student Aid (FAFSA), the application form is also used by most states to decide state scholarship awards. The purpose of FAFSA is to determine the ability of applicants to afford college tuition; to make this determination, many factors are considered beyond gross income. These include household size, whether a family has more than one enrolled college student, income from investments, savings, business and farm assets, and so forth. It is a convenient, standardized evaluation instrument that looks at the many factors that affect college affordability.

19. One can also frame this issue in the context of faculty scholarship and research. The question is whether, under my proposed financial model, universities would continue to encourage faculty scholarship, especially in disciplines that do not attract grant and contract support or for which there is no immediate practical application. Here,

too, the answer is that this ground has already been trod by private universities, which, despite the absence of state subsidy, see basic research as an important part of faculty responsibilities. Furthermore, because all universities and colleges want to recruit the best professors possible, it is essential that they maintain a supportive scholarly environment. Indeed the competitive market for faculty talent is as important to a university's success as is the competitive market for students.

POSTSCRIPT

1. *Inside Higher Education,* September 18, 2007 (www.insidehighered.com/news/2007/09/18/coache).

2. Betsy E. Brown, special assistant to the provost of North Carolina State University, presentation at the annual meeting of the National Association of State Universities and Land-Grant Colleges, New York, November 12, 2007.

3. Evan Halper, "Schwarzenegger orders plan for 10% budget cuts," *Los Angeles Times,* November 6, 2007.

4. "Higher Education Reform Bill Includes McKeon Plan to Address Rising College Costs," press release, office of Rep. Howard P. (Buck) McKeon, November 12, 2007.

5. "News Blog," *Chronicle of Higher Education,* September 16, 2008.

APPENDIX B

1. In the figure, the total cost $C(N)$ is modeled by the equation $C(N) = C_F[1 + (N/N_0)^4]$, where C_F is the institution's fixed cost, which we assume equals 50 percent of the total cost when $N = N_0/2$, the equilibrium enrollment. There is assumed to be no linear N term in $C(N)$, because for $N \ll N_0$ the institution has so few students that its marginal cost is nearly zero, i.e., $dC(N)/dN = 0$. The values of N_0 and $C(N_0)$ are chosen to be consistent with figure B2.

2. This crossing of the C_M curve at the exact bottom of the C_A curve is not accidental. So long as C_M is below C_A, every additional student pulls down the average, giving C_A a negative (downward) slope. When C_M is above C_A, it pulls up the average, giving C_A a positive slope. When C_M crosses C_A, it has no impact on the average, so that the slope of the C_A curve must be flat at that point, corresponding to its minimum.

3. Combining $N(T) = N_0 (1 - T/T_0)$ from figure B2 and $C(N) = C_F[1 + (N/N_0)4]$ from figure B1 yields $C(T) = C_F[1 + (1 - (T/T_0))^4]$.

4. How the cost curve shifts depends on how the university chooses to reinvest its excess revenue. This example assumes that reinvestment is distributed proportionately across the university's fixed costs (as might happen if the dollars are used to hire new tenured professors) and also across its discretionary costs (such as departmental travel budgets).

5. It is important to recognize that only the cost curve changes each year as expenditures rise. So long as other influences do not alter student demand, and so long as the university does not increase tuition, the revenue curve does not change.

6. There are subtleties here that go beyond the scope of this treatment. In general, the final equilibrium tuition, T_1, does not occur at the exact peak of the revenue curve, unless one makes the unrealistic assumption that all costs are fixed costs, i.e., $C(T) = C_F$. For that case, using the demand curve and notation of figure B2, the band edges occur at $T_0/2[1 \pm (1 - 4(C_F/N_0T))^{1/2}]$ and the equilibrium tuition at $T_1 = T_0/2$.

7. For purposes of discussion, I am ignoring the impact of inflation. As a practical

matter, the institution could increase both its tuition and its cost structure each year by the inflation rate and still balance its budget. However, any cost increase beyond the inflation rate would create a gap between revenue and cost. University costs have been rising at roughly twice the rate of inflation for more than a decade.

8. Although they might technically have the financial flexibility to raise tuition at will, highly selective private colleges and universities are subject to powerful nonfinancial pressures to exercise tuition restraint, less they reduce applications and thereby lower the academic quality of their entering students.

9. To illustrate the concept, I have assumed in the figure that the tuition has been lowered. In actuality, a state normally freezes tuition or sets a limit on an allowed increase, rather than dictating a tuition decrease. In either case, the general impact is the same, although the figure exaggerates the practical consequence.

10. Here I assume that all of the excess enrollment occurs in the year following the capped tuition. In reality, the additional students normally enter as freshmen and stay for four to six years, depending on the school's graduation rate and other factors. Each year, a new, larger freshman class will enroll, thereby spreading out the demand-driven enrollment increase over several years. Thus the impact of the change in demand on university finances will not be fully absorbed until steady-state enrollment levels have been reached.

Index

An f or a t with a page number indicates a
figure or table, respectively.

academic administration: buy-now-
pay-later commitments and, 68–69;
efficiency of, 77–79; faculty relations
with, 64–69, 88–90, 254n9; fundamental changes and, 113, 188; goals
of, 76–77; mutual finger pointing by
state legislatures and, 20; perspectives of, 67–68; public university
financing, and effects on, 69; shared
governance and, 79–80; time devaluation and, 77–79. See also leadership
academic culture: academic pecking
order and, 66–67; accountability,
and role in changes in, 187–88; budget oversight, and changing, 141;
cargo-cult thinking, 72; committee-
based decision-making reforms, and
changes in, 174–80, 256n2; costs and
productivity information, and role
in changes in, 186–87; decentralized decision-making reforms,
and changes in, 173–74; described,

63–64; efficiency and, 164, 165;
explanations about institutions'
future, and changes in, 166–67;
faculty and, 68, 75–76, 77, 252n3;
financial aid practices, and effects
on, 73–75, 253n2; grade inflation
case study and, 73, 253n1; group
incentives, and changes in, 169–70;
institutional research upgrades, and
changes in, 170–72; leadership, and
role in changes in, 186; personal
financial incentives, and changes in,
167–69; productivity, and resistance
in, 164–66; public university financing, and changes in, 141; resistance
to efficiency in, 165; service by
professors reduction, and changes
in, 180–85
accountability issues, 97–100, 187–88
admissions: elite private universities
and colleges and, 57–58; for-profit
universities and, 53–54; governing
boards, and role in, 136; income
dependence of SAT scores and, 52,
52t; nonselective public universities

admissions (*continued*)
  and, 54–56; Ohio State University
  statistics for, 136; private universities and
  colleges and, 57–58, 252n14; psychology
  of, 229; quality of students and, 51–53,
  52f, 60; selective public universities and,
  56–57; submarkets and, 53
Alaska, and strategic plan for the public
  university system, 192
American Academy of Arts and Sciences,
  253n1
Amherst College, 92–93
Antioch University, 90, 254n9
A. T. Kearney management consultants, 143

balance sheets, and public university financing, 13–15, 248n3
Bishop, Robert Hamilton, 147, 148
Bonaminio, Jim and Joani, 161–62
Boon, Rachel Dykstra, 258n12
Brown University, and cost of shared governance, 255n4
budget oversight, and role of governing
  boards, 138–41
business plan: economic model of public
  university system and, 3, 190–96, 257n1,
  257n10; failed, 190–92; for-profit universities, and admissions and, 53; governing
  boards and, 119; public university system, and traditional, 2–3, 7; reforms and,
  113, 198, 206, 211, 215. *See also* financial
  model for the public university system
business principles, and productivity, 162, 163
buy-now-pay-later commitments, 68–69

California, and budget issues, 217–18
California Institute of Technology, image
  of, 137
campus autonomy governing boards, 116
campus-specific governing boards, 116, 118–20
"Cargo Cult Science" (Feynman), 71–72
cargo-cult thinking, 71–72
College of William and Mary in Williamsburg, 56
Columbia University, 152
committee-based decision-making reforms,
  and changes in, 174–80, 256n2
communications, and governing boards, 138
community colleges, and six-year degrees,
  248n5

cost containment, and public university
  financing, 42–46, 251n1
costs and productivity information, and role
  in changes in academic culture, 186–87
Couturier, Lara, 257n12

Danaher Corporation, 162–63
decentralized decision-making reforms, and
  changes in, 173–74
democracy, and equal opportunity in public
  university system, 215, 218–19, 247n1,
  254n15
demographic changes, in student populations, 27, 250n7
deregulation, and financial model for the
  public university system, 7, 200–201
Duderstadt, James J., 28, 255n1, 255n4, 259n16
Duke University, 85

economic model of public university
  system: business plan and, 3, 190–96,
  257n1, 257n10; changing environment
  and, 2–3; defined, xviii, 2; efficiency and,
  7; reforms and, 113; state appropriations
  and, 2, 5, 248n6. *See also* public university
  financing
efficiency: academic administration and,
  77–79; academic culture and, 164–66; devaluation of time and, 77–79; economic
  model of the public university system
  and, 7; Miami University and, 6; public
  university system and, 6–7, 217–18
Ehrenberg, Ronald G., 15–16, 248n7
elite private universities and colleges, and
  admissions, 57–58
employment, and role of the public university system, xvi
enrollment, and effects on campus costs,
  38–39
equity, and the public university system,
  215, 218–19, 247n1, 254n15

faculty: academic administration, and relationship with, 64–69, 88–90, 254n9; autonomy of, 75–76, 77, 79; governing boards,
  and response to, 90–92; Miami University
  and, viii, xii–xiv; personal financial incentives and, 167–69; salaries and, xv, 217;
  shared governance and, 95–96; tenure for,
  68, 252n3; unions for, 56

Federal Student Aid (FAFSA), 259n18
Feynman, Richard, 71–72, 78
financial aid practices: academic culture, and effects of, 73–75, 253n2; FAFSA and, 259n18; for-profit universities and, 53–54; governing boards, and role in, 136–37; marketplace forces in higher education and, 32, 35; Miami University and, xiii, xvii, 209; Ohio and, 19
financial equity, and the public university system, 215
financial model for the public university system: deregulation, and proposed, 200–201; oversight, and proposed, 200–201; performance-based proposed, 199–200; tuition and fee strategies, and proposed, 201–3; working objectives of, 198–99. See also business plan; marketplace forces in higher education; state scholarship awards
"First in 2009" plan. See tuition plan for Miami University
Fish, Stanley, 253n2
for-profit universities, and admissions, 53–54
Friedman, Milton, 257n1, 259n13
fund-raising and development, and role of governing boards, 134–35

Garland, James, "How to Put College Back within Reach," 258–59n13
Georgetown University, 97–99
global trends, and effects on Miami University, xi–xii
governance, shared. See shared governance
governing boards: admissions, and role of, 136; budget oversight, and role of, 138–41; campus autonomy and, 116; campus-specific, 116, 118–20; characteristics of poor choices for, 120; communications and, 138; compensation for leadership on, 129–30; credentials for good choices for, 120–22; faculty complaints, and response from, 90–92; financial aid practices, and role of, 136–37; fundamental changes and, 112–13; fund-raising and development, and role of, 134–35; governor's appointments to, 117–18; knowledge of leadership on, 127–29; leadership selection and, 116–17;

Miami University and, 255n2; Ohio governor's appointments to, 117–18; Ohio State University, and elections for, 117, 255n2; political issues and, 118, 122–23; presidential oversight, and role of, 130–34, 256n4; procedures for selecting, 125; public relations and, 137–38; reforms, and leadership of, 115–16, 255n1; selection process for, 123–25, 255n4; statewide or systemwide, 116, 118–20. See also shared governance
grade inflation case study, 73, 253n1
grant and contract revenues, and public university financing, 249n9
group incentives, and changes in academic culture, 169–70

Harvard University, 59–60, 79, 253n1
Heller, Donald E., 250n7
Hennessy, John L., 132
higher education: affordability of, 3–5, 4, 249nn2–3; six-year degrees and, 248n5; student demand and options for, 4, 16, 248n5. See also marketplace forces in higher education; public university system; students
Hossler, Don, 251n15
"How to Put College Back within Reach" (Garland), 258–59n13

income dependence of SAT scores, and admissions, 52, 52t. See also middle-income students
inefficiencies. See efficiency
institutional research upgrades, and changes in academic culture, 170–72
Issue 5 (nonsmoking statute of Ohio), 172–73

Jungle Jim's International Market, 161–62

Kapoor, Vik J., 143

leadership: academic culture, and changes in, 186; governing boards and, 115–17, 127–30, 255n1; public university system changes and, 112–13. See also academic administration; presidents of universities
Lombardi, John V., 83–84
Louisiana State University, 83–84

marketplace forces in higher education: actual demand and, 30–31; competitive forces reduced by rising demand and, 49–50, 49t, 251n6; defunding state appropriations and, 28, 205–7, 250n8; dependence of revenue and cost on tuition and, 235–38, 236f, 260–61nn3–8; dependence of total, average, and marginal costs on enrollment and, 233–35, 234f, 260n2; dependence of total educational cost on enrollment and, 232–33, 232f, 260n1; enrollment effects on campus costs and, 38–39; financial aid practices and, 32, 35; future role of, 27–29, 250n8; history of public university financing and, 23–27, 249nn2–4, 250n7; impact of tuition controls on university budget and, 238–40, 239f, 261nn9–10; market pressure to control campus costs and, 39–40; shared governance and, 28–29; state regulations, and diverse, 31–33, 250nn10–11; submarkets and, 29–31, 53, 240; supply and demand in, 33–35, 34f, 231–40, 250n12; supply-demand curves and, 29–30, 30f; tuition costs and, 28; tuition dependence of revenue and enrollment and, 35–38, 36f, 250n13, 251nn14–15. See also financial model for the public university system; public university financing
Massy, William F., 252n14, 254n13, 258n12
McKeon, Howard P., 218
metric for gauging success, of public university financing, 11–12, 248n1
Miami University: affordability of higher education and, 4; cost increases and, 6; efficiency and, 6; faculty and, viii, xii–xiv; financial aid practices and, xiii, xvii, 209; financial projections and, x–xi; global trends, and effects on, xi–xii; governing board and, 255n2; historical context, and description of, vii–ix; middle-income students and, xvii; OLS and, 224–25; options for coping with fiscal realities and, xii–xiv; ORS award and, 222–24; quantitative benchmarking and assessment and, ix–x; shared governance costs case history and, 100–103; socioeconomic status of students and, xii; state appropriations and, 17–18, 207,

208; state regulations, and effects at, 31; tuition costs and, viii–ix, xi–xii, 6; tuition hike option for coping with fiscal realities and, xii, xiv; tuition primacy era and, 15. See also Ohio; tuition plan for Miami University
Michigan State University, 116–17, 137, 255n1
middle-income students, xv, xvii
minorities, and public university system, 247n1, 254n15
Morrill Land Grant Act of 1862, 1, 247n1
Murdock, Toni, 90

National Center for Education Statistics, 49t, 249n2
Newman, Frank, 257–58nn12–13
New Mexico, and strategic plan for the public university system, 192–93
New York, and public university system, xv, 194
nonselective public universities, and admissions, 54–56

Ohio: financial aid practices and, 19; governor's appointments in, 117–18; higher education student demands in, 4; Issue 5 nonsmoking statute and, 172–73; political issues, and tuition plan implementation in, 226–27; public university financing and, vii; public university system and, vii; standard of living in, 4, 248n4; strategic plan for the public university system in, 194–96, 257n10; tuition rates setting and, 18–19. See also Miami University
Ohio Board of Regents, xiv–xv, 259n17
Ohio Leader Scholarship (OLS), 224–25
Ohio Resident Scholarship (ORS), 222–23
Ohio State University: admissions statistics and, 136; applicants and, 18, 136, 249n12; author and, vii, 17, 18; described, vii, viii; governing board elections and, 117, 255n2; tuition costs and, 18, 208, 249n12
organizational efficiency. See efficiency

physical plant deterioration, and public university system, xiv–xv, 6
political issues: governing boards and, 118, 122–23; tuition plan implementation and, 226–27

presidents of universities: buy-now-pay-later commitments, and legacies of, 69; characteristics of successful, 147–49, 155; characteristics of unsuccessful, 149–51; expectations of, 143–45; fundamental changes and, 112–13; governing boards, and oversight of, 130–34, 256n4; job description of, 145–47, 256n2; perception of, 147–48; search committees for, 153–59; search consultants and, 143, 148, 256n3. *See also* leadership

Priest, Douglas M., 258n12

private universities and colleges, and admissions, 57–58, 252n14

productivity. *See* efficiency

public relations, and governing boards, 137–38

public university financing: academic culture changes and, 141; attitudes about tuition charges and, 16–17, 249n11; balance sheets and, 13–15, 248n3; cost containment, and effects of state appropriations on, 42–46, 251n1; demographic changes in student population and, 27, 250n7; fiscal situations and, xiv–xv; fundamental changes and, 112–13; goals of, 196–98, 197t; grant and contract revenues and, 249n9; history of, 247n1; marketplace forces in higher education, and history of, 23–27, 249nn2–4, 250n7; metric for gauging success and, 11–12, 248n1; mutual finger-pointing by academic administration and legislators and, 20; Ohio and, vii; options for coping with fiscal realities and, xv–xvi; privatizing, 257n12; readings, 241–45; school-to-school variability and, 12–13; six-year degrees and, 248n5; social equity and, 247n1; state appropriations and, 1, 17–18, 25–27, 60, 249n4, 259n16; tenure for faculty and, 68, 252n3; unions for faculty, and effects on, 56; unrestrained costs and, 41–42. *See also* economic model of public university system; marketplace forces in higher education; tuition plan for Miami University

public university system: acceptance of responsibility by members of, 110–11; challenging assumptions in, 108–9; competition and, 7; criticisms, and rejection by, 107–8; deferred maintenance

backlogs and, xiv–xv; deregulation, and proposed financial model for, 200–201; destructive patterns of behavior in, 109–10; experimentation and risk-taking in, 111–12; fundamental changes for, xviii–xix; history of, 1–2; readings on, 241–45; six-year degrees and, 248n5; strategic plan and, 192, 194–96, 257n10; tuition costs and, 248n7. *See also* higher education

Public Utilities Commission of Ohio (PUCO), 117

Rales, Mitchell and Steven, 162

Rosovsky, Henry, 79

SAT scores, income dependence of, 52, 52t

Saturday Night Live (TV show), 189

"Scotch Boutique" TV skit, 189–90

Scurry, Jamie, 257n12

search committees, for presidents of universities, 153–59

search consultants, and presidents of universities, 143, 148, 256n3; selection process for, 123–25, 255n4

selective public universities, and admissions, 56–57

service by professors, and changes in academic culture, 180–85

shared governance: academic administration and, 79–80; accountability of faculty and, 97–100; advantages of, 81; Brown University, and cost of, 255n4; corporate alternative to, 83–85; criticism of, 82–83; faculty unions, and effects on, 95–96; failures of, 85–88; marketplace forces in higher education and, 28–29; Miami University case history, and cost of, 100–103; at public universities and colleges, 92–96, 254n12; quantified costs of, 103; sports fans, and effects on, 95, 254n12; stress, and traditional, 25; traditional beliefs about, 81–82, 253n2. *See also* governing boards

Simmons, Ruth, 255n4

social equity, and the public university system, 247n1, 254n15

South Carolina, and strategic plan for the public university system, 192–93

sports fans, and effects on shared governance, 95, 254n12

standard of living, in Ohio, 4, 248n4
Stanford University, 132
state appropriations: cost containment, and effects of, 42–46; economic model of public university system and, 2, 5, 248n6; Miami University and, 17–18, 207, 208; public university financing and, 1, 17–18, 25–27, 60, 249n4, 259n16; social and philosophical issues about, 213–15
state legislatures: Miami University, and effects of regulations in, 31; mutual finger-pointing by academic administration and, 20; public university financing, and role of, 7, 213–15; public university system, and role of, 1, 7, 213–15, 247n1; strategic plans, and role of, 2, 192–96, 257n6
state scholarship awards: benefits of, 207–10, 259n16; evaluation of, 212–13, 259n19; financial model for the public university system and, 199, 200, 203–5, 207–10, 258–59n13, 259n18, 259nn14–16; restrictions for, 210–12. See also financial model for the public university system
State University of New York, and deferred maintenance backlog, xv
statewide governing boards, 116, 118–20
St. John, Edward P., 249n2, 258n12
Strickland, Ted, 19, 194–96
students: admissions, and quality of, 51–53, 52f, 60; demographic changes in populations of, 27; higher education demand and, 4, 16; middle-income, xv, xvii; Ohio State University applicants and, 18, 136, 249n12; socioeconomic status of, xii; state-imposed cap on tuition, and effects on, 48. See also higher education
St. Vincent College, 90
submarkets, educational, 29–31, 53, 240
systemwide governing boards, 116, 118–20

Texas A&M, 137, 207
time devaluation, and efficiency, 77–79
Trinity College, 85
tuition: attitudes about, 16–17, 249n11; costs and, 4–6, 28, 248n7; dependence of revenue and enrollment and, 35–38, 36f, 250n13, 251nn14–15; financial model for the public university system and, 201–3; Harvard University and, 59–60; Miami

University, and cost of, viii–ix, xi–xii, 6; Ohio, and rates setting for, 18–19; Ohio Board of Regents and, 259n17; Ohio State University and, 18, 208, 249n12; primacy era of, 15–16; rates setting for, 18–19; reform plan requirements for the public university system and, 225–26; state-imposed cap on, 46–49, 251nn2–3; tuition hike option for coping with fiscal realities at Miami University and, xii, xiv
tuition plan for Miami University: admissions psychology and, 229; described, ix, 221–30; fiscal realities and, xvi–xviii; marketing, 229–30; political issues and, 226–27; predicted impact of, 228–29; public relations for, 229. See also Miami University

unions, for faculty, 56, 95–96
University of California system, 79, 116
University of Colorado at Boulder, 116–17, 137
University of Illinois, xv, 35, 226, 253n2
University of Maryland at College Park, and deferred maintenance backlog, xv
University of Massachusetts at Amherst, 93
University of Phoenix, 33, 53, 248n1
University of Texas at Austin, 56
University of Toledo, 143–44

Vedder, Richard, 249n11, 250nn7–8, 250n11, 258–59n13
Videojet Technologies, 162–63, 170
Virginia, and strategic plan for the public university system, 192–93

Wegner, Gregory R., 252n14, 254n13, 258n12
West Texas A&M, 207
Wilson, Jack M., 93
Womack, Farris W., 255n4, 259n16
women, and public university system, 247n1, 254n15
Wooden, Ontario S., 249n2
Woodhall, Maureen, 257n1

Yale University, 68, 137

Zemsky, Robert, 252n14, 254n13, 258n12
Zumeta, William, 259n16